GOVERNMENT BEYOND THE CENTRE

SERIES EDITOR: GERRY STOKER

GOVERNMENT BEYOND THE CENTRE

SERIES EDITOR: GERRY STOKER

The world of sub-central government and administration – including local authorities, quasi-governmental bodies and the agencies of public–private partnerships – has seen massive changes in recent years and is at the heart of the current restructuring of government in the United Kingdom and other Western democracies.

The intention of the *Government Beyond the Centre* series is to bring the study of this often-neglected world into the mainstream of social science research, applying the spotlight of critical analysis to what has traditionally been the preserve of institutional public administration approaches.

Its focus is on the agenda of change currently being faced by sub-central government, the economic, political and ideological forces that underlie it, and the structures of power and influence that are emerging. Its objective is to provide up-to-date and informative accounts of the new forms of government, management and administration that are emerging.

The series will be of interest to students and practitioners of politics, public and social administration, and all those interested in the reshaping of the governmental institutions which have a daily and major impact on our lives.

Government Beyond the Centre
Series Standing Order ISBN 0–333–71696–5 hc
ISBN 0–333–69337–X pb
(*outside North America only*)

You can receive future titles in this series as they are published by placing a standing order. Please contact your bookseller or, in the case of difficulty, write to us at the address below with your name and address, the title of the series and the ISBN quoted above.

Customer Services Department, Macmillan Distribution Ltd
Houndmills, Basingstoke, Hampshire RG21 6XS, England

Decentralising Public Service Management

Christopher Pollitt
Johnston Birchall
and
Keith Putman

MACMILLAN

First published 1998 by
MACMILLAN PRESS LTD
Houndmills, Basingstoke, Hampshire RG21 6XS
and London
Companies and representatives
throughout the world

ISBN 0–333–69402–3 hardcover
ISBN 0–333–69403–1 paperback

A catalogue record for this book is available
from the British Library.

This book is printed on paper suitable for recycling and
made from fully managed and sustained forest sources.

10   9   8   7   6   5   4   3   2   1
07   06   05   04   03   02   01   00   99   98

Copy-edited and typeset by Povey–Edmondson
Tavistock and Rochdale, England

Printed in Hong Kong

Contents

Contents

Acknowledgements

First we would like to acknowledge the Economic and Social Research Council, which provided us with substantial financial support for most of the research that underpins this book. Our gratitude is also extended to Professor Gerry Stoker, who was a most effective yet sympathetic coordinator of the Local Governance Initiative, the larger research programme of which our work was a part. Equally, we are hugely in debt to Diane Woodhead and Sally Lane. Diane wrestled with our endless interview tapes, gained command of a rather unresponsive piece of qualitative data analysis software (which we could never understand) and even contrived to remain humorous and good-tempered. Working for us, we doubt if we would have had the same patience. Sally keyboarded most of our material, turning it into what became the last of the many books she has produced – the experience encouraged her rapidly to leave for a new life in Cornwall. We do not expect to see her equal for the speedy and meticulous production of text.

CHRISTOPHER POLLITT
JOHNSTON BIRCHALL
KEITH PUTMAN

List of Abbreviations

CCT	Compulsory Competitive Tendering
CHC	Community Health Council
DES	Department of Education and Science
DoE	Department of the Environment
DHA	District Health Authority
DHSS	Department of Health and Social Security
DMU	Directly Managed Unit
GCSE	General Certificate of Secondary Education
GM	Grant Maintained
GP	General Practitioner
IEA	Institute for Economic Affairs
LEA	Local Education Authority
LSVT	Large-Scale Voluntary Transfer
LMS	Local Management of Schools
NHS	The UK National Health Service
RHA	Regional Health Authority

1 Introduction: The Centrality of Decentralisation

The notion of decentralisation lies at the very heart of the dominant contemporary theories of public management. Decentralisation, the story goes, frees managers to manage. It makes possible speedier and more responsive public services, attuned to local or individual needs. It contributes to economy by enabling organisations to shed ('let go of') unnecessary middle managers ('downsizing'). It also enhances efficiency by shortening what were previously long bureaucratic hierarchies ('delayering'). Decentralisation even produces more contented and stimulated staff, whose jobs have been enriched by taking on devolved budgetary responsibilities and by an increased sense of room for manoeuvre. Beyond these administrative and managerial benefits, political decentralisation brings even larger rewards. It makes politicians more responsive and accountable to 'the people', less distant and more trustworthy. All in all, decentralisation is sometimes made to sound like a miracle cure for a host of traditional bureaucratic and political ills. Academics with a taste for postmodernism would no doubt refer to it as an attempt at a meta narrative – a conceptual and linguistic project designed simultaneously to supersede (and therefore 'solve') a range of perceived ills within the previous discourse of public administration. In Whitehall and Westminster almost all political factions support it – the left and right have somewhat different variants of course, but officially the Labour, Conservative and Liberal Democratic Parties all subscribe to the rhetoric of decentralisation. Tony Blair's Labour administration seems just as enthusiastic about it as were his Conservative predecessors.

Any concept that is so universally popular is bound to attract both academic interest and academic suspicion. In our case decentralisation certainly attracted both. We began with the fairly naive notion that we would go out and see whether managerial decentralisation was really taking place. As is the way with such simple projects, however, our topic complicated itself as soon as we began seriously to think about it.

1

It rapidly became clear that the concept had been used by different writers and speakers in different ways, so that a preliminary job of concept clarification would be needed. Then the idea of doing empirical research began to bristle with complexities. Where should we go to look? Which methods should we use?

Eventually, assisted by a grant from the Economic and Social Research Council, we conducted more than two years of fieldwork research in 12 British public sector organisations, four each from the healthcare, housing and secondary education sectors. This book reports that research but does more besides. It draws on government and other public documents, the general academic literature on decentralisation and the findings of many other researchers. From these ingredients we seek to build an account of both the theory and the practice of the decentralised management of public services. In this account we are able to offer at least preliminary answers to questions such as: Has decentralisation really taken place? *What*, exactly has been decentralised? What seems to have been the effect of decentralisation on the performance of the organisations concerned? And what lessons can be learned from looking at different approaches to decentralisation in different settings and sectors?

The organisation of the book is (we hope) relatively straightforward. In Chapter 2 (Theories and Concepts) we set out the theoretical and conceptual apparatus that we have found most useful in conducting our research and, more generally, thinking through the issues that decentralisation throws up. In particular we distinguish between decentralisation and devolution, and between horizontal and vertical decentralisation. Because of our strong interest in the links between decentralisation, efficiency and quality we also spend some time discussing the concept of organisational performance. Having thus clarified our conceptual vocabulary we briefly introduce the theoretical apparatuses that have informed our investigations. These include rational choice theory, a critical modernist variety of organisation theory and a rhetorical analysis of the kinds of arguments used to sell, defend and attack the different elements of management reform.

Chapter 3 (Reform Doctrines) commences with an examination of what ministers, senior public officials and other prominent 'practitioners' have said about decentralisation. This should give the reader a feel for the rhetorical usages of decentralisation and how the concept has been connected to the doctrine of the 'liberation' of public services managers, that is, 'letting managers manage', or, in its more authoritarian version, 'making managers manage'. This examination of doctrine also allows one to position decentralisation in relation to some of the other key concepts of the New Public Management (NPM), such as efficiency, competition, quality and accountability. Together these terms have fuelled a definite 'community of discourse', or rhetorical theme, which senior officials and prominent politicians of all parties have learned to participate in. The deployment of such words have permitted leaders to ascribe particular meanings to the wholesale restructuring of the British public sector that has taken place since the mid 1980s.

Chapter 4 (Roads to Freedom?) provides the policy background to the findings of research into particular institutions, which are presented in the subsequent three chapters. It delivers brief summaries and analyses of the key policy developments in healthcare, secondary education and socially rented housing from the mid 1980s onwards. This account reinforces the message of Chapter 3, namely that varying notions of decentralisation were quite central to the justifications offered for the public service policy reforms of the late Thatcher and Major administrations.

Chapter 5 is the first of three sectoral chapters. It covers the acute sector of the National Health Service (NHS) and analyses the findings of our own fieldwork research and that of others. The focus is on the scope and nature of the new freedoms, as perceived by NHS managers themselves. Compared with the bold pronouncements of ministers, what was the actual experience of decentralised management at the local level? Has the experience of early pioneers of NHS trust status differed from that of some of the later, more reluctant converts? What evidence is there that greater managerial freedom has led to a change in organisational cultures or to benefits in patient care?

Chapter 6 provides a similar account for the secondary school sector. The experiences of grant maintained (GM) schools and Local Education Authority (LEA) schools are compared. The education sector is especially interesting in that it offers a direct comparison, internal within one sector, of one decentralisation that involves devolution or 'opting out' (that is, opting for GM status) alongside another in which the service delivery unit stays within the existing organisation (LEA) but receives considerably enhanced delegations of budgetary authority (through the Local Management of Schools – LMS – initiative). It is also, of course, a sector where arguments between centralisation and local autonomy, and between different forms of autonomy, have continued to rage on into the Labour administration that took office in 1996.

Chapter 7 deals with the housing sector. Of the three sectors this is probably the one in which the most radical changes have taken place, and in which the market model has been pushed furthest. It is also one in which the policy initiative has not always lain with central government, since to some extent local authorities have been able to respond to Whitehall's schemes with reorganisation ideas of their own.

Having surveyed the impacts of decentralisation in each of our three chosen sectors, Chapter 8 addresses the task of synthesising experience across the UK public services sector as a whole. Titled 'Freedom, Performance and Accountability' it revisits some of the theoretical and doctrinal concerns of Chapters 2 and 3. The evidence is examined for a link (if any) between greater managerial freedom and improved organisational performance. Given greater autonomy, do public service managers 'bring home the bacon', and if so, what kind of bacon is it that they go for? Economy, efficiency, effectiveness and quality are not the only criteria by which the adequacy of public service organisations may be judged. Considerable concern has been expressed over the extent to which greater freedom to manage may have reduced the public accountability of the system. Does decentralisation – contrary to many popular beliefs – actually lead to a 'democratic deficit'? We also compare the three sectors, examining, in particular, the thesis of 'housing exceptionalism', that is, the suggestion that there are characteristics of the socially rented housing sector that make it fundamentally different from both secondary education and acute health care. We argue that both the local characteristics of a particular geographical area and the socio-technical characteristics of a given service are likely to influence the ways in which national policies are implemented by specific institutions. The book closes with some reflections upon both the nature of attempts to restructure our core public services and our efforts to explain and understand them.

2 Theories and Concepts

Introduction

Our principal objectives are to describe and explain a process of management reform. We achieve this mainly (though not exclusively) by analysing a mass of case study material – much of it our own, but some of it drawn from the work of others. Such analysis cannot proceed without, first, a set of organising concepts and, second, some guiding theory or theories. Occasionally commentators will claim that they are eschewing theory and offering 'pragmatic' or 'realistic' explanations, but invariably such accounts can be shown to be saturated with undeclared assumptions, undefined concepts and copious implicit theorising. In contrast we accept the usual academic responsibility to expose and discuss the abstract underpinnings of our work. This chapter is therefore taken up with an explication of our main organising concepts, followed by a discussion of how we have handled the issue of theory.

Organising concepts

It is not practicable to look at every aspect of management reform – certainly not when the reforms possess the variety and complexity of those which were undergone by the UK public sector under Prime Ministers Thatcher and Major. As indicated in the introductory chapter, we have concentrated on the concept of decentralisation. However we have also made extensive use of the related concepts of performance, accountability and control. These have been our main organising concepts.

Decentralisation is itself a complex concept with a considerable history. Its various meanings and connotations have been extensively explored by a number of writers, on whose shoulders we were grateful to be able to stand (Stanyer, 1976; Smith, 1985; Hoggett, 1996).

Common to most of these treatments is an underlying sense that decentralisation involves the spreading out of formal authority from a smaller to a larger number of actors. Thus if, say, the chief education officer of a Local Education Authority was formerly the only officer with the power to authorise expenditure of more than £10000, but after reform the power to authorise such expenditure is also held by the two deputy chief education officers, then a (modest) act of decentralisation has taken place. Notice that we are restricting ourselves here to the exercise of *formal* authority. It is conceivable, of course, that the actual ability to act could be decentralised informally, without any change to the official rules. While there were moments during our research when we encountered evidence of such informal decentralisation, it will not feature as the principal focus of our account.

There are many different ways in which formal authority may be decentralised. We have found it useful to draw three principal distinctions (see Figure 2.1). The first distinction is between *political* decentralisation and *administrative* decentralisation (Birchall, 1996b). In cases of political decentralisation the principal recipients of the decentralised authority include elected politicians and/or the directly elected representatives of some relevant public. Thus, for example, when central government decentralises authority over some particular task (health and safety inspections, transportation projects) to elected local government, then we have a case of political decentralisation. We would also classify as political decentralisation the enhancement of the authority of school governing bodies, where these include a substantial proportion of governors who are elected by parents. This second case shows that political decentralisation does not necessarily have to involve the presence of political parties or elections at which all citizens can vote. It can take the form of the allocation of increased authority to more selective bodies, elected from a sectoral rather than a universal constituency, and where the candidates may be ordinary citizens rather than professional politicians. The principle of democratic representation would still be present. In contrast, administrative decentralisation is said to occur where authority is given to a body that is appointed rather than elected, and that is primarily managerial, administrative or expert rather than political. In the UK the powers given to executive agencies by their parent ministries are examples of administrative decentralisation, as was the creation of National Health Service trusts, which are able to wield authority previously held by the District Health Authorities. One of the notable features of the UK public sector reforms of 1987–97 was that, unlike the parallel reforms in many

Three Strategic Choices

A

POLITICAL DECENTRALISATION

where authority is decentralised to elected representatives

AND/OR

ADMINISTRATIVE DECENTRALISATION

where authority is decentralised to managers or appointed bodies

---

B

COMPETITIVE DECENTRALISATION

e.g. competitive tendering to provide a service

OR

NON-COMPETITIVE DECENTRALISATION

e.g. when a school is given greater authority to manage its own budget

---

C

INTERNAL DECENTRALISATION

within an organisation, e.g. 'empowering' front line staff

OR

DEVOLUTION

decentralisation of authority to a separate, legally established organisation, e.g. when an NHS trust takes over powers previously wielded by a District Health Authority

FIGURE 2.1 Types of decentralisation

continental European states, most of the decentralisation under the British Conservative administration was administrative rather than political (Pollitt *et al.*, 1997a, 1997b). After the Labour victory at the 1997 general election the emphasis switched to political decentralisation, with referenda on the proposals to create Scottish and Welsh assemblies.

A second distinction is between *competitive* and *non-competitive* decentralisation. The kind of administrative decentralisation described in the previous paragraph is essentially non-competitive – authority is delegated from a higher tier to a lower tier within an existing organisation, or from a superior organisation to a subordinate one. Competitive decentralisation, however, takes place when competitive tendering is used. Tendering for the provision of a particular service or set of services does not transfer ownership but does transfer operational authority, within the framework of a contract. Such tendering may occur because a local authority or health authority chooses to put a particular activity out to tender or (as was widespread under the Conservative administrations of the 1980s and 1990s) because the government has decreed competitive tendering compulsory (CCT) for a particular service or activity. Of course in many cases the result of a competitive tendering process is that the contract is won by an in-house unit. This could be termed 'internal competitive decentralisation'. Alternatively, the contract may be won by an external organisation, as when a commercial firm wins a contract to manage part of a local authority's housing stock or provide refuse collection services or grounds maintenance. These cases could be termed 'external competitive decentralisation'. It is worth noting that even when competitive decentralisation results in an internal contractor, the resulting organisational relationships tend to be significantly different from those that result from a simple act of internal administrative decentralisation. The service-providing unit, although in-house, now has an arms-length relationship, through a contract, and can, in the event of unsatisfactory performance, be replaced by an external contractor at a future date.

Competitive tendering has played some part in each of the three sectors examined in this book. It has been particularly important in the field of public housing, but NHS trusts have also contracted out a number of services (for example cleaning and laundry) and under both LMS and GM status schools have been able to let contracts for tasks such as grounds maintenance, repairs and so on.

A third important distinction may be made between acts of decentralisation that are essentially *internal* to the legal form of the organisation concerned and those that entail *a transfer of authority* to a different organisation altogether. The latter tends to be rather a strong form of decentralisation, and we term it 'devolution'. Devolution may itself involve either a transfer of authority between existing organisations or the creation of a new organisation (such as Tony Blair's Scottish Assembly) to receive the decentralised powers. When, during the 1980s, the Swedish government devolved certain powers to the Swedish counties this was a case of administrative devolution from one existing authority to another. However when the NHS trusts were set up it was a case of administrative devolution in which existing, higher level authorities (in this case particularly the District Health Authority) devolved powers to a *new*, devolved legal entity, the NHS trust.

One reason why devolution tends to be a strong form of decentralisation is that it is usually more difficult to reverse than internal forms of decentralisation. If some particular authority is decentralised from a higher to a lower level within the hierarchy of a single organisation (such as a central government ministry or a local authority department) it may be a fairly straightforward process to reverse the decentralisation, that is, to recentralise the specific authority at a higher level. Indeed such recentralisation is a not uncommon bureaucratic response to crises or problems. However, when authority has been devolved to a separate legal entity its recall will probably be a more difficult, long-drawn-out and possibly contentious matter, involving fresh legislation, public squabbles or some combination of these. In the health care sector Blair's 1997 Labour government soon began to discover how difficult it was to dismantle certain aspects of the Conservatives' previous NHS reforms. Subjecting the devolved autonomy of GP fundholders and NHS trusts to greater central or local coordination and control could not be achieved without considerable public argument, and concessions to the GPs themselves.

The fourth distinction we make is between *vertical* decentralisation and *horizontal* decentralisation. This distinction, best known from the organisational analysis of Mintzberg (1979, p. 186) has not hitherto been much used in the UK public management and public administration literature. We borrowed it because it helps capture one important dimension of the evidence we collected. Horizontal decentralisation refers to the extent to which the managerial cadre in an organisation shares its authority with other groups. Thus in a horizontally centralised organisation all executive authority is exercised by managers, who direct all other categories of staff. In a horizontally decentralised organisation certain categories of staff (for example doctors in a hospital or teachers in a school) will enjoy significant areas of autonomy, where they are expected to be self-regulating and self-directing rather than controlled in any straightforward way by managers. One of the themes of many commentaries on the public management reforms of 1987–97 was that, across a variety of public sector organisations, managers were gaining power at the expense of other groups – particularly public service professionals (Harrison *et al.*, 1992; Pollitt, 1993; Fitz *et al.*, 1993, p. 68).

Moving on from the concept of decentralisation, we now turn to that of *performance*. Something of an omnibus concept, during the 1980s 'performance' became a very fashionable term indeed in public management circles (Pollitt, 1986, 1990; Carter *et al.*, 1992; Mawhood, 1997; OECD, 1997). Typically, during this period of fashionability, 'performance' has been defined in terms of the three Es – economy, efficiency and effectiveness. Some have wanted to add a fourth E – equity – but, under the Conservatives at least, equity never seemed to achieve a particularly prominent position in most major policies. 'Quality' was also spoken of as an important dimension of performance, although the term acquired almost as many definitions as performance itself, and is therefore very hard to pin down (Pollitt and Bouckaert, 1995). Given this rather messy state of affairs we will comment briefly on each of the original three Es, and also say a word about quality. However, in our own fieldwork, although we sought information on the performance of the organisations to which we had access, we were careful *not* to impose a single definition of performance on our respondents, but rather to seek to explore with them what their own definitions of performance might be.

Our own definitions of the three Es are fairly orthodox:

- *Economy*: minimising the cost of the resource inputs for an activity, for example was furniture for the hospital bought from the cheapest supplier? Did the contract for mowing the school playing field go to the cheapest contractor?
- *Efficiency*: the ratio between inputs and outputs. To be efficient is to maximise output for a given input or minimise input whilst maintaining a specified output. A school reorganisation that enables more children to be taught by the same number of teachers in the same classrooms as before yields an efficiency gain, as does a rearrangement the staffing of a set of hospital theatres that permits an overall reduction in theatre staff whilst maintaining the same number of operating sessions.
- *Effectiveness*: the extent to which the original objectives of a policy, programme or project are achieved. That is to say, the analysis of effectiveness entails a comparison between, on the one hand, the objectives set at some earlier time and, on the other, the actual outcomes or impacts of an activity or set of activities. If one of the objectives of a hospital maternity unit is to reduce the perinatal mortality rate and it succeeds in doing so, then its activities have been effective.

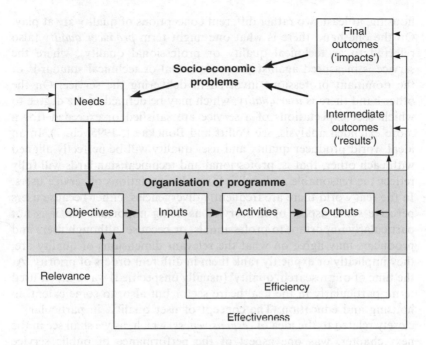

FIGURE 2.2 The input–output model

The above definitions of the three Es are presented in diagrammatic form in Figure 2.2. It should be noted that the three Es do not necessarily march together. An improved performance in one may sometimes be achieved at the cost of a poorer performance in the others. For example, if the lowered perinatal mortality rate in the maternity unit is achieved by lavishly increased resource inputs, then the gain in effectiveness may have been accompanied by decreased economy and reduced efficiency. Similarly, if school class sizes go up so that more children are taught by the same number of teachers in the same building, it is possible that this increase in efficiency could also be the cause of some loss of effectiveness if larger classes mean that individual children receive less attention and therefore the learning process itself suffers.

As far as quality is concerned it seems that, in many of the professionalised public services such as health care, education and housing, at least two rather different conceptions of quality are at play. On the one hand there is what one might term *producer quality* (also referred to as technical quality or professional quality), where the service is measured against the professional or technical standards of the dominant professions involved in delivering the service. On the other hand there is *user quality,* which may be defined as the degree to which user expectations of a service are satisfied or exceeded (for a more extended analysis, see Pollitt and Bouckaert, 1995, ch. 1). In an ideal world producer quality and user quality will be perfectly aligned with each other, that is, professional and technical standards will fully reflect the reasonable and well-informed expectations of service users. In the real world there are frequently divergencies, either because users perceive some aspect of the service as being important but it is not particularly important to professionals, or because, although users and producers may agree on what the relevant dimensions of quality are, they implicitly or explicitly rank them in different orders of priority. At the time of our research 'quality' (usually unspecified) was a much-used term, particularly in the healthcare sector but also, to some extent, in housing and education. The concept of user quality, in particular, is closely related to the idea of *responsiveness,* which, as we shall see in the next chapter, was one aspect of the performance of public service organisations that it was widely claimed would improve as a result of decentralisation.

A third main concept that we (together with many other commentators) link to those of decentralisation and performance is that of *accountability.* By accountability we mean a relationship in which one party (the accountor) is obliged to render an account of his or her actions (or the actions of a particular organisation) to another party (the accountee). In some respects, therefore, accountability is the reverse of decentralisation: in the sphere of democratic governance the allocation of authority is conventionally accompanied by the duty of giving account. Thus it is pertinent to ask, wherever decentralisation has taken place, what kind of account the new holders of decentralised powers are supposed to give, and to whom? In parallel with our earlier distinction between political decentralisation and administrative decentralisation one can think in terms of political accountability and administrative or managerial accountability (Day and Klein, 1987). Political accountability is the requirement laid on political representatives to give a broad account of their stewardship to their electors (as, for example, when ministers answer questions in the House of Commons or school governors provide parents with an annual report on the doings of the school). Managerial or administrative accountability is usually (but not always) slightly more precise. It concerns the success or otherwise of managers in achieving the targets or standards they were set within agreed resource limitations and time constraints. One strong criticism levelled at many of the public management reforms of 1987–97 was that extensive powers had been decentralised to managerially run organisations but that the managers of these were not subsequently held accountable in sufficiently clear and vigorous ways (see the debate between Stewart, 1994, and Waldegrave, 1994).

Finally we turn briefly to the concept of *control*. This we define as the ability of an actor to direct the actions of another – for the first actor to oblige the second (third, fourth and so on) to do things they would not otherwise have done or to refrain from doing things which they otherwise would have done (for an extended analysis see Dunsire, 1978). Our view of control is thus quite close to the classic political science definition of power. The role of the concept of control in public management reform is at times contradictory. Many of the decentralisations we shall be examining were accompanied by rhetoric celebrating the freeing of local service-providing units (grant maintained schools, NHS trusts) from 'bureaucratic control'. Local managers were supposed to acquire new freedoms and, through this increased autonomy, to be better able to respond to local circumstances and agendas. Yet at the same time critics expressed their anxiety that the proliferation of autonomous organisations would lead to fragmentation and loss of overall co-ordination and control. Here the concept of control is being used in a significantly different sense – closer to that frequently used by continental European academics when they refer to 'systems control' (Kickert, 1993, pp. 193–4). For example it may be harder for a Local Education Authority to develop and implement a sensible overall plan for secondary education within its jurisdiction if some of the schools 'opt out' to become grant maintained. The LEA can no longer 'optimise' the distribution of facilities in relation to the forecast population of school age young people because some of those facilities are no longer under its control.

Control is thus Janus-faced – a particular measure of control may be simultaneously regarded as a good thing by some observers and a bad thing by others. It can also be applied at different levels with rather different meanings – either control of a particular individual or organisation by another or, from the systems perspective, as a more impersonal issue of whether or not a system of institutions possesses the capacity to steer itself.

Theories: an overview

Having established working definitions of our main concepts, we now turn to the relationship between the research materials we collected and our use of theory. Case studies are a useful way of testing and illuminating theories (Yin, 1994, p. 27). They are not a reliable basis for statistical generalisation but they can assist in the process of analytical generalisation, especially if they have been appropriately designed. But which theories should we test and illuminate? Which ones are most likely to help us to understand the processes and outcomes of organisational decentralisation and restructuring?

The possibilities are almost endless. First there is a reasonably coherent (yet still diverse) set of theories of collective action, which set out to explain decisions and behaviours in terms of individuals maximising their utility in the light of their (possibly shifting) preference structures and their expectations of the choices of other actors with whom they are in interaction (Dowding, 1994; Dunleavy, 1991; Elster, 1983; Harsanyi, 1986). Second, there are many varieties of institutional theory, all of which share (however loosely) the assumption that 'institutions make a difference' – which in practice usually equates to the idea that organisational structures and procedures affect the way the staff of those organisations think, decide and behave (March and Olsen, 1989; Lowndes, 1996; Ranson *et al.*, 1997). Thus changes in structures and procedures (such as were certainly involved in the reforms we are examining) should lead to new patterns of thought, decision and action. A third body of theory focuses on the texts and arguments used to 'sell' management reform, and seeks to categorise the types of persuasive strategy that are used to convince intended audiences that change is taking place and that it is desirable or, failing that, inevitable (Hood and Jackson, 1991; Perelman and Olbrechts-Tyteca, 1971; Summa, 1992, 1993).

There are certainly other theoretical perspectives, but the above three – theories of collective action, the 'new institutionalism' and rhetorical analysis – are the ones we have chosen to deploy within the present work. We justify our choice on fairly pragmatic grounds. The new institutionalism and theories of collective action are probably the two currently most written-about bodies of theory in the field of public management, and in that sense almost select themselves. Rhetorical analysis is less well known in the English literature but appears to be a useful complement to the other approaches insofar as it concentrates on words rather than actions. Little thought is needed to prompt the realisation that texts are both the main medium and the principal product of management (Summa, 1992, 1993). A Himalayan range of pamphlets, articles, books, memoranda, presentations and speeches has been devoted to decentralisation in particular and public management reform in general. Indeed our ambition is that this book itself might become one of the minor peaks in this impressive formation. So an academic framework intended to facilitate the deciphering and classification of the characteristic arguments used in these many texts should (to adopt a typical rhetorical device) 'add some value'. Particularly so since much of the evidence we gathered came through interviews, in which the managers themselves drew heavily on current rhetorical devices in order to respond to our questions.

However a word of warning is needed before we dive any deeper into the substantive content of our chosen theories. It is not feasible, within a book of this scope, to arrive at some final, definitive judgement about the relative usefulness of the three perspectives identified above. Each perspective contains too great a variety of technical variations and nuances, and in any case a simple empirical test ('does it fit the facts?') would be regarded as crude and inadequate by at least some of the proponents of each perspective. What we are attempting is more modest than a full evaluation. Instead we select the theories put forward by one or two leading exponents of each perspective and simply ask how useful these ideas are in helping us understand the huge decentralisation efforts of the 1980s and 1990s.

Theories of collective action/rational choice

The collective action/rational choice perspective itself contains quite a wide variety of models. Most of these, however, share a number of key assumptions and emphases. These include:

- The fundamental idea that the processes of public governance and management are best explained by using models of the cognitive processes of individuals.
- That individuals possess sets of preferences, and that they can rank these preferences and compare alternative courses of action against them.
- That preference orderings of individuals are logically consistent.
- That individuals operate to maximise their utility, within whatever set of constraints they happen to be operating. Thus individuals act rationally when they make choices that realise their preferences in

the most efficient possible way, thus maximising net benefits (that is, benefits minus costs).

● That individuals are thus largely instrumental and self-interested in their behaviour (Dunleavy, 1991, pp. 3–4).

The simplest forms of rational choice model may seem crude. It appears as though some rational choice theorists envisage a world full of selfish, unremittingly calculative individuals who simply rush around maximising their own utility, free of any other considerations or constraints. However it is not fair to criticise the rational choice perspective on this basis. Theorists working within the perspective have developed sophisticated models that go far beyond this kind of over-simplified and mechanistic picture. Utility theory has been developed to deal with situations in which individuals are obliged to make their choices under risk and uncertainty. Actors are not assumed to be all-knowing and perfectly rational, but merely 'thin' rationalists (Elster, 1983, p. 3), struggling to realise their values (utilities) in conditions of imperfect information where there are many constraints (very much including those set by institutional contexts).

Game theory has been a particularly important branch of rational choice theory for those who wish to study politics, since it deals with choice structures in situations where two or more individuals are interacting in situations where the interests of the 'players' may conflict and where a variety of possible negotiations and bargains may exist (Harsanyi, 1986). A very extensive literature has grown up around the problems of collective action, focusing particularly on the interest group process and party political competition, but also with implica-tions for bureaucratic politics and public management (Dunleavy, 1991, chs 2, 3). During the 1970s and 1980s these rational choice models were brought to bear on the workings of public bureaucracies. Perhaps the easiest way of giving the reader a brief flavour of this still-developing field of 'institutional public choice' is to contrast an early but influential effort at explaining bureaucratic behaviour (Niskanen, 1973) with the more recent and sophisticated 'bureau-shaping model' (Dunleavy, 1991).

William Niskanen's rational choice approach to the behaviour of bureaucratic organisations was set out at length in his book *Bureau-cracy and Representative Government* (1971). In the UK his ideas were given additional momentum by an Institute of Economic Affairs pamphlet published in 1973: *Bureaucracy: Servant or Master?* The title of the latter gives a strong clue as to his main thesis, which is that bureaucrats are usually budget maximisers. Niskanen's ideas were repeatedly quarried by right-wing politicians on both sides of the Atlantic, to the point where some of his theoretical propositions almost achieved the status of conventional political wisdom. That is not to say, however, that Niskanen can be held responsible for all the interpretations applied to, or uses made, of his ideas.

Niskanen proposed that bureaucrats were utility maximisers and that their utility was positively and continuously associated with the size of the budget of the agency that employed them. He argued that, in the annual arguments over budgets, maximising bureaucrats had a number of key advantages over those groups which might seek to restrain budgetary growth. To begin with, he suggested that the political heads of agencies or departments were frequently judged by their success in securing and applying resources within their policy area – in other words they were frequently the allies of budget-maximising bureaucrats rather than a source of restraint. Second, bureaucrats were at an advantage because they were the only ones who really knew the true costs and benefits of producing a given level of service. The scale and complexity of bureaucratic operations in the modern state were such that very few outside the bureau could hope to equal the expertise and detailed knowledge of those who were its employees. A third major advantage was the monopoly position of most bureaucratic agencies. They did not have to face the efficiency pressures that come with competition. In combination, these advantages typically led to bureaucrats heavily oversupplying their services, that is, they produced goods and services well beyond the point at which the marginal costs of production exceeded the marginal value of the additional units of production to society as a whole. In this technical sense, bureaucracies were hypothesised as being inherently wasteful. It is worth dwelling on this point for a moment because it has frequently been misunderstood or misrepresented. As Dunleavy (1991, p. 160) points out, Niskanen was not arguing that the bureaucratic production of goods and services is always inefficient (taking inefficiency as the input–output ratio, as defined earlier in this chapter). Bureaucratic services may also be quite effective (for example hospitals may be good at curing patients and schools effective at teaching children), but even if these virtues are present the bureau is nevertheless delivering more of its product 'than society at large or the sponsor body require' (ibid.)

The conclusions that Niskanen drew from his analysis were music to the ears of new right politicians. In his IEA pamphlet he boldly stated that 'All bureaux are too large. For given demand and cost conditions both the budget and the output of the bureau may be up to twice that of a competitive industry facing the same conditions' (Niskanen, 1973, p. 33).

Although influential, Niskanen's analysis was subsequently the target of some powerful criticisms. Goodin (1982) pointed out that Niskanen's conception of the role of legislative oversight of bureaucracy was tailored much more to the US split between a powerful Congress and a relatively constrained executive than to UK executive–legislature relations. Among many other critiques, Dunleavy's (in a book that was otherwise concerned to establish the value of the rational choice approach) was probably the most comprehensive (Dunleavy, 1991, pp. 162–73). Dunleavy identifies the following weaknesses in Niskanen's model of bureaucratic behaviour.

First, Niskanen made no systematic allowance for differences between different types of bureaucracy. Generally he assumed that all bureaucracies are of the classic, unitary, hierarchical, service-delivering type. Dunleavy suggests that this bias in Niskanen's work may owe something to his own formative experiences working as an economist in the US Department of Defense. Niskanen's formulation apparently excludes the possibility of 'collective action' problems within a given bureaucracy, that is, the assumption seems to be that senior bureaucrats will pull together and speak with one voice, rather than allowing that there may be differences of preference and strategy that cause internal conflicts and waverings in the general trajectory of the department or agency concerned.

Second, following from the first point, Niskanen offered an unvarying, generic model of bureaucratic behaviour that fails to acknowledge the possibility that different bureaucrats in different types of agency might value different kinds of outcome. There is little space in the model, therefore, for significant variations in the objectives and/or strategies of different departments/agencies.

Third, Niskanen's analysis is focused on the individual bureaucratic organisation and says very little about larger interactions between such organisations, either horizontally (between different agencies operating in the same policy field) or vertically (between national, regional and local bodies). Niskanen's theory therefore says little about the whole field of interorganisational governance, although this has attracted a good deal of commentary and analysis from other academic writers over the last 20 years or so (see, for example, Halachmi and Boorsma, 1998; Kooiman, 1993). In effect, Niskanen seems to have made the dangerous assumption that one can generalise from the behaviour of individual organisations directly up to the behaviour of the state apparatus as a whole.

Dunleavy's 'bureau-shaping' model was developed specifically in an attempt to remedy some of the defects of Niskanen and other early rational choice theorists. In his book *Democracy, Bureaucracy and Public Choice* (1991) Dunleavy first sets up his bureau-shaping model and then compares it, point by point, with Niskanen's work. The key points in Dunleavy's model are set out below.

Like earlier theorists – indeed with greater rigour than some – Dunleavy assumes that bureaucrats maximise their own utilities. That is, there is little or no place in any of these models for altruistic or other-regarding behaviours. However Dunleavy's model specifies a more explicit and detailed set of bureaucratic utilities, plus classifications of types of budget and types of agency. In all these three respects, therefore, it is a more fine-grained and flexible model than Niskanen's.

With regard to bureaucratic utilities, Dunleavy assumes that bureaucrats will, *inter alia*, positively value individually innovative work, longer time horizons, a high level of discretion, relatively low public visibility, small, collegial work units, congenial personal relations, close proximity to centres of political power and metropolitan locations that are conducive (together with the above factors) to high social status. He further assumes that bureaucrats will generally wish to avoid the opposites of these utilities, that is, routine work with short time horizons, severely limited discretion, large work units, extended hierarchies, coercive and conflictual patterns of work and personal relationships, peripheral locations and so on.

Dunleavy produces a particularly interesting disaggregation of organisational budgets. He distinguishes between an agency's core budget, its bureau budget, its programme budget and its super programme budget. The *core budget* basically comprises the direct running costs of the agency. The *bureau budget* encompasses the core budget plus agency expenditures that go to the private sector through the award of contracts or through transfer payments to individuals or firms. Thus the bureau budget includes all expenditures that are directly controlled by the agency's own decisions. The *programme budget* includes the bureau budget but it also encompasses resources that the agency passes on to other public sector bodies for them to spend. The agency is accountable for these funds, but does not necessarily directly control the decisions about exactly how they are applied. For example a local education authority allocates money to schools, but cannot control the precise manner in which the schools spend much of their money. The *super programme budget* consists of the programme budget plus any spending by other agencies (from their own resources) for which the superordinate agency retains some policy responsibilities or planning controls. Thus, for example, an NHS trust may raise money through its own income-generation activities (shops in the hospital entrance, sponsorship and so on) but the Department of Health still retains overall policy responsibility for the services delivered by trusts and thus retains an interest in the way in which such income is spent. The main advantage of distinguishing between these different types of budget is that it allows Dunleavy to argue that bureaucrats at different levels are likely to wish to maximise some components of the budget more than others. For example it is argued that top-level officials are most often interested in maximising the bureau budget, whereas the interests of lower-ranking officials will be more directly served by increases in the core budget. An expanded core budget is likely to improve job security and career prospects, and possibly wage levels – all of which are of considerable salience to low-ranking officials. For top officials, however, the level of job security is already high and career positions have to a considerable extent already been achieved. For them, increasing the interest and status of their work is more likely to come from enhancing the power, influence and patronage of the bureau, all of which are served by creating slack in the bureau budget so as to be able to improve relations with clients or contractors and generally exert more influence through enhanced 'purchasing power'.

Unlike Niskanen, Dunleavy has made extensive attempts to apply his model in practice, that is, to test it against empirical data. This has involved the development of a typology of agencies. Each type of agency is defined in terms of a different balance between the four different types of budget. *Delivery agencies* produce services that they offer to citizens (or firms) using their own staff to carry through the processes of implementation. According to Dunleavy, they tend to take the form of line bureaucracies and to be quite labour intensive. Their core budgets absorb a high proportion of their bureau and programme budgets, with staffing costs a particularly prominent item. Usually there is little or no super programme budget beyond the programme budget. An NHS trust is a good example of a delivery agency, with staff costs typically counting for two thirds to three quarters of the entire budget.

Regulatory agencies have the task of controlling the behaviour of other organisations (public or private sector) or individual citizens. They tend to have much smaller budgets than service delivery agencies since they are usually able to transfer many of the costs onto those who are being regulated (for example if the water regulator – OFWAT – decides to limit the price of water then the water companies have to bear the costs and loss of revenue resulting from that decision). As with service delivery agencies, the core and bureau budgets of regulatory agencies account for most of their programme budgets, and they tend not to have super programme budgets.

Transfer agencies are responsible for paying subsidies or benefit entitlements to citizens or firms. In contrast with service delivery agencies and regulatory agencies the core budget of transfer agencies usually represents a very small proportion of the bureau budget. Here the programme budget or bureau budget may be expanded without any proportionate increase in the core budget. If, for example, the government were to decide that unemployment benefit should be raised, exactly the same Benefits Agency staff, using the same computers, could pay out larger sums to each entitled claimant.

A fourth type are *contracts agencies* whose business it is to develop service specifications or capital projects and then let contracts for the completion of such projects. Unsurprisingly, the bureau budgets of contracts agencies are usually much larger than core budgets, and there tends to be little programme budget beyond the bureau budget. Dunleavy gives the example of the US space agency NASA. It has 22 000 staff to conduct research and development and prepare contracts. The core budget is $2.2 billion and the programme budget $10 billion, the difference between the two figures being mainly accounted for by contracts with private firms (Dunleavy, 1991, p. 186).

The final main type is the *control agency,* whose main job is to supervise other public sector organisations, including specification of their terms of reference, standard operating procedures and budget rules. In these cases the bureau budget may be only a minor part of the programme budget. Insofar as control agencies supervise subnational governments or quangos, their super programme budgets may also be much larger than their programme budgets.

Dunleavy also mentions taxing, trading and servicing agencies, but these need not concern us in our present analysis. What is important for our analysis here is the fact that all three types of organisation covered by our main fieldwork are clearly service delivery agencies. Thus we will need to pay particular attention to what the bureau-shaping model predicts as typical behaviour for this type of organisation. Since our research was focused mainly, but not exclusively, on senior managers we will also pay particular attention to the predictions the bureau-shaping model makes for that specific group. In addition, however, consideration of control agencies is necessary since (as indicated earlier) we are concerned with the issue of accountability and the way in which relatively autonomous public service delivery agencies, operating within newly created quasi markets, can be controlled and held accountable for their strategies and performance.

The bureau-shaping model yields fairly definite predictions about the nature of the behaviour of different bureaucratic groups. It distinguishes between individual bureaucratic strategies and collective strategies. An *individual strategy* might be employed by a particular official to try to get him/herself transferred to a high-status policy analysis unit, located in London and working closely to a minister or ministers. However, what we are more interested in are *collective strategies*, that is, how the leaders of an organisation as a whole strive to change it so as to maximise those values they are most concerned with. Dunleavy (ibid., pp. 203–5) suggests that there are five bureau-shaping strategies that are likely to prove particularly popular:

- *Major internal reorganisations*. These can be aimed at demarcating, protecting and resourcing high-status, policy- and strategy-making functions. In other words, a stronger organisational distinction can be drawn between policy making and operations within a particular agency or, better still, routine operations can be hived off to a separate and subordinate organisation.
- *Internal work practices* can be reformed by introducing more sophisticated management and policy analysis systems. These create more work for high-level professional staff and progressively relieve them of routine operational tasks.
- *Redefinition of relationships with external 'partners'*. 'Where agencies deal extensively with external organisations – such as subordinate public agencies, contractors, regulatees or client interest groups – these relationships can be readjusted so as to cut down on routine work load while maximising the agency's policy control' (ibid., p. 204).
- *Competition with other agencies*. If agencies are in a situation where they are obliged to compete with other agencies, then a rational strategy would be to try to export low-status, routine tasks to their rivals, whilst maximising their own command of high-status tasks. For service delivery agencies this might well be translated into an attempt to capture more high-status service users and export low-

status (difficult, costly, controversial) service users to other agencies that provide the same service.

● *Hiving off and contracting out.* This is another way of increasing the proportion of non-routine, high-status activity within an agency. Dunleavy gives the example of the 1985 transfer of responsibility for housing benefit administration from the Department of Health and Social Security to local authorities. This was a complex and trouble-some system of routine benefit administration that (Dunleavy implies) the ministry was happy to be able to offload onto local authorities.

One of the obvious advantages of Dunleavy's bureau-shaping model is that it allows us to distinguish between different types of context in which public officials pursue their interests (the different agency types). This idea of institutional contexts is also important when we come to that species of rational choice thinking known as 'game theory'. As individuals strive to maximise their utilities – whether individually or collectively – their efforts are shaped and constrained by a variety of context-dependent rules and barriers. Many of these rules and barriers derive from a specific institution or organisational form. Thus, for example, if an individual wants to move from boring routine work into a higher-status post with responsibilities for evaluation and policy analysis, then he or she will need to pay attention to the specific rules governing promotion and transfer within that organisation. More broadly, the 'moves' that an organisation can make in terms of shifting resources into promising new activities and abandoning old activities will be governed by the specific legal framework for that organisation (does the founding statute permit diversification; is it allowed to cease to perform certain existing activities?), and probably by the financial regulations governing the budgeting process as well. In short, institu-tions, and networks of institutions, embody many of the 'rules of the game' within which public officials operate. Thus when institutions are reformed and restructured, and when new institutions are created, opportunities arise to change the structure of the games themselves.

Game theory was originally developed by mathematicians, and many of the publications in the field contain sophisticated quantification. We will not be using game theory in this precise, mathematical way. Rather we will be looking in a general way at the types of game that are played, and how (if at all) management reform has altered the rules. Obviously decentralisation itself (as we have defined it) embodies a potentially very significant change in the rules. It should mean that local actors gain a wider choice of options and central actors relinquish some of the controls and constraints they formerly exercised. One question that can therefore be asked is whether the local actors have actually sensed a real change in the nature of the game, and altered their tactics accordingly? A further question is whether the nature of the game itself may have changed? For example games can be thought of as zero sum (if one player gains the other must lose), bargaining (a game where the interests of players diverge but where, through negotiation, solutions can be found that will benefit more than one player) or cooperative (where active cooperation between the players can be seen to bring benefits for all). One could think of applying these concepts to, say, the annual contract negotiations between a health authority (purchaser) and an NHS trust hospital (provider). How does the game that is played between these two parties compare with the previous arrangement, where a District Health Authority allocated funds to the hospitals within its jurisdiction?

Another example of the application of a game theoretical perspective is Bengtsson's study of Swedish housing organisations (Bengtsson, 1995). In that study the author argues that games over tenure legislation have been crucial to the development of housing policy and that changes in such legislation marked 'critical junctures' at which new institutional rules afforded different areas of discretion to the key players. Like Bengtsson, we will, in later chapters, explore the value of a game theoretical perspective as a descriptive metaphor for the decentralisation reforms that are our focus.

To conclude our consideration of Niskanen and Dunleavy it may be useful to summarise some of the predictions of bureaucratic behaviour that their versions of rational choice theory generate. In later chapters we can then attempt to assess how far these predictions have been borne out in the empirical research that we and others have carried out into recently-decentralised service delivery agencies.

The predictions that can be made on the basis of Niskanen's model are fairly simple and can be summarised as follows:

- Public managers will consistently seek to maximise the total budgets of their organisations.
- They will also seek – as far as possible – to conceal or obscure the true costs of their operations and the fine detail of exactly how they produce the goods and services which their organisations are responsible for delivering.

- The budgets and outputs of such organisations will be much larger than would obtain in a truly competitive environment. Therefore one might expect to see any increases in the competitiveness of the environment resulting in reductions in either budgets or service output, or both.
- 'Among the several variables that may enter the bureaucrat's motives are: salary, perquisites of the office, public reputation, power, patronage, output of the bureau . . . all are a positive function of the total budget of the bureau during the bureaucrat's tenure' (Niskanen, 1973, pp. 22–3).

Unsurprisingly, the more sophisticated bureau-shaping model yields a richer menu of predictions. Bearing in mind that our focus is on senior managers within local service delivery agencies, we may interpret Dunleavy's work as pointing towards the following.

First, top-level staff are more likely to be interested in boosting the prestige of their organisation, improving relations with clients or contractors, protecting or creating slack within the bureau budget, increasing their powers of patronage and reducing conflict within the work place.

Second, some of the most obvious ways of doing this will be to delegate or hive off routine work in order to concentrate on strategy-making 'policy analysis' and 'diplomatic' relations with other bodies. The latter are all high-status, high-discretion and intrinsically interesting tasks relative to routine operations (incidentally the performance of these tasks is also usually more difficult to measure, which is one reason why they tend to involve high levels of discretion).

Third, since, in delivery agencies, the core budget may take up most of the programme budget, senior officials in this type of agency are likely to be found arguing for programme budget increases. In this sense the leaders of service agencies are likely to behave differently from those in control agencies or transfer agencies. For leaders in the latter two types of organisation few direct personal benefits are likely to follow from increases in the programme budget – senior officials are more likely to look for ways of maximising the core or bureau budgets.

Fourth, the bureau-shaping model also predicts that, in pursuit of their interests, the leaders in service delivery agencies are likely to indulge in extensive internal reorganisations and transformations of working practice in order to increase the proportion of high-status work undertaken at the top of these organisations and delegate routine work to staff lower in the hierarchy, or even contract it out altogether.

The new institutionalist perspective

Having dealt with the implications of rational choice theory at some length, we can now turn to the work of the 'new institutionalists'. In two interconnected ways this corpus is more difficult to summarise and adapt to our present purposes than is the rational choice approach. First, the new institutionalists are a diverse group and do not share a set of common assumptions and simplifying hypotheses to the same extent as do the adherents of the rational choice approach. Second (and partly as a consequence of the first characteristic) it is harder to extract (at least from most institutionalist texts) a clear set of testable propositions about organisational behaviour (Dowding, 1994). As exemplified by leading writers such as Di Maggio and Powell (1991) or March and Olsen (1989), this approach is more a question of concept building, taxonomising and the advancement of interpretive strategies than it is a matter of generating firm predictions. Because it has this nature, the new institutionalism can be both rewarding and frustrating for those who – like us – wish to apply it empirically. It is rewarding because of the richness of interpretation and the wide range of organisational phenomena it appears capable of encompassing. It is frustrating, however, because the generality of much of the writing makes it difficult to formulate tests that could convincingly confirm or falsify the ideas that are being put forward.

We are not able to cover all the varieties of new institutionalism here but will confine ourselves to two of the main sets of ideas. The first is that of seeing the activity of public management not as a process of maximising utilities but rather as one mainly characterised by norm-governed activities. March and Olsen (1989, p. 22) put it like this: 'Action is more often based on identifying the normatively appropriate behaviour than on calculating the return expected from alternative choices.' They suggest that most behaviour in organisations (both public and private) follows a 'logic of appropriateness associated with obligatory action' rather than a 'logic of consequentiality associated with anticipatory choice' (ibid., p. 23). This view leads the authors to be suspicious of claims that organisations can be radically reengineered and transformed within short periods of time. They attempt to show how efforts to restructure organisations are easily and frequently diluted, absorbed or reshaped so as to conform with prior norms and patterns of behaviour. March and Olsen also point to the extent to which attempts at change generate unexpected consequences, which then require further attention and may divert the efforts of reformers from their original goals. In short, the picture of organisations that March and Olsen offer is a fairly conservative one: organisations are fairly solid bodies with well-established routines and norms, and can usually be changed only incrementally.

A second set of institutionalist ideas stresses the need that managers have for legitimation. From this point of view restructurings and the adoption of new management concepts may be undertaken as much in order to 'look good' and to 'keep up with the others' as to achieve defined performance gains in efficiency or effectiveness. It is suggested that organisations are driven to incorporate practices and procedures defined by prevailing rationalised concepts of organisational work and institutionalised in society, and thereby increase their legitimacy and survival prospects independently of the immediate impact of the acquired practices and procedures.'

Similarly Di Maggio and Powell (1991) identify a process of 'isomorphism', whereby organisations follow fashions and copy each other. They classify isomorphism into three categories:

- *Coercive isomorphism*, where the state obliges organisations to adopt certain forms (for example when the government decided that certain local government services must be subjected to compulsory competitive tendering, or that the 'Investors in People' programme will be adopted right across the civil service).
- *Mimetic isomorphism*, where organisations voluntarily copy each other in the hope that identifying themselves with prevailing trends will bring legitimacy. Countless waves of management fashion could be cited to illustrate this process – management by objectives, total quality management, reengineering and so on.
- *Normative isomorphism* is driven by professional and occupational socialisation. Again, many examples could be given of the attempts of managers to turn themselves into a profession, with its own institutes, journals, training programmes, awards and accreditation.

All these activities are seen not so much as substantive attempts to improve organisational performance (although many of those involved may believe that that will be one of the results) as a strategy for building new forms of meaning and status. The world of management reform is seen as full of myths and stories, told with the purpose of validating certain types of attitude and behaviour whilst devaluing others. Most organisations tend their own crop of tales of victories and disasters. In the (frequent) absence of hard evidence of management reforms achieving their stated goals (Pollitt, 1995), myths, tales and symbols may become the normal currency of everyday organisational life. Whether these stories are strictly accurate (or even true at all) is not the main point. For they are 'cautionary tales' that have the function of illustrating and reinforcing current definitions of appropriateness and inappropriateness, legitimacy and error.

Rhetorical analysis

Although they do not come from the same intellectual stable, there is a link between new institutionalist views of management as a legitimising process and those of other theorists whose prime focus is on rhetoric and argumentation. The founding writers on 'the new rhetoric' saw that argument and persuasion were central to human affairs, but also that strict demonstration-by-logic-and-evidence was far from the only means by which persuasion could be accomplished. 'Rhetorical argumentation, as another strategy of reasoning and persuasion besides demonstration, aims at conclusions that are acceptable not only intellectually but also socially and emotionally' (Summa, 1993).

Rhetorical analysis is fundamentally different from the rational choice approach (and from other theories that attempt to uncover the 'objective' factors that produce given behaviours or changes in the performance of public sector organisations). Hood and Jackson (1991, p. 10) put it like this: 'Rather than looking only at the objective truth or falsity of administrative doctrines as recipes for better performance, we can treat them as objects of study *in themselves*, deserving to be carefully mapped and catalogued as a set of available ideas. To look at administrative argument in this . . . way, is to start from the proposition that the impact of administrative doctrine is a function of its credibility, not necessarily of its truth.'

Credibility and persuasiveness are at the heart of rhetorical analysis. The aim of such analysis is to uncover the basic forms and mechanisms that allow those producing speech and text (the rhetors) to convince their audiences that what they say is right. In this theoretical perspective the term 'rhetoric' is used in a neutral way: it denotes processes of selecting and shaping arguments that are present not just in the speeches of politicians but in *all* those written and spoken texts which have a persuasive purpose (Hood and Jackson, 1991, p. 11; Fischer and Forester, 1993; Summa, 1993, p. 219).

There are a number of different approaches to rhetorical analysis. One, based on the rather disparate group of writers sometimes referred to as representing the 'new rhetoric', is of a generic type and can in principle be applied to any piece of text. Summa (1992, 1993) has attempted to make use of these ideas within the specific field of bureaucracy and planning. She identifies at least four important elements which require attention.

First, there is the question of the identity of the audience. To what audience is the rhetor directing his or her arguments? Sometimes it may be a 'universal' audience – an appeal to common sense or popular sentiment. Sometimes a more specific audience may be in mind – managers, taxpayers, newspaper correspondents and so on. The intended audience is not necessarily the actual audience in front of a speaker. For example a minister may make a speech in the House of Commons that is much more intended to capture the attention of journalists and grab headlines than to convince or impress the other MPs in the chamber ('playing to the gallery'). We are all likely to use a different mixture of arguments and styles when addressing a group we know well and believe to be friendly than when addressing an audience that is relatively unknown or believed to be hostile.

Second, it is often important to look for the starting points in an argument – those assumptions on which the overt elements of persuasion are based. One might think of these as attempts at 'prior agreements' between the rhetor and the intended audience. Examples in the field of public management reform are not hard to come by. Ministerial speeches during the 1980s frequently assumed that the private sector was more dynamic and efficient than the public sector. Another common starting point was that the current levels of spending could no longer be afforded, and that savings had to be made. In the late 1980s and early 1990s a third assumption that was often articulated was that change was inevitable – nothing could stand still (an idea popularised by management gurus such as Tom Peters with his book *Thriving on Chaos*). These sorts of assumption were very rarely justified by any detailed presentation of evidence – indeed the available evidence on all three of the starting points identified above was highly contestable.

Third, most rhetors make frequent recourse to metaphors and other types of analogy. Famously, Margaret Thatcher likened public expenditure to a housekeeping budget. In the specific field of planning examined by Summa, 'efficiency' and 'flexibility' were frequently used dormant metaphors (Summa, 1993, pp. 227–9). They were terms with positive connotations, but in metaphorical rather than substantive ways, that is, some arrangements would be referred to as 'efficient' although no information on input–output ratios would be given (and might not even be available). We certainly encountered a very similar use of 'efficiency', 'responsiveness' and 'quality' in our own research. It would not be over-harsh to say that 'efficiency' and 'quality' were much more talked about than measured.

A fourth principle element in the 'new rhetoric' approach is an examination of the way in which three different aspects of communications are intertwined. Following Aristotelian notions of rhetoric these are:

- *Logos*: the abstract, logical content of an argument (for example does each statement follow logically from the assumptions of the preceding statement?)
- *Ethos*: how does the rhetor present his/her intentions and moral position? For example does the rhetor present him/herself as an improver, seeking to redress an injustice visited upon a particular group (such as taxpayers or people on NHS waiting lists)? In short, what kind of moral authority is claimed for the text?
- *Pathos*: involves orchestrating the audience's emotions in order to increase its receptivity of the text. For example a minister for education addressing an audience of school teachers may make fond reference to her experiences during her own school days, or a chief executive announcing his departure for another, more highly paid post elsewhere may stress how happy he has been at his present establishment and how much he has valued the sense of trust and teamwork that has obtained. The main point here is that virtually no text – even the driest piece of bureaucratic prose – relies on logos alone. It is always worth looking for the strands of ethos and pathos that are likely to be there, enhancing and modulating the purely rational components of the argument.

The approach of Hood and Jackson (1991) to rhetorical analysis is more specifically geared to the field of public administration. They point out that a number of prominent policy theorists have acknowledged the role of general argument and general advocacy over and above 'pure' rational or scientific analysis (citing both Lindblom and Cohen, 1979, and Majone, 1989).

Hood and Jackson go on to identify a large number of administrative 'doctrines', some of which are highly relevant to the present book. They point out that these doctrines often come in opposing pairs, for example in one period the dominant argument will be that large-scale organisations have powerful advantages, whilst in the next it will be held that 'small is beautiful' (Hood and Jackson, 1991, pp. 71–5). Of course these – and other – doctrines do not just float free of any support. Each is buttressed by a set of typical justifications. Each justification emphasises some particular value. The number of these value-laden justifications is much smaller than the total number of administrative doctrines, that is, a relatively small stock of justifications must be mixed and remixed to support a population of doctrines that runs into three figures. Hood and Jackson classify these crucial justifications in terms of the types of value they promote:

- *Sigma-type justifications* emphasise the need to match resources to tasks. They include arguments for avoiding waste, increasing efficiency, minimising confusion.
- *Theta-type* justifications, in contrast, stress the importance of fairness, honesty, integrity, transparency and democratic accountability. Bias, corruption and secrecy should be eliminated.
- *Lambda-type* justifications are those relating to reliability, robustness, the capacity to withstand pressures and shocks, adaptivity and so on (ibid., p. 14).

Take for example the doctrine that 'small is beautiful'. A common justification is that size brings about waste and diseconomy (sigma-type). It may also be argued that small organisations are more easily held accountable and are more 'accessible' and transparent to local citizens and users (theta-type). Similarly, the doctrine that it is good to encourage a diversity of types of public service delivery organisation rests on the 'sigma-type claim that there is no single uniform best way of organisation irrespective of time and context' (ibid., p. 76).

When a dominant doctrine ('big is best') is displaced by a very different doctrine ('small is beautiful') this is seldom because some conclusive new piece of evidence has just appeared. On the contrary: 'Administrative doctrines "win" over potential rivals by a social process which labels them as the received view, accords them prominence and ignores competing doctrines or treats them as heresies or outdated ideas. Conviction is achieved mainly by timing, packaging, presentation, not by objective, conclusive demonstration of the superiority of one doctrine over its rivals' (ibid., p. 17).

Concluding remarks

In this chapter we set out the main concepts used in our research (decentralisation, accountability, performance, control) and summarised three bodies of theory that appear potentially useful for 'explaining' the evidence we have collected. The three perspectives from which we have selected the ideas of prominent theorists are rational choice, the new institutionalism and rhetorical analysis. Each perspective has a number of important subvariants, but since we are focusing only on chosen elements that seem, *prima facie*, relevant to decentralisation, we do not need to burden the reader with the full complexity of all the possible variants. It is, however, important to understand that each of our three perspectives 'explains' in a different way. Rational choice theory seeks to model direct changes in behaviour, and therefore in outcomes. It postulates that, under given conditions, certain causal processes will lead to specific results. The approach of the new institutionalists is more oblique and interpretative. They offer a way of seeing public management as much more than just dealing with behaviour, decisions and results. They lay stress on the fact that managers (and even more so politicians) are continually concerned not merely with events, but with assigning *meaning* to events. Certain events (and persons) will be mythologised – selected to act as symbols and representations of larger purposes. Thus the management of meaning becomes as important as the management of resources. Performances are seen to consist of reputations and styles as well as of tangible achievements. Finally, rhetorical analysis directs our attention to the manifold ways in which arguments are put together and 'won'. Here the focus is on the constituent parts of an argument – how rational, emotional and ethical strands are woven together in order to convince a specific audience that reform (or resistance to reform) is the right course of action. Rhetorical analysis and institutional interpretation are thus less directly open to empirical falsification than are rational choice approaches, since they yield less definite predictions of what will happen in a given situation. According to intellectual taste, one might therefore say that this makes our second and third perspectives less powerful or more subtle!

It will not have escaped the reader's attention that this book is itself a management text. No academic author can claim to stand entirely outside the processes of narrative construction, argument and persuasion. However we will leave it to you, the readers and reviewers, to form your own interpretations of our 'performance'!

3 Reform Doctrines

Introduction

The previous chapter dealt with academic theories and concepts. It is not unusual for such theories to influence public policy makers. For example Nicholas Ridley, a minister who had an important role in shaping some of the policies discussed in this book, was certainly acquainted with, and sympathetic to, Niskanen's theory of bureaucracy. However it is most unusual for policies to be *determined* by theories, that is, to be the direct expression of a coherent set of abstract ideas. Far more common is the situation where policies bear the traces of theories, but are also heavily influenced by short-term practical and political constraints, overarching ideological prejudices, chance contemporary events and a host of other possible factors (see, for example, Dunsire, 1995, p. 29).

In the UK, the central expression of 'policy' has usually been thought of as the ministerial speech or the government White Paper (in contrast to many European countries where 'policy' is more usually identified with the process of making and implementing laws). Media and other commentators search the fine print of ministerial utterances looking for 'changes in policy'. It is in these speeches that one can sometimes discover traces of theories, mixed in with broad statements of ideology and headline-catching 'sound bites'. It is this rich, rhetorical material that we refer to as 'doctrine'. Doctrine is therefore policy that is enunciated, but not necessarily yet programmed (that is, specified as a set of specific actions or procedures), still less implemented (that is, actually carried out). In this chapter we will focus on doctrine or, to put it less ceremoniously, ideas and talk. Then in Chapter 4 we will look at the programming stage – the way decentralisation policies developed as they encountered pressures from within the relevant policy networks, and as practical issues increasingly demanded solutions. In Chapters 5, 6 and 7 we will explore the actual implementation of policies in the health care, education and housing sectors.

The management doctrines of the Conservative government: main themes

Although the history of public management reforms under the Thatcher and Major administrations contains its fair share of twists, turns and *ex post* rationalisation, there was a certain consistency and continuity in the objectives identified by ministers as being of principal importance:

• Greater efficiency.
• Services that were more user-focused and user-responsive.
• Greater political control.
• Tighter control over expenditure.

A number of ministers appear to have shared a Niskanen-like belief that monopoly public services were inherently inefficient, and therefore that considerable efficiency gains should, in principle, be available if these monopolies could be dissolved. Alongside this there was a belief that many of these services were producer-dominated (a belief that the 'new right' shared with the 'new left') and therefore reforms were needed to break through this inflexibility and make services more responsive to users. The belief that public services were essentially run by and for the benefit of those professionals who provided them was also a stimulus to calls for greater political control – though in practice this seemed to mean control by central government rather than by local authorities. The fourth objective – tighter control over expenditure – also has a Niskanen-ish flavour to it. More obviously, perhaps, it was simply the preoccupation of a government that, from the moment it took office in 1979, struggled vigorously, if often unsuccessfully, to restrain the powerful forces fuelling public expenditure growth (Thain and Wright, 1995).

These four themes – together with the assumption that the private sector was inherently more efficient than the public sector – reappeared again and again in ministerial speeches. We may now examine their particular manifestations in the sectors that are to be analysed later in the book.

The National Health Service

In the case of the NHS, the title of the first major policy document issued by the new Thatcher government – *Patients First* – was indicative of the tone it wished set (DHSS and Welsh Office, 1979).

The rhetorical implication, of course, was that some other group had been able to put their interests first, but that this distortion was now about to be remedied. However this concern for the patient was soon allied with a concern for management. The speech of the then Secretary of State for Health and Social Security to the Conservative Party Conference of 1982 was typical:

We want manpower directed at serving the patient, not at building new empires of paper and bureaucracy . . . I intend to establish a small team, headed by people from private industry, to achieve it. Their job will not be to produce a lengthy report – there is no shortage of lengthy reports in the health service – but to help us produce results, not in years, but in months. (Norman Fowler, speaking at the Conservative Party Conference, 7 October 1982)

Note the ingredients of the argument here – bureaucracy must be defeated if the patient is to be served, and the best opponents to set against bureaucracy are private sector managers. This speech was actually the announcement of the setting up of the team that produced the first Griffith Report (National Health Service Management Inquiry, 1983). The report recommended that general managers should be introduced at pivotal points at each main level of the NHS hierarchy. The general managers who began to be appointed in 1984 were to become the chief executives that would run the NHS provider market of the 1990s.

Another feature of this body of doctrine was the assumption that a sense of individual responsibility was lacking in the public services, and that if it could be introduced it would have a cathartic effect. The Griffith Report recommended that the general management function should be the responsibility of one person. In a much-quoted passage the Griffiths team argued that: 'it appears to us that consensus management can lead to *lowest common denominator decisions* and to long delays in the Management process. . . In short, if Florence Nightingdale were carrying her lamp through the corridors of the NHS today, she would almost certainly be searching for the people in charge' (National Health Service Management Inquiry, 1983, pp. 17, 22) The Secretary of State enthusiastically endorsed this view: 'We accept this view; and believe that the establishment of a personal and visible responsibility . . . is essential to obtain a guaranteed commitment . . . for improvement in services' (DHSS Press Release, no. 84/173, 1984).

A later echo of this doctrine is to be found in the 1989 *Working for Patients* White Paper, where it is stated that the managers of trusts 'will be expected to carry more direct responsibility for running their affairs', and that this would 'stimulate greater enterprise and commitment, which will improve services for patients' (Department of Health, 1989a, paragraphs 3.10–3.14).

A more general expression of the desire for individuals to carry greater responsibility came from another senior minister, Michael Heseltine, who, in the 'high Summer' of Thatcherism, wrote that what he wanted of public servants was 'fewer of them, carrying more personal accountability, in a climate of less certain careers' (Heseltine, 1987, p. 57).

The year 1989 was a watershed for the NHS. The publication of *Working for Patients* marked the introduction of a new and untested market-type mechanism, the purchaser–provider split and its associated regime of contracts and competition. The programmatic aspects of this radical reform will be covered in the next chapter, but for the moment we can note how, on the rhetorical level, two new themes were now added to those of the primacy of the patient and the superiority of managers over 'bureaucracy'. These were 'efficiency-through-competition' and 'responsiveness through local autonomy'. The emphasis on competition proved unpopular in the country at large, and was soon put on the back burner. However the issue of local autonomy was linked with that of responsibility, and these, together with the familiar faith in management, were presented as the keys to a better future:

> The separation of purchaser from provider, a particularly acute requirement in a service of such size that the necessary debate about priorities easily gets lost, is being achieved through a system of locally managed hospital trusts, while delegation of financial responsibility has been taken to its logical conclusion by devolving fund holding to individual GPs. (Speech by the Chancellor of the Duchy of Lancaster, 1993 – see Waldegrave, 1994, p. 82)

Once more, the theme of personal responsibility raised its head:

> However devoted and professional the staff, multi-tiered levels of administration [in the NHS] inevitably encouraged buck-passing and discouraged responsibility or personal involvement. As in education, accountability to the citizen, clear enough in theory, was dissipated between too many half-responsible interests. . . Our reforms have

retained the Secretary of State's ultimate responsibility to Parliament for the service as a whole . . . the purpose has been to clear up the confusion below. We have established a firm division between purchaser and provider, which has been absolutely fundamental in clarifying responsibility. And we have delegated the responsibility down to individual units. As a result, management accountability has actually never been clearer. Where there are problems in an individual hospital, it is now the Chairman or Chief Executive of the Trust Board who answers. Not surprisingly, this encourages the feeling of local ownership. (Waldegrave, 1994, p. 85)

Local authority services: schools and socially rented housing

On the whole Conservative ministers were willing to be more out-spoken in their criticism of local authority control than of the NHS. In the latter case their critique was perhaps muted by their knowledge of the enduring public popularity of the service, and the generally high esteem in which the citizenry held doctors and nurses (much higher than that accorded to politicians – see Harrison, 1988, pp. 88–9). In respect of local authorities, however, ministers knew no such restraint: 'Monopoly provision by local authorities has not succeeded. There have been serious problems of management. Thousand of dwellings are left empty. Performance on repairs is poor and insufficient attention is paid to the wishes of the tenant' (Ridley, quoted in Malpass, 1990).

Prior to a 1987 White Paper on housing (Department of the Environment, 1987) there had not been many pronouncements by government ministers on the subject of council housing. What there had been had tended to contrast renting unfavourably with home ownership, using rhetoric stemming from the successful 'right to buy' policy, which had been introduced in 1980. There was also recognition of the particular difficulties caused by the mass housing estates built in the 1960s and 1970s to house people from slum clearance schemes. In 1986 the government 'top sliced' funding from local authority housing subsidies to set up the Priority Estates Project, which worked with authorities on hard-to-let estates and experimented with a concentrated form of local housing management (Power, 1987). The work of Alice Coleman became influential among government ministers and her radical prescription for the redesigning of mass housing estates was accepted: 'estate action' schemes were set up with capital that had been top-sliced from local authority housing investment progrmames (Coleman, 1985). In 1986 an Audit Commission report found that roughly 10 per cent of local authorities were in crisis, in need of funding to deal with the mistakes made in building these systems-built and high rise estates, and in need of a radical improvement in housing management (Audit Commision, 1986). Pamphlets began to be published by Conservative think tanks that were critical of local authority management (Henney, 1985; Bailey, 1987). In particular Alex Henney, having reviewed the progress of the policy of selling council houses to the tenants, concluded that it had its limits and that a million and a half homes were in poor condition and virtually unsaleable. He recommended four objectives: to 'give people more responsibility for and control over, the houses in which they live'; 'to 'reduce the opportunities for patronage and electoral engineering'; to 'introduce more choice and competition'; and to 'lighten councils' burden of managing housing on a large scale' by taking it off them and allowing them to concentrate on core problems (Henney, 1985, p. 19). He proposed a model of a housing management trust that would allow estates to opt out of council ownership.

Behind these objectives were assumptions about the nature of the problem that were at last spelled out in the 1987 White Paper. It declared that the council housing system was 'often not in the tenants' best long term interest', being too large, distant and bureaucratic. The combination of poor design and bad management had alienated tenants, and the quality of the housing and environment had declined. Rents were unrealistically low, leading to inadequate maintenance. One aim was to give 'more opportunity for tenants to control their own destinies' by opting out of local authority control by voting for a new landlord (Department of the Environment, 1987, p. 2). Another was 'a more pluralist and more market oriented system' giving wider choice, more effective use of public money and so on. The role of the local authorities was to change from provision to enabling: 'Local authorities should increasingly see themselves as enablers who ensure that everyone in their area is adequately house, but not necessarily by them' (ibid.)

A new financial regime for council housing would encourage 'more businesslike management of the stock', while new central government agencies known as housing action trusts would take over some of the worst estates, bringing private sector skills and finance to bear on the problem. The rhetoric of the White Paper was quite restrained, but it was the most radical rethinking of the assumptions underlying public sector housing since the beginning of government subsidy in 1919. As we will see in Chapter 7, it was seen by housing managers as a complete undermining of the legitimacy of local authority housing. The forced takeover by housing action trusts was a humiliation for the authorities, which had been attempting to improve their worst estates. The 'Tenants' Choice' mechanism was seen as a way of allowing private developers to pick off estates in areas where land values were high and to asset strip them. The ring-fencing of housing revenue accounts was seen not just as a move towards more business-like accounting but as a way of levering up council house rents. Finally, the whole discourse of the housing policy community was changed from 'providing' to 'enabling'. The stage was set for a battle over doctrine that was to culminate in the local authorities developing their own opt-out me-chanism – the large-scale voluntary transfer to housing associations (LSVT).

Throughout the above there had been a persistent, public choice-ish implication that the local authority bureaucracy was tending to pro-mote its own 'producer interests'. The suggestion was that, in doing so, it increased the cost of local government and reduced the effectiveness of the service to the user. Michael Heseltine made a similar point in a much more sweeping and colourful fashion than the restrained lan-guage of White Papers would permit: 'By 1979 local government had become a barely controllable, free-wheeling employment machine which for year after year had been run largely for the benefit of the machine-minders' (Heseltine, 1987, p. 43).

Freedom from local authority control was also seen as benefiting the education sector. In a speech to the Grant Maintained Schools Foundation in September 1995, the then prime minister, John Major, claimed that 'The liberating effect of independence within the state sector affects the whole atmosphere of the school. Better motivated staff means better motivated pupils. And that means better results. Those of you who run self-governing schools know that' (Major, 1995). Commenting on how the number of grant maintained schools con-tinued to grow (though actually at a very slow pace by that time), Major added that:

> It is against that background of success and expansion, that I set out last month my ambition that all state schools should gain the benefits of becoming self-governing, independent schools free to parents. This is no distant aspiration. Gillian Shepherd and her

Department are now looking at the details of the implications of this policy and the practical options for how we might bring this about. (Ibid.)

Four years earlier another senior minister, Kenneth Clarke, had drawn a parallel between GM schools and NHS trusts: 'The initiative and creative thinking I want to see pervading the whole education service is exemplified, above all, by those schools that go on to seek and achieve grant maintained status . . . The parallel model in the health service is the NHS trusts' (Clarke, 1991).

The similarity of ideas between the creation of NHS trusts and the conversion of schools to GM status was also picked out by the chancellor of the Duchy of Lancaster: 'In education, a parallel process has seen the establishment of grant maintained schools which are helping empower those most concerned with each particular school – the governors, teachers and parents – as opposed to the more distant, and, at times, politically motivated, control of local authorities' (Waldegrave, 1994, p. 83).

Thus in both housing and education the themes of user-responsiveness and empowerment were given great prominence. In both cases ministerial rhetoric suggested that control by an elected local authority was actually dangerous for users' interests – in the case of housing because the local authorities could be remote and inefficient and in the case of schools because they could be remote and/or politically motivated. Later in the book we will attempt to show how and to what degree the new arrangements the Conservative administrations introduced were in fact conducive to the 'empowerment' of which Waldegrave and his colleagues spoke.

The broad perspective: management as the key

Underlying all the rhetoric about the importance of personal responsibility, clearer accountability, weakening producer monopolies and decentralising power there ran a profound belief that better management (rather than, for example, politics) would bring a better future. This founding doctrine was expressed from the early days of Margaret Thatcher's first government: 'Efficient management is the key to the [national] revival . . . and the management ethos must run right throughout national life – private and public companies, civil service,

nationalised industries, local government, the national health service'
(Heseltine, 1980).

More than a decade later, when Thatcher had been succeeded by
Major, the chancellor of the Duchy of Lancaster (then the minister
with responsibility for the public service) reaffirmed this inspirational
vision:

> It took some time for the reform movement to become comprehen-
> sive. But I now believe it has become pretty well comprehensive and
> total. Achieving something like what Osborne and Gaebler [Amer-
> ican authors of the popular 1992 book *Re-inventing Government*]
> have written about . . . However . . . it is a reinvention designed to
> produce responsive management and to raise standards of service
> within existing resource levels – essential if we are to cope with the
> pressures. . . It has increased, not diminished, the individual's prac-
> tical control over the public services provided to him or her. It has
> replaced a system where the control, exercisable in theory, was
> routinely subverted in practice by producer interests. (Waldegrave,
> 1984, p. 83)

This speech powerfully combined three of the four main themes
referred to at the beginning of this chapter: greater efficiency (raised
standards within existing resources), increased user-responsiveness and
tight control over expenditure ('cope with pressures'). The dangers of
monopolistic groups of public service providers are also alluded to. The
only missing theme is that of greater political control. This was an area
of seeming inconsistency within the government's position, in that
improved political control by central government (for example in the
creation of execeutive agencies operating within a ministerially determined framework agreement) was generally portrayed as a good thing,
but improved political control by local authorities tended to be
portrayed as a bad thing ('politically motivated', and so on). In both
cases, however, better management was seen as essential. This was
neatly summed up by the then secretary of state for education (later
chancellor of the Exchequer) in 1992: 'A measure of the success of our
first ten years is that we have restored management to its proper place
in our society' (Clarke, 1992).

It is this prospect of autonomous management as a galvanising force
that the remainder of this book subjects to close scrutiny.

4 Roads to Freedom?

Our task in this chapter is to tell three interrelated stories of how similar forms of decentralisation emerged through a process of policy making in very different sectors of the public services: health, education and housing. The key policy questions have been well expressed by Marsh and Rhodes (1992b) in relation to 'Thatcherite' policy in general: how much change has there been, to what extent has this resulted from a distinct policy agenda, and (particularly pertinent for our three sectors) why has there been less change than expected? They suggest that systematic comparison of different service sectors is necessary if we are to assess the degree of change, and so this chapter will not only be setting the scene for the more detailed study of each sector in Chapters 5–7, but also aims to make its own small contribution to the assessment of the impact of Conservative government policies.

The similarities between the three sectors are interesting, because they confirm that it is possible for an ideologically driven central government to impose its will on a variety of local forms of service delivery agency – despite inherent differences between service characteristics – and to do so remarkably quickly. The differences are interesting because they point to the limits of central power and the problems of implementation, and also because they raise a further question: to what extent are the different outcomes from the policy process in each service area explained by the differential power and interest of the participant organisations, or by inherent differences in service characteristics? We shall explore these questions further in Chapters 5–7, but in this chapter we will take a more conventional view that the outcomes of policy-making are the product of the interaction between different levels of government, pressure and interest groups, individual politicians and professional leaders, the parliamentary process and so on. We provide a micro-level analysis, tracing 'the role of interests and government in relation to particular policy decisions', and concerning ourselves with the 'personal relations between key actors rather than structural relations between institutions' (Marsh and Rhodes 1992a, pp. 1, 7).

In Chapter 2 we identified game theory as a useful theoretical framework; it can be used, as Bengtsson suggests, 'together with empirical observations as a means to reconstruct and clarify historical processes of decision making' (Bengtsson, 1995, p. 231). Policy is not made within stable networks, characterised by routine and shared values and regulated by accepted rules of conduct. It is made in an arena where organisations play an 'iterated bargaining game' in which the decisions of one actor depend on the decisions of other actors in an evolving set of strategies. There are games of 'institutional design', in which the outcome of one game determines the players and what alternatives are open to them in the next stage in the game, and in which there is bargaining over the rules as well as over outcomes. It may be going too far to picture our three policy arenas of education, health and housing as 'nested games', in which the outcome of one affects that of another – the three policies are more independent than that – but we will be noting the points at which actors themselves see parallels between them. Whether the opting out of service delivery agencies can be seen as marking a critical juncture, a 'site of non-reversible change' triggering institutional transformation (Bengtsson, 1995), is arguable; in the case of housing the change probably is irreversible but, as we shall see below, in the other cases the new forms of organisation are highly dependent on central government statute and funding for their continued existence.

These insights from game theory are suggestive, and we will be applying them in the next three chapters in our accounts of each service area. Here, we merely use 'game' as a metaphor and concentrate on telling the three interrelated stories in some detail. We do, however, draw on the insights of a 'power-resources' model of central–local government relations. The players in this 'game' are not equals. They have different levels of resources and require different types of incentive in order to cooperate. Rhodes (1981) identifies five types of resource upon which the players can draw: financial, constitutional and legal, hierarchical, political, and informational. While central government departments are dominant in the first three, considerable informational power rests with the service agencies. They have some political weight as well; they are closer than is central government to the users of services and to local public opinion, and may be able to get these on their side. We might also expect that their relative power and dependency will vary over time, and differ from one sector to another. The strategies of each organisation will also affect their need for resources and incentives; a local authority that is politically in tune with the central department will need fewer resources than one whose ruling group is determined to fight central government policies, and will need fewer incentives to cooperate. We will find that in relation to opting out, those in control of schools, hospitals and housing departments vary in their attitudes.

We shall organise the three accounts into a series of stages. There is 'no agreed characterisation of the stages of the policy process' (Rhodes, 1981, p.109), for instance Hogwood (1987) provides a nine-stage plan of agenda setting, processing of issues, selection of option, legitimation of option, allocation of resources to policy, implementation, adjudication, impact and evaluation. However our plan is simpler. We distinguish four phases: emergence of the idea, development of the policy, implementation and impact. We have to bear in mind that 'Legislation is not the end of the policy process, merely a step en route', that the impact of a policy can be quite different from its intent, and that there can be unintended consequences (Marsh and Rhodes, 1992b, p. 4).

Emergence of the idea of opting out

In education, the early 1980s were a relatively quiet time for policy making. The 1980 Education Act strengthened the role of parents on the governing body, a series of position papers set out good practice for schools, there was an attempt to tighten control over the content of teacher training, and an assisted places scheme was set up to send children to private schools. Underlying these were a desire to promote the consumer interest of parents over the producer interests of the LEAs and teacher unions, to raise standards in education, and to encourage excellence even if this meant greater inequality in provision.

The idea of grant maintained (GM) schools fitted well into this framework. Its genesis can be traced back to 1985. At first it was confused with the idea of direct-grant schools: these were private schools that up until 1976 had received a grant that enabled more than 25 per cent of pupils to take up a free place. A Labour government had abolished the grant, and now Margaret Thatcher was interested in looking again at the question, along with ideas for independently owned primary schools, and centrally funded elite secondary schools which would take the lead in each area (see Fitz *et al.*, 1993). The implication was that state schools, as presently constituted, were unable to meet the needs of the most able pupils.

A logical alternative might have been to free up the funding of education, allowing parents to choose between the private and state sectors. In 1982 proposals for education vouchers were given serious consideration by the Department of Education and Science, but a pilot scheme found it to be 'mostly impractical' (ibid., p. 21). One major problem was that schools had to become cost-centres before they could begin to price their services and so create a market for vouchers. Several publications by new right think tanks then outlined proposals for centrally funded schools that would be independent of LEA control (for details see ibid., p. 22). Despite the lack of enthusiasm for the idea by the education secretary, Kenneth Baker, and officials within the DES, the idea received support from the prime minister and other ministers. The pledge to introduce GM schools was in the 1987 election manifesto, and legislation was enacted the year after. GM schools were to take their place in a quasi-market of LEA schools, new city technology colleges and private schools operating the assisted places scheme.

There are interesting parallels in the health sector. Again, in the early 1980s there was no foretaste of the radical changes to come during the Conservatives' third term, beginning in 1987. There had been compulsory competitive tendering (CCT) of support services, which was reputed to have saved £73 million by 1987, but which seemed to have reached its limits due to a lack of interest from the private sector. There had also been the general management initiative, which broadly had failed to establish managerial control of medical-led expenditure and cash limits were being used as a way of controlling spending. The first pilot projects on clinical budgeting had floundered and were to be rerun (Pollitt et al., 1988). Early in 1987, doctors and nurses had received large pay awards, and the Institute of Health Service Managers (IHSM) had set up a working party on funding, born of managers' frustration with the persistent underfunding of the NHS.

As in education, there was a desire among government ministers to do something radical, but an equal difficulty in doing anything at all about the funding side of the service. There was talk of a move towards the use of vouchers, to an insurance-based system, to levying more charges, but the enduring popularity of an NHS free at the point of use was too powerful a political obstacle. As in education, the government turned to internal changes designed to make the service more responsive and cost-effective. The idea of an internal market had been explored in a Nuffield study by an American, Professor Alain Enthoven, but at this stage it was more an experiment with management contracts – a kind of extension of CCT - than the devolution of entire provider units. By the end of 1987 Margaret Thatcher had given her personal backing to the idea of an internal market, which by now included allowing hospitals to opt out of the NHS and be managed privately (*Health Service Journal*, 15 October 1987). The reaction of the policy community was wholly negative: the Institute of Health Service Management opposed it on the grounds that the market would be 'bureaucratic or random' (*Health Service Journal*, 8 October 1987). The British Medical Association was concerned about the possible restriction of clinical freedom.

The then health and social security secretary, John Moore, would reveal little of the government's intentions for the NHS, but a report from the Centre for Policy Studies (CPS) called for a debate. There is some evidence that the radical plans for housing and education were indirectly putting pressure on those charged with health to come up with something similar; the author of the CPS report, John Peet, declared that 'Education and housing have been put on the agenda but not health' (*Health Service Journal*, 17 March 1988). There were calls for a series of demonstration projects to test out the idea. Comparisons were made with US health maintenance organisations, and the principle derived that purchasing should be split from provision. Independent provider agencies became a precondition for such a market to emerge. They were regarded as a next step from general management; as one expert put it, they would 'give general managers greater freedom in terms of financing and organising locally' (Nick Bosanquet, quoted in *Health Service Journal*, 17 March 1988). John Moore promised a wide-ranging and fundamental NHS review, but Conservative MPs were impatient; a private member's bill introduced by Ann Widdecombe would have abolished the regional health authorities on the ground that in an internal market they would be superfluous. Managers were also beginning to see advantages, expecting that the proposed review would force a relaxation of Treasury rules on capital spending.

As in education, so in health, a radical idea needed a strong political will to bring it to fruition. That willpower came from the prime minister. Stung by continuing adverse media attention, Thatcher chose the TV programme 'Panorama' to announce a wholesale review of the NHS. This review was conducted mainly by politicians and in strict secrecy (Griggs, 1991; Harrison, 1994). The resulting White Paper, *Working for Patients* (Department of Health, 1989a), declared a wish for as many acute hospitals as possible to seek self-governing status as NHS hospital trusts.

In housing, again the early 1980s were a quiet period, with the exception of the 'right to buy' scheme. The 1980 Housing Act had given council tenants the right to buy their homes at a discount, which varied according to how long they had lived there. The policy was outstandingly successful, and it led to the loss of some of the best council stock, particularly in rural and suburban areas where later the idea of voluntary transfer would prove attractive, partly because new housing association tenants would no longer have this right. In 1986 a new Housing Act allowed local authorities to enter into partnership agreements with private developers and this led to a few interesting schemes, but only in those areas where run-down council estates coincided with high land values, so that spare land and buildings could be traded for new or renovated council homes. However, behind what looks like a relatively quiet time the government was using its revenue subsidy to local authorities to force up council house rents, and was also using a housing investment programme inherited from the Labour government ruthlessly to cut back spending on new building. The statutory duty of local authorities to house those deemed homeless under the 1977 Homelessness Act had to be fulfilled, yet expensive bed and breakfast accommodation was being resorted to because local authorities had fewer and fewer new lettings of their own with which to meet the growing need. There was a growing sense of frustration among housing managers and local politicians.

The immediate catalyst for the development of voluntary transfer was the 1987 White Paper on Housing (Department of the Environment, 1987), which made it clear that the government no longer saw local authorities as natural providers of social rented housing, but as enablers who would stimulate and coordinate local housing markets in favour of provision by other agencies (notably, in the case of social rented housing, the local housing associations). This rhetoric of enabling would not have been sufficient on its own to spur local authorities to get rid of what had been one of their primary functions (and in the case of district councils, *the* primary service function). But it signalled an intention, backed up by the introduction of the 'tenants' choice', to allow private landlords to purchase council estates. Nicholas Ridley, who claimed to be the originator of the GM schools idea, was also behind the tenants' choice legislation. This was seen as a very real threat. It was also felt to be a turning point in that the government was obviously concerned more with changing the terms under which housing was consumed than with the problem that dominated the local agenda – the construction of new housing.

On the other hand, for housing providers the effects of transfer to a housing association would all be positive. First, it would preserve most of the housing stock, since new tenants would be assured association tenants and would not have the right to buy. Second, providing the valuation of the stock was right, rents could be kept down while major repairs could be funded. Third, the capital receipt obtained by the local authorities could be used, after paying off the remaining housing debt, for the construction of new homes by housing associations.

Development of the policy

In education, though the GM schools idea went quickly into legislation in 1988, there were differing views on the ultimate goal. Thatcher thought that most schools would want to opt out and that the policy would allow them to become selective, but Kenneth Baker, Education Secretary, was more cautious about the initial impact and had reservations about allowing them complete freedom on admissions. As Fitz *et al.* (1993, p.25) note, it was Baker's view that prevailed. However, in a speech early in 1991 Kenneth Clarke, Health Minister, made explicit links between GM schools and health trusts, saying that trust status would become the 'natural organisational model' for providers, and that there were 'similar possibilities' for schools, especially secondary schools (quoted in ibid., p. 13). During the short period of consultation in the summer of 1987, almost all those who responded and who wrote in the education press were against it. Some saw it as a route towards selective schooling, with GM schools only needing to control their own admissions to become, in effect, grammar schools; at the very least they would become an elite and increase inequality between schools. Others were worried about the loss of LEA control over strategic planning; GM schools could not be closed even if there were a surplus of places locally, and their opting out would lead to difficulties in placing pupils with special needs or behavioural problems.

The more cautious approach politically, and the influence of those civil servants who were anxious to make the GM initiative complement rather than cut across other policies, was reflected in the initial rules contained in the 1988 Act: only schools with over 300 pupils could apply (effectively excluding most primary schools), they were to be funded at no extra cost and at a level roughly equivalent to LEA schools; they would not have the power to change their character, in particular via changing admissions policies; and there had to be a

ballot of parents. It was to be, as Fitz *et al.* (ibid., p.27) put it, 'limited
autonomy'. The differences between GM and LEA schools were
deliberately minimised in order to show up the advantages of managerial efficiencies arising directly out of institutional autonomy. Also, the
influence of the Treasury was shown in the determination not to ask for
new money. A Grant-Maintained Schools Trust was set up to promote
opting out: by 1991–2 it was receiving a £600 000 grant, and had
become an important element in the process of persuading schools to
become GM.

In health, as the above quotation from Kenneth Clarke makes clear,
the government was all along aiming for trusts to become the 'natural
organisational model' for the provision of patient care. The White
Paper promised 'a range of powers and freedoms not available to the
NHS generally'. In return trusts were expected to 'encourage a stronger
sense of local ownership and pride, building on local goodwill . . .
stimulate commitment and harness skills, fostering local initiative and
greater competition' (Department of Health, 1989a). It was expected
that there would be a substantial number of trusts by the launch of the
provider market in April 1991. They were empowered to employ staff,
enter into contracts and raise income from a variety of sources,
including GP fundholders, health authorities and private patients.
The initiative for the opting out was expected to come from the
secretary of state, the health authority, the management, groups of
staff or even people from the local community, though in practice it
was the management, and occasionally the clinicians, who were most
interested. Unlike education and housing, there was no ballot, and so
bids were assessed by the secretary of state on three criteria: that the
management, supported by consultants, had demonstrated sufficient
management skills, that the trust would be financially viable, and that
self-government was not being sought as an alternative to hospital
closure (a criterion that did not seem to be so stringently applied in the
case of schools nor, in some cases, in relation to hospitals).

Reactions to the White Paper proposals were, like those to the GM
schools, mainly negative. There were worries about whether, with
resource management being so insecurely rooted in the organisational
culture of the NHS, and with management budgeting having failed to
enlist consultant support, the managers were really up to the challenge
(Pollitt, 1989). There were rallies against the reforms, with nearly a
hundred organisations backing a charter drawn up by the Health
Rights pressure group as an alternative to the White Paper. There
was a nationwide lobby of MPs against the 'devastating implications'

of the plans (*Health Service Journal*, 23 February 1989). Critics foresaw that trusts would be able to use their local monopoly power to increase costs, or could opt out of health authority control altogether, or alternatively that some could go bankrupt. They criticised the lack of accountability of boards dominated by business people and managers. Responding to these pressures, Clarke declared that each and every hospital could become a trust, but probably not in his lifetime. He assured them that local people would be consulted, but ruled out the use of ballots. A working paper set out the details of the new managerial freedoms, but made it clear that the reverse side of these was an obligation to treat their assets as if they were private companies; they would start with a debt equivalent to these assets, and have to pay interest on it. In this respect the government was responding to pressure from the private hospitals for a 'level playing field' within the market.

On a tight timetable, the health authorities were asked to identify likely trusts for the first cohort, to be transferred in April 1991. The opposition was formidable. The Institute of Health Service Managers chose to highlight the funding problem, which would still remain, and criticised the lack of pilot testing of the proposals. It forecast that health authorities would have to negotiate with monopoly suppliers in some cases, and that the less successful hospitals would be caught in a spiral of inefficiency but, for political reasons, not be allowed to close. The British Medical Association and the Royal College of Nursing came out against the proposals and began high-profile campaigns against them, sending out 11 million leaflets and declaring that opting out could pull apart the structure of the NHS. A vote among junior doctors was decisively against, surveys of consultants showed widespread opposition, and a Gallup Poll of the general public showed that 71 per cent of those who knew about the White Paper disapproved of its proposals. A team of backbench Conservative MPs had to be set up to counter local opposition, and government ministers took pains to emphasise that trusts would not be opting out of the NHS, but, as Michael Forsyth put it, would 'have greater freedom of management to do their job better' (quoted in *Health Service Journal*, 24 August 1989). Yet almost immediately cracks appeared in the opposition. Managers and some doctors in London teaching hospitals, which had had self-governing status until the 1974 reorganisation, saw the advantages of 'getting clear of bureaucracy' and having a board of governors again. A community campaign was organised to put forward the Queen Victoria Hospital in Sussex for trust status, against the health authority's attempts to run it down. Despite uncertainty about what the advantages might be, and despite claims that the exercise was unlawful in advance of legislation, by mid 1989 there had been 178 expressions of interest, including interest by two ambulance services, which took the government by surprise.

In housing, the tenants' choice mechanism went into law in 1988 with a minimum of consultation. The idea was universally unpopular, and although a vital concession had been made to allow tenants a vote, this had not helped to legitimise the idea: the 'negative vote' upon which Ridley had insisted – counting those who did not vote as being in favour – was condemned as undemocratic. Despite the Housing Corporation actively taking up the development of tenants' choice, providing promotional funding and encouraging tenants' groups to use it to take over ownership themselves, the expected rush of applications for tenants' choice transfers did not materialise. This was partly because the Housing Corporation did a good job – intentionally or not – of putting off prospective private landlords with a very difficult registration process. Even more crucially, tenants had associated the legislation with an attempt at privatisation that would lead to the loss of their security of tenure and, urged on by local authorities whose 'dominant coalition' were adamantly opposed to the idea, they began to organise actively against it. In the end, the combined effect of tenants' choice and a parallel policy of housing action trusts (which were designed forcibly to take six large estates in inner city areas away from local authority control) was to galvanise a new tenants' movement into being. In the end only six tenants' choice schemes went ahead, each with a unique set of circumstances that made it impossible to see it as a model with a general future. Six housing action trusts were eventually declared, though these had conceded to a tenants' ballot and had been set up in a much more cooperative way than originally envisaged.

However the threat of tenants' choice rapidly led some local authorities to develop their own form of opt-out, large-scale voluntary transfer (LSVT). At first it was reported that 150 local authorities were interested. The legislation was in place, under the 1986 Housing and Planning Act, to transfer housing stock to a new landlord, subject only to the secretary of state's approval (it was originally intended to enable local authorities to transfer tenants to other accommodation if they were holding up the work of a developer). In the event, the logic of accountability to consumers won out over the logic of the market, and the secretary of state insisted that a ballot of tenants be held before a transfer was approved. Distaste for the discredited 'negative ballot' of tenants' choice meant that nearly all opted for a straight majority vote. Three possible scenarios opened up: that local authorities would opt for wholesale transfer to new landlords, that they would develop an initial surge of interest but then settle back to a more modest interest over time, or that they would look at the idea and mostly reject it. In the event, the second of these scenarios proved the most accurate.

Transfer involved several quite difficult stages. First, there was the process of setting up a new housing association; nearly all LSVTs were to new agencies, because the existing local associations were often too small to cope with the transfer, and because tenants were more reassured by the idea of the council staff transferring to a new organisation that would really be a continuation of the old one (no transfers to existing associations were successful until 1993). Second, there was the task of negotiating over a purchase price. A local authority would want to get the best price it could, in order to pay off the housing debt and use the remainder for the development of new housing (usually in the form of grants to the new housing association) or of non-housing capital works such as a local swimming pool. But, on the other hand it would not want to put up the price so much that tenants would vote against the transfer, or that new tenants would be saddled with an impossibly high rent. Third, there was the organising of the campaign to persuade tenants to vote in favour. At Chiltern District Council, the first to transfer, this was unashamedly a pro-transfer campaign orchestrated by the housing staff, who would transfer with the tenants. It was only after this transfer was under way that it was realised that there might be a conflict of loyalty among the staff, a need for a balanced campaign that would put both sides of the argument, and a need for an independent advisor to tenants.

Unlike other privatisation initiatives, this was not the government's idea but a reaction by local authorities to the restrictions they were under. At first the government was content to let the idea develop. There was growing concern that transfers should not simply replicate council housing empires, but should be to smaller organisations, including some existing housing associations. A ceiling of 10 000 homes was put on any one transfer. Nevertheless there was reluctance to stop Conservative councils intent on divesting themselves of their stock. Bromley was allowed to transfer 12 393 homes on the ground that with right to buy sales this would anyway fall to 10 000 in time. At that stage government ministers were not prepared to put too many obstacles in the way of the local authorities. As Sir George Young, the housing minister, put it, 'The tortoise of voluntary transfer is overtaking the hare of tenants' choice' (quoted in *Housing Magazine*, January 1992).

Characteristics of the devolved agencies

It is worth pausing at this point in the narrative to look in more detail at what kinds of organisation were being set up. The health trusts were incorporated as private trusts, corporate bodies with their own legal personality, but they were constrained by the duties and limitations placed on them by the 1990 NHS and Community Care Act and further orders and instruments stemming from it. They were given the power to enter into contracts, to acquire and dispose of assets, and to retain their operating surpluses. In addition the board was given the freedom to raise private finance, though within limits set annually by the Department of Health. They were essentially creatures of statute, dependent on the government for the space in which they operated. They were further weakened by the decision taken early on in the new Major administration to backtrack on the idea of markets; their contracts with NHS purchasers were not to be made legally enforceable. Commentators concluded that trusts were 'a notoriously imprecise and difficult concept' whose life expectancy was uncertain because they could be dissolved by the secretary of state, that they were 'subject to a degree of direct government control that no ordinary trust ever experiences' and should really be called NHS corporations (Hughes and Dingwall, 1990). All appointments to the board had to be approved by the secretary of state. There were to be a maximum of ten members, with four executive members and a chair appointed by the secretary of state. Any accountability they had towards consumers or the local community was indirect and uncertain, and the local authority role, which had always been small, was eliminated.

The GM schools were also constituted by statute as 'autonomously incorporated institutions directly funded by central government' (Fitz *et al.* 1993, p. 9). Their governing bodies were designed to exclude party political nominees. Enhanced powers were given over admissions, finance and staffing, and they were enabled to invest money, acquire and dispose of property and enter into contracts. Fitz *et al.* (1993, p.9) sum up the advantages of autonomous status as follows: 'a GM school has greater flexibility than an LEA school to deploy income, manage its local reputation and employ teachers and other staff'. They were different, but not that different, since local management of schools (LMS) schools also had delegated budgets. Accountability to consumers was through parents, to producers through teacher representatives, and the wider community was no longer represented directly by the local authority.

Most of the housing transfers were to new housing associations, set up in the same way as existing ones with dual registration with the Registry of Industrial and Provident Societies and the Housing Corporation. The former registration ensured that they were legally autonomous with an identity that allowed them to trade and make surpluses, but to have a nominal shareholding that did not receive dividends. One early transfer, in Rochester, was to a company limited by guarantee (which provides a similar identity), but as it had no obvious advantages most took the tried and tested route. The second form of registration, with the Housing Corporation, was based on the applicants being competent housing providers, and it provided access to housing association grant funding in return for regular Corporation monitoring. They had no trouble in becoming registered since they had already demonstrated their competence as providers, and Corporation officials were glad to welcome them as potential large-scale developers who could compete with existing associations for grant funding, providing further coverage of areas previously dominated by council housing, driving down development costs and potentially being able to keep down the rents of new homes through rent-pooling with their large existing housing stocks. Accountability was through a board, the composition of which was affected by two rulings. The first was a rule in the 1989 Local Government and Housing Act that limited the local authority share of representatives on independent agencies to less than 20 per cent. This meant the local authorities had two or three appointees. The second was a Housing Corporation preference for limiting the share of tenant representatives to the same level, a preference that was successfully challenged in one case, Torbay, where it was planned to have a majority of tenants on the board; in the event the tenants voted it down so the issue was never tested. All other directors were appointed to the board by the members, who could be a small clique of founder members or a wider group consisting mainly of tenants; it all depended on the policy of the founders towards advertising and encouraging a broad membership. Because they were non-charitable housing associations, registered as friendly societies, there was a potential for their democratisation through the signing up of new members.

Implementation of the policy

In all three sectors, the framework for opting out was an enabling one. The task of implementation was one of providing incentives, persuading organisations to opt out, and managing and regulating (in the case of housing rationing), the process. It was a task delegated by the government to various intermediaries: the NHS Management Executive and Regional Health Authorities, the Grant Maintained Schools Trust and the Housing Corporation. In all three cases, central government departments retained the right to decide who should be allowed to opt out; for instance the Department of the Environment would publish an annual list of those applicant housing departments which were entitled to go ahead with the process of persuading tenants to vote in favour.

In education, the pace of opting out was quite slow. The first GM school opened in September 1989, but after the first 50 ballots the number of applications dropped. Gradually the policy of minimising the differences was changed to one of providing incentives. In January 1990 preference was given to GM schools in capital projects, and 29 schools were allocated 6.3 million compared with 410 million spread among the other 24 000 schools. From then on about a third of the capital expenditure was diverted to schools within the GM sector, rising to 77 million in 1993–4 (Fitz *et al.*, 1993). Calculation of the GM revenue budget also favoured them against LEA schools. In 1990 Baker's successor, John MacGregor, announced the abolition of the size limit (allowing even small primary schools to opt out), a 50 per cent increase in transitional and annual specific grants payable to GM schools and, on incorporation, a one-off payment of £30 000 plus £30 per pupil. Not surprisingly the number of applications grew sharply in 1991. GM schools were then allowed to change their admissions policies so as to specialise in some areas. By the beginning of 1993, 836 schools had begun the process, of which 337 were operating as GM schools, and a further 26 had been approved. Seventeen per cent of secondary schools had begun the process. The government then introduced new incentives in the 1993 Education Act that were designed to keep up the pace of change.

In health, the pace was faster than anyone had expected. Kenneth Clarke remained wary of setting targets, declaring 'I have no targets for either the first round in 1991 or for the ultimate total' (*Health Service Journal*, 15 May 1989). Two hundred draft application forms were sent out and a Department of Health roadshow began actively to sell the idea. By the end of 1989 a third of the 200 (71 submissions, including two ambulance services and eight district health authorities) had been allowed to progress. Despite vigorous local campaigns against every one of these, 66 went ahead to the final stage, of which 56 were approved, eight rejected and two told to wait another year. The motives for applying were mixed: some were attempting to escape from the dangers of eventual closure, while others, such as the ambulance service chiefs, could see ways in which autonomy could be used to reorganise their services. There was an expectation of extra financial help, which persisted despite government insistence that there would not be any extra funding. The first wave put in bids of £900 million for capital spending, a wildly unrealistic figure since the current spending by the whole of the NHS was only £1.25 billion. They received only £8.8 million more than if they had remained directly managed units. According to one manager, 'trusts led themselves down the garden path' in their expectation of funding (*Health Service Journal*, 14 February 1991). A second blow came with the decision to allocate half of the trusts' capital debt to the private sector rather than the one third many had built into their calculations when applying. This forced them to raise more revenue to cover the interest payments on the debt, and it made several business plans go into deficit. As another manager put it rather plaintively 'it is little use having freedom if you do not have the money to exercise it' (ibid.). Guy's Hospital ran into financial trouble and announced 600 job losses, while the Bradford NHS Trust announced that it expected 300 jobs to go over three years. By the time of the second wave, there was more information available and there were fewer misconceptions about the benefits and drawbacks, but there were still 120 applications.

In housing, interest remained steady over time, sustained by the reaction to financial pressures brought about by the 1989 Local Government and Housing Act and then by the introduction in 1992 of plans for compulsory competitive tendering for housing management. The earliest ballots, at Chiltern, Sevenoaks and Newbury, aimed to predate the 1988 Housing Act and tenants' choice, and they set the pattern for the future. Tenants would lose their secure tenancies and become assured tenants, but they would keep their right to buy and have rents pegged to a little above inflation for five years. New tenants, on the other hand, would face significantly higher rents in order to pay the new association's mortgages. In contrast, it was claimed that if tenants rejected the transfer they would face much higher rents. By April 1995, 40 housing departments had carried out LSVTs, transferring 180 000 homes and generating more than £2.6 billion in private finance. A further 13 were in the pipeline. Nearly all were district councils with a housing stock of between 1 600 and 8 000 homes, mainly in rural areas and predominantly in the South of England, and under Conservative control or with no overall control. To date Bromley's transfer of over 12 000 homes to Broomleigh Housing Association has been the only one by a London borough. Over 30 attempted transfers have been voted down, while several others did not proceed because opinion polls indicated substantial opposition.

There were five main success factors. First, it was important that there should be no local opposition, either from tenants or from the local Labour Party; where there was such opposition, transfers were voted down or never reached the ballot stage. Second, transfer was more likely to succeed if it was to a new association controlled by people the tenants already knew; they were highly resistant to transfers that involved an existing association. Third, tenants had to be convinced that there were steep rent rises in store if they did not make the move; in the case of some obviously well-run housing departments with few repair problems they simply did not believe the warnings. Fourth, it was important to have stable political control; when Walsall District Council fell to Labour in the 1992 election, the new council suspended the director of housing and ordered a rerun of the (successful) ballot on the ground that the information given to tenants was biased. At Cherwell District Council, the new Labour/Liberal Democrat administration imposed rent restrictions on the new association, with the result that the transfer had to be abandoned, again after the tenants had voted in favour. Lastly, it was important that the capital receipt received by the council was up to the expectations of councillors; in at least two cases an LSVT was vetoed because councillors were disappointed with the promised outcome.

There was some evidence in this first wave of transfers of undue pressure being put on tenants. In several cases tenants complained about inadequate or late consultation. In Rochester the sale to a company caused controversy because it was not going to be registered with the Housing Corporation and because tenants were not allowed independent advice. Thirty-six MPs signed an early-day motion in the House of Commons in an attempt to block the transfer, but it went ahead because tenants in general seemed satisfied with the deal. Rochford twice postponed its ballot, and was threatened with legal action by opposition councillors after 'well-informed and vociferous tenants' campaigns' (Bright, 1988, p. 29). In Salisbury tenants' associations formed a federation to resist a transfer, amid rumours of intimidation by the Council and housing association at public meetings; not surprisingly in such an atmosphere they rejected the proposal. In Torbay a tenant-led transfer was voted down after acrimonious battles between the new association and the council lasting several years.

The government began to intervene to regulate the process. The Department of Education (DoE) delayed a ballot at Ryedale District Council to allow more time for tenants to consider it, and insisted on the rent guarantee being set at a (by now standard) rate of 2 per cent above inflation. In Torbay the Council caused controversy by using the discredited 'negative ballot' system, but the DoE insisted on a new ballot with straight majority voting – a surprising turn around for a government that had originally introduced the idea. More generally, the Government accepted the criticism that tenants were not being given any other alternatives, such as transfer to a tenant-led body under the tenants' choice legislation. It was made mandatory for local authorities to point out to tenants that they had this option (see Birchall, 1992). One issue the government chose not to tackle was that of the cost of transfers, which fell, whether or not they were successful, on the housing revenue account. This meant that tenants had to pay for what was, more often than not, a management-led exercise. In Bromley, for instance, some tenants mounted an unsuccessful legal challenge concerning the £650 000 set-up cost for the Broomleigh Housing Association. Nor would the government interfere in the question of how the proceeds were spent, beyond its ruling that up to 75 per cent should be used to pay off existing debts. By the end of 1991 it was estimated that more than £650 million had been raised in transfers, but only £75 million of this had found its way back into new housing investment (*Housing Magazine*, November 1991).

In their 1992 election manifesto the Conservatives gave notice that there would be an upper limit of about 5 000 on the number allowed to transfer, that transfer to existing housing associations would be favoured, and that the Treasury would be clawing back part of the transfer proceeds to pay for the increased housing benefit bill faced when council tenants become association tenants (since the 1989 Act, council tenants' benefits have been paid out of the housing revenue account, and so are less directly a cost to the Treasury). In 1993 the new rules were announced: the Treasury clawback was to be 20 per cent of capital receipt, the top limit for number of homes transferred to one agency was set at 3–4 000, with a limit of 5 000 from any one local authority (which meant a split transfer to at least two agencies). Because it was felt that the large sums raised on the capital markets might imperil the housing associations' housing development programmes, an annual limit was put on the total number of homes transferring under the initiative.

Clearly, the government had decided to take much greater control over the whole process and make it potentially less attractive. Pressure from the Treasury meant a slowdown in the numbers being allowed to transfer: 14 in 1994–5, 11 in 1995–6. There was no lack of willing participants, especially with the prospect in 1996 of another major challenge to local authority housing departments from compulsory competitive tendering. At the moment, even with the demise of CCT under the new Labour government, the interest in transfer remains because it allows housing agencies to concentrate on one service and to raise money in the capital markets. This means that large-scale voluntary transfer may have a new lease of life under the Labour government.

Impact of the policy

In education, the government hoped that most secondary schools would have opted out by 1995. Clearly the pace has not been nearly so quick. The impact of the policy has been modest, though in some areas (such as the outer London Borough of Hillingdon) a concentration of GM schools has meant a much reduced role for the LEAs. They were also meant to introduce competition so as to raise standards more generally, but it is difficult to isolate the GM effect from other initiatives such as open enrolment, city technology colleges, LMS and the national curriculum.

In health, the policy has been a complete success, in that after the fourth wave virtually all hospitals had achieved trust status. Yet the very success of the policy may be due to the fact that being a trust is not as radical a change as originally predicted. Trusts are the creature of statute and their autonomy is circumscribed by government control. The internal market has not been the radical free market originally envisaged, as contracts are not enforceable by law, core services are protected, natural monopolies are recognised and so on. All this may mean that what seems a very successful policy is in fact empty of some of its original content.

In housing the impact has been steady, but only operates at the margins of the very large housing stocks held by local authorities. The policy has not yet had any impact on that area where a crisis was first identified in housing management (Audit Commission, 1986): the inner cities. One vital development has been the Treasury's agreement that authorities that are still carrying debts on their stock, and whose stock valuations are low or even negative (because of the need for large-scale repairs), may transfer their housing and yet continue to receive subsidy on it. A new transfer model, the Local Housing Company, has been developed, and this may breathe new life into what has been a minor policy development, taking it from the district councils in rural areas right to the inner city authorities with the largest stocks, and the largest problems (Zitron, 1995).

Rationality, resources and strategies

One problem with providing an account of policy development is that, with hindsight, it can appear more rational, more single-minded than it really was. Hence we have to add an important caveat: the selection of devolution as a policy option was only one of a variety of policies that were being developed at the same time, and some of these were to collide with it. We can see an underlying rationale for the policy in each sector in the more general belief in markets and competition and the drive for privatisation, but these beliefs did not dictate the form policies would take. As Marsh and Rhodes (1992b, p. 3) point out when reviewing the more general record of Conservative policy making in the 1980s, 'there is no constant set of Thatcherite policies' and 'the relative priority accorded to particular policies did not remain the same over the decade'. Consistency in policy making cannot be assumed. In our cases, some of the other policies that were introduced around the same time as the devolution policy cut across it and made it less attractive. This can be seen most clearly in education, where the same 1988 Act introduced local management of schools, giving to all state schools most of the autonomy that grant maintained schools would obtain: they also held their own budgets, calculated on a capitation system, and had local control of staffing and employment through the board of governors. The incentives for opting out were diminishing even as it was being introduced. In housing, council and housing association tenants benefited from a strengthening of their legal position through a tenants' charter introduced as early as the 1980 Housing Act, giving them security of tenure and the right to consultation, succession and so on. In an attempt to attract private finance for development of the housing association sector, the government, in the same 1988 Act that introduced tenants' choice, changed the housing association tenure to one with less security of tenure. This enabled access to private finance but at the same time made it much less likely that council tenants would opt to become tenants of a new or existing housing association. That some did was due to the efforts of the housing association policy community to reinstate, by contractual agreement, most of the rights the Act had taken away.

It may be useful to compare the strategies of the different participants. The government's strategy varied between the sectors. In health, trusts were a logical application of the idea of a market, though as ministers backpedalled from the implications of a free market they progressively restricted themselves to selling the idea as an exercise in managerial freedom. In education and housing, devolution was a way of circumventing the local authorities and enabling single-purpose organisations to deliver services free of political 'interference'. These initiatives can be seen as part of a long and bitter struggle throughout the 1980s to take power away from local government. At the back of all three initiatives was the assumption that private was better than public, even if the private organisations were only quasi-private: dependent on the state for funding, non profit-making and tightly regulated. The strength of this preference can be seen in the naive view of the then secretary of state, Nicholas Ridley, that council tenants would prefer to opt for private, profit-making landlords rather than the local authority.

The strategies of the service delivery agencies were dependent on local circumstances and a changing assessment of the attractions and risks of opting out. They wanted more freedom, but there is no evidence of a widespread desire to escape from local or health authority control, more a desire to find ways round restrictions on funding. They wanted to do what they were already doing, but to do it more effectively, or with a more secure future, or in the case of housing to do again what they had recently been stopped from doing. They were prepared to weigh up the alternatives on a quite rational basis of estimated advantages, but in the case of health it seems that they overestimated these. Some managers did seem to be convinced that there would be further funding, even when told that there would not be, and their inclusion of a more favourable ratio of public to private debt in their business plans proved to be wishful thinking. If their strategy was to 'bounce' the government into giving away more than the ministers intended, it was not successful.

We have noted the ease with which the government was able to persuade individual schools and hospitals to opt out, despite the almost universal clamour among their wider policy communities against the policy. In health and education, almost all the representative bodies of managers, professionals and consumers were implacably opposed to the policy. In housing this was true of the government's opt-out policy of tenants' choice, but in relation to voluntary transfer the policy community was much more neutral or supportive. This is not surprising, since the initiative had come from them rather than from the centre.

What kind of resources did the participants bring to the 'game' of opting out? Clearly the government had most of the financial resources, though we should not underestimate the extent to which local authorities and hospitals were able, through consultants and secondment of their own staff, to conduct their own policy development that at times challenged government interpretations. It might have been expected that the government would hold all the constitutional and legal resources and use them to good effect. In education and health, the government had to legislate to create new forms of organisation, while in housing a new form of tenure was not needed – there were already a variety of tenures, including private renting, housing associations and cooperatives. The problem was finding a way for landlords to target council estates and begin the process of persuading tenants to vote for privatisation. The 1988 Housing Act set out the complex tenants' choice option. However not all legal resources were on the government's side. In the case of housing, local authorities also had a resource, ironically in the shape of the Housing Act of 1986, which had also encouraged privatisation by allowing local authorities (subject to the permission of the secretary of state for the environment) to sell estates to other landlords. Unexpectedly, this enabled local authority managers to devise a strategy of transfering their stock to a new housing association; they still needed the permission of the secretary of state, but they did not need new legislation.

It might be expected that in a unitary state such as the UK the central government would have had no problem in imposing its will hierarchically, using its administrative arms to instruct service delivery agencies to opt for devolution. This was the case in health, where the secretary of state could issue commands through the national management executive that passed down through the regional and district health authorities to the hospitals and other service delivery units. Because patients were not an organised group of consumers, and because their representatives – the community health councils – were not part of the chain of command and were effectively sidelined, there was no effective push for consumers to have a say in the decision. However in education and housing the consumers were more easily identifiable, and had more regular contact with the providers of the services. In education, the legislation of 1980 and 1988 strengthened the role of parent governors, who gained a direct say in how their schools were run. In housing, tenant participation was more patchy: the 1980 Housing Act provided the right to be consulted about any significant change in management, and good practice in local authorities led to all the inner city authorities, and a majority of the rest, having a well-developed system of tenants' associations and federations, with various mechanisms for gauging consumer opinion (see Birchall, 1992). There were even a small, but influential, number of tenant management cooperatives, which had established consumer control of some estates. Under these circumstances the policy communities of education and housing found it relatively easy to insist on a ballot of consumers before any transfer could go ahead.

In housing and education, then, the local players possessed a key political resource: the constitutional power of the users of their services. Of course, for those who did want to transfer, this was also a constraint, because they had to persuade service users of the merits of the case. This was also a resource they could turn against the government, because they could demand assurance of extra benefits before encouraging users to agree to the opt-out. Political resources were also needed at the local level by those wanting to opt out. They had to persuade their tenants and parents that it was a 'good thing'. The key resources here were a good relationship between the head teacher and the parents and between the director of housing and the tenants, and the absence of political opposition within the local authority. If either of these conditions were not met then the transfer tended to be voted down (see Mullins *et al.*, 1992).

Finally, almost all informational resources were held by the local players, which meant that not just their compliance but, to some extent, their enthusiastic cooperation were needed. In order to gain such cooperation, the government had to resort to the provision of incentives. In the health sector not too many were needed because the government minister already had the hierarchical resources necessary to drive the policy through. In the education sector, considerable resources were held by the locality: the producers had the information and the consumers had the ultimate political power to make the transfer happen. This meant that, over time, the policy would only work if the local players were given enough incentives. In the housing sector, almost all the resources were held by the locality, because it was their initiative. The government confined itself to regulating and rationing the process. On the other hand the power of the government was felt indirectly: housing providers were being driven to transfer their stock in order to avoid the cumulative effects of other central government housing policies. This also confirms that the resources brought to the game by the central player were dominant.

In health and education the policy networks surrounding the local provider agencies seem to have been sidelined: Even as they were protesting, deals were being done by the government and local providers. Their resources, mainly consisting of expertise, advice and information, were largely ignored, which meant that though the policies were driven through, in the long run their eventual impact may have been less radical than government ministers had hoped. The lack of consensus between opted-out agencies and their wider policy networks, and between professional and managerial networks, may have damaged the sector's ability to operate as a policy community. Fragmentation may prove to be the main policy outcome.

5 Decentralised Management of NHS Trusts

Introduction

In January 1989 the Thatcher government published a White Paper on the future of the health service, entitled *Working for Patients* (Secretaries of State for Health, Wales, Northern Ireland and Scotland, 1989). Seven 'key changes' lay at the core of the government's proposals, the second of which was: 'To stimulate a better service to the patient, hospitals will be able to apply for a new self-governing status as NHS hospital trusts' (ibid., p. 4). In the same White Paper the government spoke of 'enabling as many hospitals as are willing and able to do so to run their own affairs, whilst remaining in the NHS' (ibid., p. 22). Those hospitals which decided to put themselves forward for trust status would have to convince the Department of Health that they were financially sound and capable of self-management.

Thus at the time when our research was designed, we envisaged a situation in which some NHS hospitals would be trusts and others would continue to be directly managed units (DMUs) under District Health Authorities (DHAs). This would have enabled us to compare the experiences of managing trusts and managing DMUs. In the event, however, the creation of trusts developed very rapidly. As we explained in Chapter 3, the government was able, by a mixture of pressures, to create a situation in which virtually all provider units felt it necessary to apply for trust status, whether local clinicians and managers were enthusiastic about the idea or not. By as early as April 1994 more than 90 per cent of NHS services were being managed by a total of 440 trusts. In the end, there were virtually no DMUs for us to use as comparators! We therefore modified our design so as to conduct detailed fieldwork in two acute hospitals that had fairly enthusiastically embraced trust status in the second wave (commencing as trusts on 1 April 1992), plus two further acute hospitals that had been reluctant to apply for trust status until the final main wave of applications, which had led to them achieving autonomous status on 1 April 1994. There were significant differences between our four hospitals, very briefly summarised as follows (the pseudonyms will be used throughout the remainder of the book):

- *Pigeon*: a medium-sized NHS acute hospital in an urban and economically depressed part of northern England. A fairly enthusiastic second-wave applicant for trust status.
- *Starling*: a small acute hospital in the same subregion of northern England as Pigeon. A cautious fourth-wave applicant for trust status.
- *Duck*: a medium-sized acute hospital in the south of England. A fairly enthusiastic second-wave applicant.
- *Eagle*: a large acute teaching hospital in the south of England. A fourth-wave applicant for trust status.

It is worth bearing in mind that most acute hospitals are large and complex organisations – certainly much larger in terms of staff numbers and diversity than housing associations or secondary schools. At the time of our research, for example, one of the selected trusts (not the largest) had an annual budget of £45 million and employed 2 700 staff. One implication of size and complexity is that the effects of a fundamental change such as achieving self-governance are likely to be perceived and experienced in a variety of ways in different parts of the organisation. This was certainly true for our fieldwork. In very general terms, senior managers were more consistently positive about the changes than senior clinicians, with some of the latter maintaining to a highly sceptical position. In this respect our research repeated the findings of a number of earlier projects investigating management change in the NHS, for example the introduction of general managers in the mid 1980s (Harrison *et al.*, 1992). It also matched the initial stances of the various national associations concerned, with those for doctors and nurses being very critical of the 1989 White Paper while only managers' associations broadly welcomed it.

More generally, the history of management change and restructuring in the NHS reflects a number of continuing tensions and paradoxes. From a political point of view, one of the paradoxes is that, although the NHS has never been democratically accountable to local authorities, and has never contained any directly elected element, it has nonetheless been the focus of intense public and media concern.

Change in the NHS has therefore long been an intensely political issue, and as the financial pressures of the late 1970s and 1980s unfolded, the Labour opposition maintained strong pressure on the Conservative government to preserve this very popular public service in more or less its existing form.

A second tension was that between NHS managers and senior doctors (consultants). Since the founding of the service, consultants had enjoyed a high degree of autonomy: for more than 30 years they were, in essence, administered but unmanaged (Harrison *et al.*, 1992). But as the squeeze on public expenditure tightened during the 1980s, the government was obliged to reexamine a situation in which consultants had, *de facto*, the authority to commit considerable expenditures without the full scrutiny and control of senior managers. Acute hospitals were therefore particularly interesting places in which to look for possible changes in the degree of *horizontal* centralisation (that is, the extent to which managers were able to control the performance of other occupational groups).

A third issue directly concerns the nature of decentralisation within the NHS. In a minute to his cabinet colleagues on 5 October 1945 Aneurin Bevan, the principal political architect of the NHS, stressed that 'We have got to achieve as nearly as possible a uniform standard of service for all' (Minister of Health, 1945). Indeed from the outside the NHS did appear to become a fairly uniform national service: after all, there was a ministry, an executive at national level and a hierarchy of regional and district authorities. Yet a series of academic studies during the 1979s and 1980s confirmed what many people who worked in the NHS already knew, namely that priorities, resource levels and patterns of service varied considerably from one locality and one region to another (see, for example, Department of Health and Social Security, 1976). Furthermore, some of these studies showed that senior doctors (consultants) often appeared to have considerable influence over the way in which facilities and services were planned and developed in particular localities. In short, the implementation of what appeared to be national policies took on a wide variety of forms locally and real decision-making power about the shape of services was effectively quite decentralised (see, for example, Elcock and Haywood, 1980). Thus the rhetoric of the 1989 White Paper declaring that 'as much power and responsibility as possible will be delegated to the local level' (Secretaries of State for Health, 1989, p. 4) was directed towards a situation in which there was already considerable *de facto* decentralisation of power and influence.

Reasons for opting out (or not)

At the time of the *Working for Patients* White Paper the DHSS was quite clear about what the benefits of trust status would be. In their original working paper (Department of Health and Social Security, 1989b, p. 3) it was stated that trusts 'will have far more freedom to take their own decisions on matters which affect them most without detailed supervision from above. This new development will give patients more choice, produce a better quality service and encourage other hospitals to do even better in order to compete.'

Later in the same document (ibid., pp. 5–6) a list of more specific benefits was presented:

- 'The power to acquire, own and dispose of assets to ensure the most effective use of them.'
- 'The power to borrow, subject to an annual financing limit.'
- 'Freedom to retain operating surpluses and build up reserves.'
- 'Freedom to set their own management structures without control from district, regions or the NHS management executive.'
- 'Freedom to employ whatever, and however many, staff they consider necessary.
- 'Freedom to determine pay and conditions of services for staff, and to conduct their own industrial relations.'
- 'Freedom to employ and direct their own medical and nursing staff.'

What struck us most during our interviews at the two trusts that had achieved self-governance during the (early) second wave was how *infrequently* most of this range of alleged benefits were cited as reasons that had significantly influenced the decision to apply for trust status. The most emphasised and most frequently cited motive at both hospitals was the more negative one of simply escaping from the control of the DHA and/or Regional Health Authority (RHA): 'The driving force behind the move towards trust status was a desire to gain independence and the opportunity to be able to develop without the interference of the local health authority' (*Duck*). 'Traditionally the health authority had meddled and involved itself too much in the planning and management of the hospital' *'Duck'*. 'Most of the medical staff . . . saw the transfer as an opportunity to escape from the bureaucratic style of the former District Health Authority' *'Duck'*. 'The principal reason was not a great deal to do with theoretical freedoms, it was to do with the freedom from the health authority'

(*Pigeon*). 'Management wanted to manage the hospital as its own business. They wanted to move away from control by Region' (*Pigeon*). Thus the single most important motive seemed to be the desire to escape from 'interference from above'. We shall explore later how far this was a realistic aspiration.

This finding needs to be qualified by a recognition that other motives, though not so frequently stated, were certainly in play. It was clear that a number of consultants had ambitions to develop particular services. It was also clear that, although escape from close control by the health authorities was a popular theme, opinions certainly varied as to whether it was a sufficient argument to justify becoming a trust. At *Duck* opinions among the medical staff were divided and a secret ballot resulted in a vote of almost 50/50. In this case the sensitive leadership of the then chief executive was widely recognised as having been decisive. Open debate had been encouraged, and most of the key staff felt as though they had least had the opportunity to express their views. At *Pigeon* too, there were differences of opinion among the consultants. The medical staff committee had run two ballots on the desirability of trust status, and the outcome had been very close on both occasions. There had been considerable concern about future security of employment and possible changes to terms and conditions. The nursing staff (who at the time were stuck in the morass of clinical regrading) and some ancillary groups had also been apprehensive. Nevertheless the chief executive had been able to persuade a sufficient body of opinion that an early application was justified. One issue had been that, because of the merger of the pre-existing health authorities, *Pigeon* was now faced with a purchasing authority that appeared to have less of a specific commitment to that particular hospital than the previous, more 'local', DHA.

Turning to the two fourth-wave trusts, we asked why they had refrained from applying during the first three waves. In one case there had been no particular enthusiasm for trust status (despite some irritation at the perceived bureaucracy of the DHA and RHA) but eventually moves by other hospitals in the area had kindled a fear of being left out. The Conservative victory at the 1992 general election had been important in removing the last hope on the part of some of the staff that the NHS reforms would lose momentum or fade away. As one consultant said, after that election trust status 'was merely an inevitable outcome of the political situation beyond the hospital boundaries'. The other fourth-wave trust was situated in the middle of a strongly Labour area, where there was considerable suspicion about trust status on ideological grounds. There was also concern about the financial viability of the hospital, and a desire to complete a substantial capital programme before leaving the shelter (as it was perceived) of the RHA and DHA. Furthermore the hospital was a relatively small one and did not see itself as a trail blazer. The interviewees there distinguished themselves from early trusts by saying that they were not a 'flagship' or a 'glamorous outfit'. In these circumstances the then chief executive had pursued a cautious, consultative style. This had helped him establish widespread trust among the staff but had probably not helped him when the fourth-wave bid finally came to be made - he had not been chosen to lead the shadow trust. The 1992 general election had been significant here too. After the conservative victory it had been seen that there was no viable alternative to trust status: indeed staff jokingly referred to the fifth wave as the 'remedial wave'. For both fourth-wave applicants, therefore, despite the very great differences in their local circumstances, the feeling that, politically, trust status was now unavoidable had been an important factor in finally overcoming local doubts and uncertainties.

The perceived benefits of trust status

Unsurprisingly, becoming a trust gave rise to benefits and drawbacks that had not necessarily been fully foreseen or appreciated at the time the applications had been drafted. The list of benefits mentioned by our interviewees bore some relationship – but not a particularly strong one – to the 'official' benefits listed in the previous section (Department of Health and Social Security, 1989b). In particular, financial regimes were generally perceived as restrictive, the freedom to borrow was heavily circumscribed and the freedom to set local pay and conditions was being explored only slowly, and in some cases reluctantly. The most pessimistic view was that of one chief executive who told us that 'there are virtually no benefits'. A clinical director at the same hospital remarked that 'financially, it has been very austere'. Asked about the freedoms of trust status the manager of a clinical directorate at *Pigeon* said 'It has been like wading through treacle.' A clinical director at the same hospital opined that 'there is no point having freedom in financial matters if you have no money'. At *Starling* another doctor explained that 'the improvements have not been made because there isn't any money for anything except more managers'. His frustration was made obvious by his further remark that 'We are asked to run the hospital as a business but we are not allowed to make a loss, we are not allowed to make a profit, and there are so many constraints on what we can do.'

At *Duck* it was explained to us that the atmosphere was 'much more money-orientated than in the past', that this was associated with a greater demand for accountability, and that these two factors in combination made staff feel more constrained. More than one chief executive or manager grimaced when we referred to the DHSS's original list of supposed benefits and indicated that these were no longer regarded as realistic, if they ever had been.

In relation to personnel freedoms even the more optimistic interviewees seldom claimed more than that there was a potential for greater movement in the longer term. *Duck* was the hospital that appeared to have made the greatest use of its power over issues relating to personnel. During the first round of our fieldwork the management had succeeded in persuading about 40 per cent of the staff (excepting medical staff) to join a performance-related pay scheme. The remainder continued to hold fast to the Whitley terms and conditions. It was suggested to us that a lot of the staff had who joined the new scheme had already been at the top of their Whitley scale and therefore the only opportunity they had had to increase their pay was to transfer to performance-related pay. At *Pigeon* discussions on a new incentives package were in (slow) progress, but the chief executive nevertheless described the pay and rewards side of the 1989 reforms as thus far 'a total flop'. However it needs to be said that this fieldwork was undertaken before the 1995 push for local pay. Paradoxically that initiative came strongly from the central government, which tried hard to orchestrate the responses of trusts, causing no little frustration among the latter.

In other respects, however, the promises of 1989 seemed closer to fruition. Our fieldwork showed that the trusts in question had already taken advantage of their freedom to reshape their own management structures, and in many places we encountered a sense of relief that proposals for minor or modest initiatives no longer had to be negotiated through the DHA/RHA hierarchy. We were given a number of examples of hospitals' abilities to go their own way. For example at *Duck*, trust status had enabled the hospital to keep its local kitchen service and escape involvement in the RHA's strategy of developing a centralised cook-chill facility. Also at *Duck*, we were told that it had been possible to spend 1 million refurbishing the main hospital entrance to 'four star hotel standard', (we didn't have the nerve to

ask why not five star). It was claimed that this kind of expenditure
would never have got through DHA scrutiny had the hospital remained a directly managed unit. At *Pigeon* the managers had bought
new uniforms for the midwives and the medical secretaries and it was
said that these had been popular. Also at *Pigeon* a clinical director
praised the way in which the hospital was now able to market its
services to local industries and to the independent sector. Physiother-
apy packages were being offered to prisons, nursing homes and private
hospitals: 'We have been able to conduct our own business.'

At *Eagle* a new chief executive had been able to effect considerable
internal decentralisation. This included what one consultant described
to us as 'medical devolution' – a process of breaking down the pre-
existing medical hierarchy. Another consultant at *Eagle* told us that the
new arrangements had obliged medical staff to think more about
money – 'I never thought about money at all until at least the mid
1980s.' Greater cost consciousness was mentioned at all four hospitals,
though in some cases this was a trend that had existed before the
acquisition of trust status and seemed to be most closely connected
with the establishment of clinical directorates with budgetary responsibilities. At *Duck* we were told that, under the new system, 'hospital
managers have for the first time taken on the management of medical
staff . . . Now the medical staff are not only under the control of the
trust management, but are required to make a commitment to its
successful operation.' In terms of our key concepts (Chapter 2) this
seems a fairly clear example of horizontal centralisation. It would be
wrong, however, to suppose that this necessarily meant that trained
managers were exerting direct authority over doctors. More commonly
within clinical directorate systems, it was a matter of an emerging
group of doctor–managers gradually gaining greater influence over
their colleagues (Harrison and Pollitt, 1994, especially Ch. 6).

A further benefit identified by staff at *Eagle*, *Duck* and *Starling* was
that many hospital staff now identified more strongly with their
particular institution. Territorial and functional antagonisms within
the hospital had been somewhat muted by a heightened awareness of
external risks. Although these assertions were based on impressions -
no-one could offer us any hard survey evidence of such shifts in
attitude – the suggestion seemed quite plausible.

One freedom that had certainly been exercised was the power to
reorganise management. In the new situation it was easier to 'let go' of
managers who were no longer regarded as particularly effective. In one
case an incoming chief executive had moved rapidly to replace almost

all senior managers, forming a quite new management team within a few months of achieving trust status. More common was the rearrangement of organisational structures. Typically, clinical directorates had been strengthened, and as the contracting process in the new provider market developed the trusts had been able to decentralise contractual negotiations so that those actually providing services within the clinical directorates were able to play an increasingly direct part in the negotiations with the purchasing authorities (*Pigeon* and *Duck*).

Finally, there was evidence in *Pigeon, Starling* and *Duck* that trust status had encouraged hospitals to forge closer and more responsive links with local GPs. Sometimes consultants had undertaken this process in a grudging, complaining way, but all recognised that the introduction of GP fundholding had given GPs real clout. At *Duck*, for example, a GP satisfaction survey had been carried out, and as result action had been taken to ensure that discharge notes arrived at GPs' surgeries within 48 hours of patients being discharged. At *Starling* a consultant told us that relations had even been enhanced in pathology, where GPs had long enjoyed open access to the laboratory services. Within some of the acute divisions of the hospital the cultural shift towards responsiveness to GPs had been even greater. At *Eagle* we were again told that relations with GPs had improved, and that 'GPs are now thought of as being part of the hospital and no longer outsiders'. All the trusts had set up regular meetings with GPs, and newsletters and other specifically targeted communications were widely in evidence. Broadly speaking, these claims of improved relations were confirmed by the GP fundholders we spoke to. Unsurprisingly, however, these GPs took a slightly less enthusiastic view of what had happened, recognising that the new warmth shown to them by their consultant colleagues probably had more to do with the latter's recognition of their market power than with a sudden shift in fundamental attitudes. It was obvious that GPs were much less concerned with the newsletters and wine and cheese parties than with the speed and quality of clinical services they could obtain for their patients. The following comment from a GP within *Eagle's* catchment area, was fairly typical:

> GP fundholding has meant that we have been able to purchase better service – not better treatment. For example, in the past patients had to wait for up to six months for urology treatment, but now they only have to wait two or three weeks as we are able to buy in treatment from private hospitals.

The drawbacks of trust status

We asked all our interviewees whether they thought there were any disadvantages to trust status. Quite a few of them – both managers and consultants – chose to respond by talking about the failure of financial freedoms to materialise. Technically, we do not classify this as a disadvantage *caused* by trust status – rather it was a disappointment that a promised benefit had not come about, and we have already discussed this in the previous section. A second, fairly frequent response to our question about disadvantages was to complain about the 'intefering' behaviour of purchasing authorities. However these criticisms were little different (except insofar as they were more muted) from the dislike voiced of the behaviour of DHAs and RHAs *before* trust status had been acquired. In other words, these complaints sounded like echoes of an old disgruntlement rather than anything new and attributable to trust status.

A rather more novel complaint concerned fragmentation and self-seeking behaviour within the NHS. We heard this from virtually every group on every site, but most frequently from consultants. For example one argued that greater autonomy was encouraging 'a parochial and localised attitude to health policy'. A senior manager at a purchasing authority that contracted with two of our case study hospitals emphasised that mutual suspicion between rival providers was a real issue. However the hope was expressed that this was a transitional phase: lack of co-operation 'reached a peak last year [1994] but now maturity was growing'. At several of the hospitals consultants suggested to us that it was not only mutual suspicion that was the problem but the resource climate combined with the way the new interrelationships were structured. It was argued that, with the purchaser–provider split, trusts were generating ideas but could not develop new services as they lacked the money, while the purchasers had the money (the purchasers themselves tended to disagree with this!) but lacked the expertise to identify the opportunities for growth. Furthermore, two of our four case-study hospitals derived a significant proportion of their contract revenues from second or subsequent purchasers, and in this context we heard a number of complaints about the difficulty of getting multi-stake-holder agreement, since any proposal was inevitably more in one purchaser's interest than another's. Of course these claims referred as much to the consequences of the purchaser–provider split as those that derived from trust status *per se*. Once more, we heard echoes here of grievances that hospitals used to voice against each other and against the previous DHA/RHA superstructure. Our general conclusion was therefore that trust status alone, although in many ways yielding disappointingly modest benefits, did not appear to produce significant direct drawbacks. Certainly we couuld hardly find anyone who was interested in a return to the *status quo ante*.

Concepts of performance

When asked what signs would denote a well-performing hospital, the majority of our respondents were able readily to cite several 'performance indicators'. Most mentioned both 'hard' and 'soft' types of measure. Furthermore most mentioned both existing indicators – ones already measured – and possible additional ones for the future. There was no discernible difference in the items mentioned by the second-wave trusts *Pigeon*, *Duck* and the fourth-wave trusts (*Starling*, *Eagle*). Managers were slightly more likely to mention financial indicators. Doctors were slightly more likely to mention staff morale and patient satisfaction, but the overlap between the two groups of respondents was quite extensive.

The main indicators of good performance that were suggested to us included the following:

- Clinical outcomes (though most of the people who mentioned these also admitted that there was as yet very little reliable data in this area).
- Rates of unplanned readmissions (as a proxy for clinical outcomes – again most of our interviewees were carcful to emphasise that this indicator would require careful interpretation).
- Infection rates.
- Financial stability (for example whether the hospital was 'able to sustain its present purchasing level').
- Staff morale/commitment (including proxies such as 'whether the staff were talking to each other' or 'whether consultants were talking to local GPs').
- Sickness, absenteeism and turnover rates among staff.
- Trends in the number of complaints and how these were handled.
- The physical environment ('not so much the front door as the working spaces').

- Average length of stay by procedure and individual consultant (everywhere the average length of stay was falling, but this reduction had begun long before trust status had been acquired).
- Waiting times (though a considerable number of consultants criticised the measure of waiting times laid down in the Patients' Charter as being crude or misleading, and some of them asserted that patients were much more interested in the quality of care they eventually received than in small differences in waiting times).
- A survey of community opinions of the hospital involving patients' Community Health Councils (CHCs). (Interestingly, this idea was put forward by two consultants, but was not spontaneously mentioned by any manager.)

We also asked what the signs of a poorly-performing hospital would be, in case the indicators for the 'downside' were different from those for the 'upside'. No such asymmetry was discovered – most respondents simply said that a poor performance was the reverse of a good one.

We were impressed by the alacrity with which doctors, managers and nurses replied to our questions about concepts of good and poor performance. It was evident that this was a topic to which they had given some thought and which had already been the subject of previous discussion within their hospital and/or profession. This state of affairs stood in contrast to that which obtained in secondary schools (see Chapter 6) where thinking about performance and performance indicators seemed less extensively developed.

In addition to our questions about concepts of a well-performing hospital, we also asked our interviewees what they thought would be the key factors in stimulating performance change (that is, significantly improved performance). The answers to this question were disappointing, at least in the sense that we obtained few answers that could be described as coherent descriptions of potential processes of performance change. Perhaps our question was phrased in too abstract a manner. We tend to believe, however, that there was more to it than this – that most of our interviewees simply did not customarily think in these terms. They were perfectly willing to suggest particular, concrete things that could be done to improve their institution's performance, but to theorise about how purposive change could best be achieved – that is, to model the process of that change – was evidently a form of thinking they were not accustomed to or particularly comfortable with.

Probably the most popular response (in all four hospitals) was that 'leadership' was necessary if people's attitudes were to change. A large majority were either cool towards or strongly critical of the possible use of performance-related pay. On the other hand, the minority who thought that performance-related pay might be worthwhile was probably slightly larger than in schools (see Chapter 6). Virtually nobody saw performance-related pay as more than a minor and marginal aid to motivation.

Thus fairly 'soft', 'human relations'-type comments predominated. Yet we also heard a less frequent voice of a very different tone. One non-executive trust director with a business background said that 'We need to have a Wapping . . . if I had my way consultants would have heart failure. They still think they run the hospital.'

Less dramatic was a suggestion from one chief executive who saw the process of change as directed at the creation of a much more 'generic, consumer-focussed' type of health worker. It was management's job to convince staff that this form of generic working was worth achieving, and to foster support for a common set of quality controls. The chief executive concerned clearly saw that it was management's responsibility to arrange the necessary training and to explain what was going on more widely and thoroughly than had been done in the past.

Performance in practice

Again, there was no discernible difference between the two second-wave trusts and the two fourth-wave trusts. For all four hospitals, existing measurement at the institutional level was heavily focused on finance and Patients' Charter measures (especially waiting times). As one manager said, 'The bottom line is still money.' Average length of stay was another much used management measure (as it had been for many years) and there was widespread awareness of the importance of the appearance of the physical environment (although the physical improvements under-way seemed to be concentrated more on the public spaces than on the working spaces). An important general point was made by the chief executive at *Duck*: 'Managers now know far more about their businesses than they did previously. Contracts, and especially GP contracting, has driven this.'

Although most of our respondents were able to give clear accounts of what performance information was actually collected, they tended to be quite vague about to whom this information was circulated. Chief executives usually knew where the information went, but most of the managers and consultants were not too sure. There seemed to be some differences of practice among the four case-study hospitals in the supply of performance information to the CHCs, GPs and other potentially interested local institutions, but these differences did not display a particularly striking pattern. None of our respondents were prepared to confess to having been particularly surprised by any of the performance indicator data that had appeared since trust status had been acquired. The general attitude was that such data had either confirmed what was already known or (particularly in the case of waiting time data) had tended to be superficial and potentially misleading.

In April 1995, when the initial round of interviewing was complete, we wrote to all four hospitals formally requesting a range of specific performance data from the period from 1991 onwards. Our hope was to construct some before-and-after time series that might reveal any discontinuities in performance consequent upon the advent of the provider market and the acquisition of trust status. The response to this part of our research was illuminating. Two of the hospitals responded rather slowly, but eventually sent us packs of assorted performance data. The other two – despite a number of reminders – took even longer. The main characteristics of the information eventually sent to us were as follows:

First, it was dominated by financial and process data – very little information related directly to issues of clinical effectiveness. Nor was there much patient satisfaction data except, in one case, an annual review of complaints (we had specifically asked for patient satisfaction data where that was available). There were no measures of equity at all (for example as between different ethnic groups, or different parts of the hospital catchment areas, or different purchasers).

Second, the data was dominated by those items which, since the advent of the provider market and the Patients' Charter, the government had insisted that trusts should measure. Essentially these items comprised three basic financial measures (rate of return on assets, the degree to which the external financing limit had been met, and the balance of income and expenditure), plus activity levels (the number of finished consultant episodes, day cases, and so on, by specialty) and patient waiting times.

Third, we were presented with a number of performance information briefings prepared for top management within the hospital. These briefings fully reflected the balance indicated in the types of data described above.

Fourth, most of the clinical data (such as it was) was marked 'confidential', especially when it could be used for comparative purposes (say, between different provider trusts) or to identify individual clinicians.

Finally, two of our case studies were involved in a quality indicator project (although, surprisingly perhaps, only one of them had mentioned this during the interviews or supplied any data generated by this project). This was a US-developed system that generated information about clinical indicators such as hospital-acquired infection rates and in-patient mortality. The contractual position for those participating in the project was that they were forbidden to release any data that would enable their performance to be compared with that of the other participating hospitals.

Our interpretation of this state of affairs was that, while NHS trusts had been obliged to construct information systems to meet the governments demands, and they could produce the information required by the government fairly readily, anything beyond that was still experimental, sensitive or non-existent. Of course it was probably the case that the hospitals took such a long time to respond to our requests because, as outside researchers, our requests were (understandably) seen as low-priority. However the documentation we eventually received exhibited clear evidence that our low-priority status was far from being the only factor. It appeared that the hospitals were simply not yet used to being asked about their performance in any detail and that they had found it difficult to put together a coordinated response. They were able to show that their activity rates had been increasing and that their waiting times had been falling, but none of our four hospitals could – at that time – produce systematic data about trends in the effectiveness of their clinical care. Neither were they able to demonstrate how equitably they treated different users with similar clinical needs, or different purchasers. More surprisingly perhaps, only one of the hospitals in our set appeared to possess systematic, centrally collated patient satisfaction data, although this comment should be qualified by recognition that particular *ad hoc* studies of patient satisfaction with individual services or aspects of services had been carried out in all four hospitals.

On the whole, the findings of other researchers seem broadly compatible with our own. A careful review of trust performance using an economic approach revealed major barriers to the formulation of a clear answer to the question 'Do trusts perform better?' (Bartlett and Le Grand, 1994). The authors pointed out that it was difficult to distinguish between the impact of the creation of trusts and the installation of the purchaser–provider split on the one hand, and other, longer-term trends on the other. They also noted that the picture was blurred by the fact that the government significantly increased the resources going to the NHS during the first two years of operation of the provider market. Finally, their research makes it clear that the available data is almost exclusively concerned with costs and activities, and that while it is therefore in principle possible to measure efficiency, effectiveness and clinical quality are beyond the analyst's reach. They summarise their findings as follows:

> The first wave trusts did, on the whole, succeed in meeting their financial objectives; however, this is not very surprising, given that the market in which they were operating was very heavily managed and that they were a self-selecting group of hospitals that were significantly more efficient than their non-trust equivalents. In addition, there has been growth in various forms of hospital activities since the introduction of the reforms; however, this may be due to a variety of factors unconnected with the reforms, notably the substantial increases in resources that has accompanied their introduction. (Ibid., p. 71)

Whilst the authors were not able to find conclusive evidence that the reforms had led to a widespread improvement in performance, they were relatively confident that the conditions were in place for efficiency gains to be achieved in the future. On the basis of our own fieldwork we would make only two final comments on this broader analysis. First, the difficulties that Bartlett and Le Grand had in interpreting performance trends within the system as a whole were more than matched by the difficulties experienced by senior managers and doctors locally. Whilst many of our interviewees could point to highly specific improvements in particular services (shorter waiting lists, more intense use of operating theatres and so on), it was by no means clear to them to what extent such improvements could be attributed to trust status and the purchaser–provider split. Second, the available information on the quality and effectiveness of services were so patchy as to make it quite impossible accurately to assess whether increases in activity and efficiency had been paid for (as some have alleged) by a reduction in quality.

Finally, at the time this book was going to press there were some signs that these issues were being addressed by the new Labour government. In July 1997 the health minister, Baroness Jay, was reported to have promised the addition of 15 new clinical indicators, including death in hospital within 30 days of admission with a heart attack, infection rates and readmission rates (*Independent*, 10 July 1997, p. 8). Significantly, however, it was quite clear that the new government intended to preserve and improve the system of centrally orchestrated performance tables (which include more than 70 indicators per hospital). Indeed the commitment to better clinical indicators represented a continuation of work done under the Conservative government, which had piloted these new measures during its last year in office.

External factors

In trying to understand the new NHS provider market and their place within it, many of our interviewees were struggling with essentially the same attribution problems that face us as academic researchers, trying to construct explanations for observed changes. In the health care sector, as in secondary schooling and public housing, the move towards self-governance was only one of a range of reforms that both constituted and stimulated organisational change. Indeed, in the case of NHS acute trusts it would be wrong to presume that the attainment of trust status was necessarily the factor with the largest impact on the internal workings of the hospital. In many ways the purchaser–provider split and the advent of explicit competition were more keenly felt. A manager at *Pigeon* said 'I have never seen trusts as the key issue. The key issue is the contracting process and particularly the rise of GP fundholding.' The finance director at the same hospital opined that 'I detect in the health service as a whole a great and growing irritation with the contracting process. . . .. It has become very tight and arguably bureaucratic.'

Frequently mentioned were national initiatives such as the change in junior doctors' contracts and the Calman Report on medical training. For example the Director of Finance at *Duck* explained that the hospital was in the middle of a major strategy review, not so much because of the opportunities now open to it as a trust, but rather because of the combined impacts of an emerging strategy by the dominant local purchaser, the change in junior doctors' hours and the Calman Report. The chief executive at the same hospital said that these developments had 'massive implications for all trust status hospitals'. More broadly still, government policies designed to give priority to primary and community-based services, combined with demographic and technological changes, held strong implications for the future shape and size of the acute sector. A clinical director at *Pigeon* put the matter succinctly: 'We mustn't pretend that hospitals will grow. Hospitals will decline.' Elsewhere we were told that 'beds are closing all over the country', and there was a good deal of fatalistic acceptance that a considerable number of mergers and closures of acute trusts was inevitable in the medium term.

These external, national pressures combined with financial stringency to create a particularly difficult context in which to test the potential of self-governance. Overall we gained the strong impression that the circumstances and tasks that senior managers faced in the NHS were, by an order of magnitude, greater than those to be found in secondary schools and housing associations.

Fragmentation, system coherence and equity

It would be misleading to suggest that either fragmentation or equity considerations loomed particularly large during our interviews with hospital managers, consultants and nurses. But neither were they absent. Equity considerations were clearly of considerable concern to a number of our interviewees, and both this issue and the related one of fragmentation seemed to generate rather more comment across our four hospitals than our four secondary schools (see Chapter 6). At *Duck* the medical director expressed the view that GP fundholders had become too powerful: the rules of the game would have to be changed so that they could be held responsible as a group, and at present the divergent behaviours of individual practices were causing problems. At *Pigeon* the chief executive said that the NHS had indeed resulted in a degree of fragmentation: 'The so-called market actually inhibits your ability to address some of these issues.' He went on to speak with feeling about the reality of 'collaboration': 'It is just so complicated. It takes up an incredible amount of time. And GP fundholding is an extra level of complication . . . I saw no real dialogue taking place. The public health dimension was totally absent.'

At another trust the chief executive unwittingly echoed these words. Arguing that the best measure for the hospital's performance would be its ability to improve the population's health status, he commented that to be able to use such a measure would require much wider recognition of the need for a multi-agency approach. At present in the NHS, 'we still play at that – I get very frustrated at the difficulty of getting co-ordinated action between social service departments, housing, education and the NHS'. The same chief executive also had concerns about equity: 'We don't have a two tier system, we have a multi tier system.' Different standards could be set by the Patients' Charter, the main purchasers and GP fundholders. A third chief executive was slightly less critical of the workings of the market, but still registered significant reservations: 'There is clearly a tension between competition and planning.'

Trusts received conflicting messages from the centre, some in favour of entrepreneurialism and competition, while others (such as the Calman Report on Cancer) envisaged a planned pattern of specialist centres. Nevertheless one interviewee believed that coordination and collaboration was possible. Whilst he complained about different purchasers applying different standards to the same service ('a real nuisance') he was enthusiastic about the possibility of creating 'stable strategic alliances' with neighbouring hospitals: 'Within our situation the market has allowed us to pursue that strategy.'

The opinions we encountered among senior managers were widely echoed elsewhere in the service. Fragmentation and inequity were the central issues behind the decision of the finance director at the Radcliffe Infirmary NHS Trust in Oxford to resign. She gained some notoriety by telling the reporters

> that the spirit of co-operation between hospitals has gone. Working in the health service has become very unpleasant because you end up fighting over everything. That can't be good for patients . . . 'I have looked consultants in the eye and told them to see fundholders' patients in advance of health authority patients . . . it's the inevitable consequence of having an internal market: in order to achieve financial targets you end up doing that. It warps you. (Quoted in Brindle, 1996)

Unsurprisingly, this was not the view of the market that Conservative ministers wanted to hear. During the mid 1990s the government and the NHS executive put considerable energy into trying to control the kind of 'news' and interpretations of the workings of the market that reached the mass media. The candid expressions of opinion that were shared with us were forthcoming only with the protection of non-attributability (together with the knowledge that academic publishing timescales were lengthy).

Overall it could not be said that we found a well-functioning and smoothly coordinated market. A more accurate description of the situations we witnessed in 1994–95 would be one of a partly regulated and partly unpredictable quasi market in which funds were desperately short in relation to demands and where uncertainty, frustration and complaints about a somewhat baroque contracting system were widespread. The Conservative government's original concept of a highly competitive market in which trusts would behave innovatively and entrepreneurially had certainly not come to pass. Indeed the Conservative government was subsequently to offer various sorts of *de facto* acknowledgement of the problems, such as its 1995 efficiency scrutiny of the burden of paperwork in NHS trusts and its 1996 drive to reduce management costs.

Whilst the above features may be fairly clear, it is almost impossible to give any confident and final judgement on the issues of fragmentation and equity. Whilst a number of well-placed interviewees told us very clearly that fragmentation was a problem, it also has to be borne in mind that the NHS was hardly immune from such divergencies before 1991. Furthermore – and more significantly – our fieldwork took place during a period in which it could reasonably be argued that the NHS provider market was still 'finding its feet'. It was not brand new, but neither was it fully 'mature'. This dynamic condition offered opportunities for critics to point to examples of the downside of competition and apparent failures of coordination, but it also enabled more optimistic commentators to point out that 'the NHS has a unique opportunity to reshape primary and secondary care boundaries and relations' (Øvretveit, 1995, p. 226). Our own detailed local researches certainly yielded ammunition for both camps.

The incoming Labour government of 1997 was quick to issue a White Paper that appeared to echo some of the concerns we identified above (Secretary of State for Health, 1997). The Secretary of State told the Commons that 'We will keep the separation between planning and providing services. But we will end competition and replace it with a new statutory duty of partnership so that local health services pull together rather than apart' (Sherman, 1997). Large groups of GPs and community nurses were to become the main purchasers of hospital and community care – thus replacing (and going beyond) the Conservative governments' GP fundholding schemes.

The lessons offered by our research for this new situation seem fairly obvious. First, some reduction in the degree of fragmentation that took place during the mid 1990s will be welcomed by many NHS staff. Second, the White Paper's proposals for simplifying the contracting procedure (partly by moving to a system of three-year contracts instead of an annual round) have the potential to please both managers and clinical staff. Third, however, it will clearly take a great deal more than a 'statutory duty of partnership' to persuade all the different groups and interests within the NHS to work smoothly in partnership. Finally, and probably most importantly, the envisaged reorganisation by itself will do little to address the chronic funding shortage that was so often apparent during our research.

With respect to equity, definitive conclusions are even more difficult. Certainly there were many inequities within the NHS prior to the 1991 reforms, but it is equally certain that concern for equity did not shine out from the foundational documents that laid the basis for the reforms. Efficiency, competition, managerial autonomy and customer responsiveness were the government's priorities, and each of these held a potential threat for equity. In a careful review of the research evidence, Whitehead came to the following conclusions:

> First, there is no overall picture of what is actually going on. Above all, it shows how painfully incomplete our information is, particularly in relation to equity . . . Second, examination of these fragments and individual pieces of evidence indicates that there are reasons to be concerned about whether an equitable service can be maintained under the new conditions set in place under *Working for Patients*. Yet there are also some rays of hope. (Whitehead, 1994, pp. 239–40)

Fieldwork at our four case study hospitals tended to confirm Whitehead's conclusions. There were certainly rays of hope. Worryingly, however, we found that equity did not seem to be high on the agenda of most of our interviewees – it was not a topic that most of them spontaneously referred to. There were also some disturbing specific examples. In summarising these, we cannot improve upon the words that Whitehead used to describe the national picture: 'In the new contract culture, deals have been struck which deliberately give preference to some patients above others, on financial rather than clinical grounds. This has come to a head with contracts between fundholders and hospitals or consultants, but it is more pervasive than that' (ibid., p. 240).

Whether the new Commission for Health Improvement announced by the Labour government, combined with the official disfavour of 'competition', will be enough to eradicate these practices remains to be seen (Secretary of State for Health, 1997).

Accountability

When we asked about the advantages and drawbacks of trust status, accountability was hardly ever mentioned at any of the four hospitals. Partly because of this, we decided to make it a special focus of our second round of interviews between September 1995 and February 1996.

In one sense the absence of comments about accountability can be easily explained – not much had changed. The long line of account-ability up to the Secretary of State for Health remained. Accountability to local elected representatives had never existed. Local councillors had been nominated as members of DHAs, but that practice had been abolished by the 1989 White Paper. We encountered no expressions of regret about their departure – on the contrary, the one or two interviewees who mentioned the previous activities of local councillors on the health authorities were clearly pleased that they had gone. In short, what was there to comment about?

From a different perspective, however, the apparent absence of interest in accountability issues was curious. After all trust status had created, for the first time, freestanding statutory corporations run by boards of executive and non-executive directors. On the face of things, this was a major change. Relations with the District Health Authorities were now conducted through contracts. There had also been change in the detail of hospitals' obligations to CHCs. To probe these issues further, in our second-round interview schedule we included a specific question about changes in accountability.

Perhaps our most optimistic interviewee was a director of finance, who told us that, as a trust, the hospital was much more accountable than it had been in the past. Previously hospital management had always 'hidden behind the health authority'. But now 'you are no longer able to hide behind the authority – your standards have to be higher and are examined publicly'. Non-executive board members had brought useful new business techniques and knowledge and the trust was accountable both to the government and to the people living in the locality. A contrasting view was provided by the director of finance at a different hospital: 'I don't think we are locally accountable at all.' To balance this he pointed out that 'trusts are just as accountable to central government as we ever were'. This particular individual was also critical of the chairperson of and non-executive directors on the board of the trust. He saw them as 'merely another group of people who put controls on the system', and he followed this up with critical comments about the qualifications and backgrounds of the individual non-executives.

Clearly there was a difference between the views of these two finance directors. However the contrast may not have been as great as it appeared at first sight. If we distinguish between *political* account-ability and managerial accountability (Day and Klein, 1987), then one can see that both interviewees were arguing that *managerial* account-ability had, if anything, intensified while political accountability had not greatly altered. Where their views clearly conflicted was over the value of non-executive directors. To some extent this may simply have been due to differences between the personalities and abilities of the individuals concerned.

The chief executives in our case study trusts were possibly the best-positioned individuals to comment on issues of external accountability. When asked, this was a topic they warmed to. One suggested that the mere presence of local authority councillors on District Health Autho-rities had hardly been enough to make them democratically responsive. He added that 'I suspect that we make a much greater effort to get alongside local people [now]'. The hospital made a point of making annual presentations to local and county councils. In the ensuing discussion we put it to this chief executive that it might be thought inappropriate that such a large volume of public resources should pass through a series of health care organisations that had only one remote political representative: the Secretary of State for Health. In response to this he made three points. First 'the NHS was more private than it was public', and had always been so. GPs were the foundation of the service and they had always been private contractors. Second, there wasn't a single line of accountability. Different lines ran to staff, patients, the local community and central government. Perhaps differ-ent accountability mechanisms were needed for each relationship. Third, there were possibilities in the future for further developing the nature of trusts, in a variety of ways. One possibility would be to establish them as mutual ownership organisations.

A second chief executive began by saying 'It is a question of what is your own view of democracy'. He then launched a scathing critique of the influence of councillors under the old DHA system, for example 'The councillors who were on the DHAs didn't understand the issues, weren't capable of understanding the issues.' Unfortunately, he was of the view that the non-executive directors on trust Boards, though, possibly of a slightly higher average intellectual ability, hadn't brought any major added value as far as decision making was concerned. Nevertheless, 'I think that trust Boards are more effective than health authorities used to be.' Invited to speculate on ways in which greater democratic accountability could be achieved within the NHS in future, he said that, although he recognised the strength of the argument, he was unable to think of a suitable form of elected representation.

Very few of our interviewees – in both the first and the second rounds of fieldwork – made any spontaneous mention of the CHCs. Evidently these were not seen as powerful players, or as important foci for public accountability. The basic opinion seemed to be that they were a group of people to whom one had to give information and with whom it was generally a good idea to cultivate friendly relations – but no more. This attitude was typified by the remark of one manager, who said of the local CHC: 'They are OK – their average age is about 76 – they are not a rebellious lot.'

The self-governing hospital: concepts

Our research yielded a veritable cornucopia of richly varied data. The problem is to try to make sense of the variety. We shall tackle this task in two stages. First, we shall apply the conceptual apparatus developed in Chapter 2. Second, in the final section of the Chapter we shall deploy the theoretical perspectives which were introduced in Chapter 2, and use them to try to make sense of our findings.

Within the overall concept of decentralisation we made four major distinctions. The first was the distinction between political and administrative decentralisation. On this score, the creation of NHS trusts was clearly an act of administrative decentralisation. Formal political control had remained unchanged. The hospitals had gained managerial autonomy, but the powers of the Secretary of State for Health were undiminished and no new elected element had been introduced to the system (this was equally true for the reforms announced by the incoming Labour administration – see Secretary of State for Health,

1997). The only vestigial element of indirectly elected representation (the councillors on the old DHAs) had been eliminated as part of the same reform package that introduced the trusts.

Our second distinction was between competitive and non-competitive decentralisation. The process of achieving trust status was non-competitive. It was not a situation in which rival organisations competed to run the trust. Existing hospitals, or amalgamations of them, bid for trust status, which they were awarded if the government believed they met certain minimum standards of manageability and financial viability. Of course once trusts existed they had then to compete within the new NHS provider market. The strength of competition clearly varied from locality to locality and from service to service, within the hospitals. Opinions differ as to how intense or weak competition within the provider market has been, but it would be a fair generalisation to say that an awareness of the need to compete had certainly touched all the hospitals we visited, although this need was felt and expressed more acutely by some parts of the service than others.

Our third distinction was between the strong form of decentralisation that we term devolution, and the weaker form in which no new organisation is created and decentralisation remains internal. Trusts are clearly a form of devolution. They require the transfer of legal authority from one organisation (the DHA) to another (the trust). However constrained, trusts are legally self-governing institutions, with their own boards of directors.

Our fourth distinction was between vertical and horizontal decentralisation. Here the picture is complicated. On the horizontal dimension it certainly seems as though managers have strengthened their authority over other groups of staff, including doctors. However there are different breeds of manager within the NHS. Some are ex-administrators or professional managers who have been trained as such. Others are doctors who have taken on some managerial responsibility, for example by becoming clinical directors. Many are nurses who have pursued a career in management. All three categories seemed to have gained some authority, but in many ways the most interesting category is that of the doctor-managers. The extent to which these 'hybrids' behave like professional managers remains an open question. Very few are willing to give up their clinical duties entirely. Unsurprisingly, given the nature of the medical career, most of those we met seemed to retain a predominantly 'producer' approach to quality rather than a 'user' perspective (Pollitt and Bouckaert, 1995).

Turning to the issue of vertical centralisation, no simple answer can be given. Certainly there was a downward, devolution of authority from DHAs to trusts. But at the same time central government strengthened its hand. By the mid 1990s there was a degree of programmatic intervention and regulation by the Department of Health and the NHS Executive that would have seemed novel 15 or 20 years previously. The Patient's Charter, with its attendant league tables and starred performances, represented a major (and a Major) intervention in hospital life. The waiting list initiative had been another. The reorganisation of junior doctors' hours and training was a third. All these signified centralisation rather than decentralisation. Furthermore the provider market itself, originally envisaged by some politicians as an engine of freedom and diversity, was subject to increasing central regulation. A number of commentators have documented the ways in which the Conservative government felt more and more obliged to orchestrate what economic textbooks sometimes refer to as a 'spontaneous order'. By the end of our research there was little that was genuinely spontaneous in the NHS provider market. One authoritative observer summarised the national picture thus:

> Far from the changes leading to more devolution and decentralisation . . . the changes paradoxically led to more central control in the NHS than has existed at any time in the Service's history. Not only were trusts directly accountable to the centre rather than to local health authority control but the centre kept very close reins on what was happening within the Service at all levels in order that no political embarassment should occur prior to the general election which took place in April 1992. (Hunter, 1993, p. 35)

As made clear in the 'Performance in Practice' section above, issues of performance and quality were very much on the agenda at all four hospitals. The concept of 'quality', in particular, was the focus of many initiatives and a good deal of discussion. The dominant conceptualisations of performance appeared to be those of efficiency (maintaining or increasing outputs while holding steady or reducing resource inputs) and clinical quality (still largely conceived of in terms of adherence to professional procedural standards). However there was also extensive evidence of more user-oriented concepts of quality coming into play – not least because the introduction of the Patients' Charter had obliged hospital managements everywhere to pay attention to waiting times and waiting lists. In short, the terrain of 'health service quality' was occupied by a variety of actors and groups, each with its own specific conceptualisation and set of mechanisms. The director of quality at *Pigeon* explained to us, with a touch of despair, that some parts of the hospital were subject to four or five different types of quality procedure, running in parallel. The nurses had their nursing quality procedures, the purchasing authority insisted on audits of its own, the doctors conducted medical audits, attention had to be paid to Patients' Charter measures, and so on. As we have suggested elsewhere (Harrison and Pollitt, 1994, pp. 94–112), there has been a struggle for control of the concept of 'quality' in health care, and one of the manifestations of this struggle has been a proliferation of terms, labels and procedures. The contestations over definitions, titles and meanings can be related to lines of occupational demarcation, at least in the sense that the major professional groupings within the NHS have now all acquired explicit quality procedures of their own. These particular schemes are overlaid by attempts on the part of the government or NHS managers to establish more generic and/or user-oriented forms of quality assurance, such as total quality management (TQM – see Joss and Kogan, 1995).

Finally, we turn to the concepts of accountability and control. The sheer diversity and complexity of the NHS is directly reflected in the somewhat confused and variable responses we encountered when we asked about accountability (see the section on 'accountability' above). Doctors spoke in terms of accountability to their patients, senior managers were clearly conscious of their accountability to the NHS Executive for the stewardship of funds, and several respondents offered the opinion that, in practice, trusts were not effectively accountable to anybody. Certainly the Secretary of State for Health, although politically accountable for the whole of the NHS, featured rarely in our discussions – this was a very remote form of accountability. On the other hand, the doctors' claims of accountability to patients, although appealing in principle, seemed somewhat short of substance in practice. There was no systematic obligation on doctors to explain themselves to their patients (although, no doubt, many did so), and patients are notoriously short of quick, effective sanctions when they receive medical attention that they regard as being of poor quality. In many ways the most tangible and immediate form of accountability was that expressed through the basic measures of financial performance of the hospital. Chief executives knew that if they repeatedly fell short of these requirements their careers (not to speak of their performance-related pay) were likely to suffer. In short our fieldwork indicated that 'accountability' was not a term that came readily to the lips of most of the senior staff of the four trusts, but that in practical terms the most obvious and concrete manifestation of external accountability was the managerial requirement to achieve a 6 per cent return on capital and stay within the prescribed external financing limit.

The self-governing hospital: theories

We have now arrived at the point where we can take the theoretical perspectives outlined in Chapter 2 and apply them to the evidence unearthed by our fieldwork. Beginning with theories of collective action, we would argue that whilst Niskanen's theory of budget maximisation appears to be of only very limited value in discussing hospital self-governance, the bureau-shaping approach generates some useful and interesting interpretations.

Niskanen proposes that the utility of bureaucrats is positively and continuously associated with the size of the budget of their employing organisation. Such bureaucrats are able to conceal the true costs of producing a given level of service and are usually able to ensure that their organisation produces a much larger volume of services than is actually required by society at large or those directly purchasing their services. This picture does not fit the post-1991 NHS provider market at all well. To begin with, one has to make allowance for the fact that the managers of trusts share power with the senior members of the medical profession. For many of the latter, and probably many of the former too, increasing the size of the hospital's budget is by no means necessarily the top priority. Indeed many consultants are blissfully ignorant of whether the aggregate hospital budget has increased or decreased in a given year. Although (as our fieldwork confirmed) such doctors appear to have become somewhat more 'cost conscious' in recent years, their main interest still lies in the type and quality of clinical work that they get to do. As is widely attested in the medical sociology literature, doctors like to have 'interesting cases'. Their careers are advanced by establishing reputations in particular specialties or subspecialties, innovating new services or techniques and publishing in medical journals.

In a less direct way these considerations also influence senior trust managers. There is a status pecking order of hospitals, and this is determined as much by the type of work undertaken as it is by the overall size of the hospital budget. Furthermore the idea that hospitals can relatively easily bamboozle their funders into a situation of gross and growing over-supply of services bears little relation to the reality of the NHS in the late 1990s. In the real world purchasing authorities have strict, hierarchically determined budget limits, and usually there is very little 'left over' with which to finance schemes proposed by the trusts for the development of new and additional services. As we have made clear in our discussion of the benefits and drawbacks of trust status, with the possible exception of *Eagle*, all our case-study hospitals were desperately short of money, and a clear majority of the managers and consultants we interviewed were sceptical (if not cynical) about the prospects for significantly increasing revenues by developing new services. In short, the three principal weaknesses in Niskanen's model we identified in Chapter 2 (no systematic allowance for differences between different types of bureaucracy; no allowance for the possibility that bureaucrats in different types of agency may value different kinds of outcome; lack of attention to interorganisational issues) all handicap the budget-maximising model as a vehicle for explaining the behaviour of NHS trusts.

At first sight Dunleavy's bureau-shaping model also appears somewhat inappropriate. After all, hospitals are intrinsically service delivery agencies and their leaders could not hope to transform them into small policy-making units, even if they wanted to. But this is too crude: there are more subtle ways of applying the model. If we look again at the five bureau-shaping strategies that Dunleavy identifies, at least some echoes of each can be found in our evidence (Dunleavy, 1991, pp. 203–5). The first strategy proposed by Dunleavy was that of major internal reorganisation aimed at insulating high-status policy- and strategy-making functions. There was certainly some evidence of this, particularly in the larger hospitals *Eagle* and *Duck*, but also to some extent at *Pigeon* and *Starling*. In each case there had been (to a greater or lesser degree) some internal decentralisation of operational decision making and an attempt to establish a clear strategy-forming function at the top of the organisation. There was also some evidence of the hiving off of routine and ancilliary tasks such as laundry, catering and cleaning, although the policy of contracting out was driven as much by the government as by local initiative.

Dunleavy's second proposition was that it would make sense for bureau-shaping managers to introduce more sophisticated management and policy analysis systems that would create more work for high-level professional staff, yet distance them from routine operational tasks. Again, we did find signs of this kind of process taking place. More sophisticated systems for monitoring clinical workloads, the condition of the hospital estate and (most saliently) the achievement of contract targets, were common factors across all or most of our four case studies.

Dunleavy's third strategy was that of redefining relationships with external partners so as to maximise policy control. It appeared that (with varying degrees of success) all four chief executives were trying to do just this. Autonomous status, combined with the introduction of the provider market, had made senior managers more sharply aware of their relationships with other key organisations in the healthcare sector. This was perhaps most apparent at *Eagle*, where much effort was being put into establishing a partnership with a range of other hospitals that would pass on specialist cases to *Eagle* in return for various commitments and cooperative arrangements. In the early days of trust status there had also been a good deal of boundary redefinition between each of the four trusts and their respective health authorities. The trusts had been vigorous in rejecting what they saw as attempts by the health authorities (now purchasing authorities) to interfere in detailed operational issues as they had done under the previous regime.

The fourth strategy suggested by Dunleavy was for an agency to try to export low-status, routine tasks to their rivals whilst capturing more high-status work for itself. Again, we found some evidence of this, although the scope for both 'capture' and 'export' was generally rather limited, given the tight funding climate, the long timescales involved in developing new services and the geographical considerations that made some hospitals natural local monopolies in particular services. The partnership strategy launched by *Eagle* was perhaps the clearest example of this kind of strategy. In contrast *Starling* and *Pigeon* were struggling to hang on to their existing services whilst a larger hospital in their subregion tried to 'capture' new regional and subregional specialisms. It should be added, however, that whilst the advent of the provider market and the autonomy of trust status probably made such strategic games easier to play, a version of this kind of game had existed within the NHS for a very long time. Under the old system of RHAs, DHAs and DMUs a great deal of 'bureaucratic politics' had taken place over the location of new services, especially high-status specialties (see, for example, Elcock and Heywood 1980).

Dunleavy's fifth strategy (hiving off and contracting out) has already been mentioned. Under central government compulsion, hospitals had been contracting out ancilliary functions since the early 1980s. This activity was continuing during the time of our fieldwork, but we found no evidence to indicate that achievement of trust status had either accelerated or reduced the amount of it.

Elements of bureau-shaping could therefore be identified at each of our four case study hospitals. Furthermore, what we were told about the manner of decision at each hospital to apply for (or refrain from applying for) trust status fitted quite readily into a game theory format. The 1990 National Health Service and Community Care Act was, in Bengtsson's terms, a 'critical juncture' at which the institutional rules of the game underwent fundamental change (Bengtsson, 1995). Interestingly, our fieldwork seems to show that the players' conceptions of the new game tended to evolve from a predominantly zero sum model through a bargaining model and towards a cooperative ideal. At the time when trust status was being considered, much of the thinking was essentially zero sum, that is, 'let's escape from interference by the DHA/RHA'. In the immediate aftermath of the acquisition of trust status, considerable resentment was generated by the perception that DHAs were still 'interfering' and that GP fundholders had received overgenerous allocations (sometimes referred to by trust managers and doctors as 'our money'). However, by the final stages of our fieldwork we found that chief executives and other managers at three of the four hospitals were talking much more in terms of partnership and cooperation with other hospitals, local GPs and – though somewhat despairingly – local social services departments. (The despair with respect to social services departments arose from the perception that they were drowning in the 'redisorganisation' of the new community care legislation, and were under resourced, over politicised and somewhat under managed.) At the fourth hospital, *Pigeon*, there was still a considerable degree of antagonism towards the main local purchaser and the other main providers. There was also some resentment that, whereas it had once been the most modern, dynamic hospital in the subregion, the passage of time plus the NHS reforms had now left it in many ways the weakest.

Yet despite the fact that much of the 'story' we encountered can be neatly repackaged into the vocabulary of bureau-shaping and game theory, this perspective ultimately seems narrow. For example to say that many doctors want to get rid as much routine work as possible, to concentrate more on their specialism and to develop new services is perfectly true, but it ignores a large part of what it is to be a doctor. Unless one is to discount as pure window dressing a great deal of what consultants (as well as many managers and most nurses) say, there is a large element of other-regarding behaviour in their activities that is hard to accommodate within a perspective founded on an assumption of individual, calculative utility maximisation. By the same token, a straightforward application of a collective action perspective runs the risk of significantly underplaying the amount of uncertainty, fear and confusion that accompanied the early days of the NHS provider market. Although strategic thinking undoubtedly did go on, any suggestion of key decision makers coolly calculating alternative strategies and pay-offs would misrepresent the evidence we collected. Many of the decisions and debates our interviewees informed us about were as much concerned with vague fears and old rivalries as they were with maximising utility under the new rules of the game.

Of course it would be possible for the afficianados of rational choice theory to argue that all these things could be taken into account. In principle, game theory approaches certainly allow for elements of uncertainty and calculations of the cost of obtaining better information. It might even be argued that helping others (that is, other-regarding, altruistic behaviour) could be incorporated for by including it as an additional 'utility' that individuals would wish to maximise, subject to constraints. But there are problems with this kind of defence of the rational choice approach. First, there is a serious conceptual problem, once it is admitted that other-regarding behaviours are frequent and important. If self-interested calculation is redefined so as to include altruism, then the concept of utility maximisation seems to lose all its shape and precision. If 'maximising utility' can mean absolutely anything, then in effect it means nothing. Yet even if other-regarding behaviour is excluded from the definition and a tighter concept of self-interest continues to be employed, there are severe practical difficulties in applying the approach to a process of policy implementation as complex as the one with which this book is concerned. Of course it is theoretically possible that a history of the development and implementation of a policy for creating trusts could be assembled in strict, game theory terms. But the information requirements of such an exercise would be huge. For each key player (chief executive officer, finance director, medical director, chairman, chief executive of the local purchasing authority, key officials in the NHS Executive and so on) one would need to know their own preference structures, what information they possessed about the preference structures of each of the other key players, and what they perceive as the strategic options open to them and the constraints within which they have to operate. Furthermore, one would need all this information not just at one point in time, but at many points, so as to chart shifts in information levels and constraints as the situation unfolded, both locally and nationally. Even the most intensive and high-quality case studies seldom manage to collect information of this quality and breadth. Thus, whilst the collective action perspective can be used in a loose and metaphorical way – dealing crudely with aggregated entities such as 'doctors' or 'the LEA' – it can seldom, if ever, be applied rigorously on a large scale and/or over a substantial period of time. It seems strange that, in all the vigorous theoretical debates for and against (and within) collective action/rational choice theory these very considerable practical difficulties are only infrequently discussed.

Moving on, we may now consider the value of new institutionalist approaches in casting light on our case-study materials. New institutionalists stress historical development, the pressure to behave 'appropriately', the need for legitimation and the role of symbolism in organisational life. As noted in Chapter 2, this body of theory is weak in generating specific, testable propositions, but strong in identifying issues of style, ethos and conformity.

It was actually quite hard for senior NHS trust managers to behave 'appropriately' during the early days of the provider market. On one level, so much had changed that the traditional role of diplomatic and deferential administrator was, in effect, simply no longer available to them (Harrison *et al.*, 1992, pp. 26–41). They were under fierce and contradictory pressures from the government. On the one hand they were supposed to behave dynamically and entrepreneurially, but, on the other, strong messages from the centre told them not to do things that might cause adverse media attention. The first of April 1991 represented a genuine historical discontinuity. New norms for acceptable behaviour had to be established, and the intensive cycle of management conferences and seminars that was still continuing during our fieldwork may be partly interpreted as an attempt to network in order to establish a common understanding of what was now 'appropriate'. In this sense, therefore, it could be argued that institutionalist approaches are of limited value. They find it hard to explain the wide-ranging, radical change the government was able to impose on the NHS through the 1990 Act. Yet it would be premature to dismiss this approach entirely. In some ways what was remarkable was how quickly new norms were built up. By the end of our fieldwork (early 1996) there was already a sense that incremental evolution had taken over from radical change. New styles and patterns of bargaining had established themselves, and the wilder fears about trust status that were still abroad when our project began in 1993 had largely disappeared. Quite soon after the launch of the provider market the Secretary of State for Health began to talk about a 'steady state', warning both purchasers and providers to be cautious about making sudden or dramatic changes to previous patterns of service and referral. Presumably, therefore, institutionalists could argue that the strength of their model was demonstrated by the speed with which a new normality was established after a temporary 'blip'.

In any case, the most dramatic changes in relationships took place *outside* the trusts – in relationships with purchasing authorities and GP fundholders. Although we found evidence of various forms of internal decentralisation and restructuring, on the whole the pace of change inside trusts seems to have been more incremental. The crucial relationship between managers and doctors did seem to shift, but only incrementally. At none of the four hospitals did we find evidence of managers taking the opportunity to have a 'showdown' with doctors (or for that matter, *vice versa*).

Predictably, the establishment of new behavioural norms went hand in hand with the construction of new strategies for legitimation. In a sense the creation of a provider market with free-standing trusts to some extent competing against each other, itself provided a powerful legitimation for management. There was a sense in which everyone knew that, in a market with firms that produce things, you needed managers to run them. There was also some evidence in our fieldwork to suggest that the mood of 'sink or swim together' inside trusts strengthened management's hand in taking action against those who appeared to be obstructing progress or dragging down efficiency. This was particularly visible in the relationship between managers, the most striking example probably being the complete change in the senior management team by the new chief executive at *Starling*. But even among consultants there was perhaps some strengthening of peer pressure against those who appeared to be falling short of local 'productivity norms'. A clinical director at *Pigeon* expressed this slightly cynically when he said: 'I often feel we are mainly ciphers. We are here mainly to control our consultant colleagues.' In some of our case-study hospitals, waiting-list and waiting-time information was broken down by consultant and this permitted senior managers and doctors managers to exert greater leverage against those who appeared to be out of line.

Finally, if we look for evidence of organisational isomorphism (Dimaggio and Powell, 1991) we can see that, within the space of four years, the NHS went from a situation where there were no trusts to one in which almost every provider unit had converted to the trust format. Surely this was therefore a striking example of isomorphism. What type of isomorphism it was, however, is less obvious. In the beginning, one might have classified trust applications of the second and third waves as examples of mimetic isomorphism, in which individual hospitals voluntarily copied what others had done in the hope of gaining greater autonomy and, possibly, resources. But by the time of the fourth-wave applications (including those from *Starling* and *Duck*) the process had become, *de facto*, more coercive. The government left the remaining DMUs in no doubt that they were supposed to move to trust status as quickly as possible.

In all these respects, therefore, institutionalist approaches are helpful in deepening our understanding of the early development of the NHS provider market. They draw attention to features that are different from those highlighted by a collective action perspective. But the instititionalist lens is not one that yields a particularly sharply-focused picture. It does not seem very useful in producing convincing explanations of why specific decisions went one way or another, or, indeed, why government policy itself developed in the way it did.

Management reform in the NHS offers a rich field for rhetorical analysis. Along with the provider market there developed a new managerialist vocabulary – one that evolved quite quickly, according to the prevailing political mood. Hunter (1993, p. 40) describes the three-year period following the publication of the *Working for Patients* as follows:

> Tough talk about competition began to give way in the face of mounting public and professional hostility to the reforms to a new language which did not contain words like 'markets' and 'competition'. It was quite noticeable that with the change in the Secretary of State [the replacement of Kenneth Clark by William Waldegrave] a marked shift in the vocabulary describing the reforms was discernible. William Waldegrave sought to play down all talk of markets and competition, and tried to shift the debate onto new ground, in particular by articulating the need for a strategy for health that would provide a framework to guide all the activities for purchasers and providers at local level. However, the shift in language did not constrain him from announcing a second wave of National Health Service Trusts in April 1992 or from increasing the number of GP fundholding practice.

In our fieldwork we certainly found that the vocabulary of business was in fairly common usage and had begun to spread beyond managers to consultants. A number of the latter talked in terms of how the hospital should be managed 'as a business' or suggested that certain aspects of the current arrangements were still too 'bureaucratic' and not sufficiently 'businesslike'. The sense of playing with a new vocabulary was well encapsulated in an interview with the manager of a clinical directorate at *Pigeon* who, describing the joys of operating a delegated budget for the first time, told us that: 'It was wonderful going out with your little shopping list and thinking, it's our money and we can spend it.' It was noticeable, however, that clinical staff tended to keep business terminology well away from their references to patients. They would use business language when discussing hospital finances but switch into a different, more traditional discourse when discussing patient care.

A crucial question in any analysis of rhetoric is that of the presumed audience towards which the argument in question is being directed. There was an interesting difference here between NHS trusts and secondary schools. As we shall see in the Chapter 6, the intended audience of much of the argumentation we heard from head teachers and their senior colleagues seemed to be parents or other teachers. In contrast most of the arguments deployed during our interviews in the four hospitals seemed to be directed upwards – towards purchasers or, beyond them, the NHS Executive and the Department of Health. There was a sense in which many of our NHS managers seemed to be trying to convince their colleagues higher up the hierarchy rather than addressing patients or a wider public audience. There was a strong assumption that the trusts were still part of a much larger and interconnected system, and the arguments to which we were exposed were often attempts to propose improved solutions for the whole of the NHS system rather than ideas that were justified solely in terms of the local interest of the particular trust.

We will close the chapter with the words of one chief executive who attempted to summarise the reality of the provider market as he saw it at the end of 1995:

- 'The best that has happened has been to do with creating coherent organisations.'
- 'The financial regime is pretty tightly constrained.'
- 'I have not come across a purchasing authority that has made a purchasing decision.'

- 'In the real world we only get judged on narrow and short-term criteria.'
- 'There is clearly a tension between competition and planning.'
- 'What we actually have is an opportunity to enter into deals with people.'

6 Decentralised Management of Secondary Schools

Introduction

The schools sector has a particular significance for our analysis because it is the only sector where – perhaps by accident rather than design – the Conservative governments of the 1980s and 1990s afforded local service-providing organisations a genuine choice between opting for independent self-managed status or remaining within a locally coordinated yet managerially 'liberated' system. As we have seen, by the end of 1992 NHS acute hospitals were faced with a situation in which there seemed to be no viable alternative to applying for self-managed (that is, trust) status. Equally, as will be explained in Chapter 7, the 'choice' facing local authority housing departments was a powerfully constrained one. The large-scale voluntary transfer (LSVT) route offered housing managers strikingly more freedom and a far more flexible set of financial arrangements than they could possibly hope for if they remained in a local authority housing department. In the schools sector, however, the development of LMS during the late 1980s meant that there was much more of a real choice. On the one hand schools could 'opt out' by applying for grant maintained (GM) status. This would bring an immediate financial boost plus considerable managerial autonomy. On the other hand, however, it was possible to stay within the LEA sector whilst achieving – through Local Management of Schools – a significant enhancement of managerial autonomy, including far greater control of the school budget. Delegation to schools of at least 85 per cent of initial school budgets (as defined by the Department for Education and Employment) became mandatory. Many LEAs decided to delegate an even higher percentage than this. As the Local Schools Information Unit put it: 'As a result of LMS all schools are far more autonomous than they used to be and the differences between GM and LEA schools have diminished greatly' (Local Schools Information, 1996, p. 5).

Thus, it was really only in the schools sector that there was anything approaching a 'level playing field' between the legally independent self-managed option and the modernised and liberalised version of the traditional system. Even here the field was somewhat tilted, but it was not the steep incline that prevailed in respect of NHS trust status, nor the veritable ski slope faced by local housing departments.

In this context the pattern of opting out over the period since the first wave (September 1989) is instructive. The flow of applications for GM status appears to have fluctuated quite markedly, mainly in accordance with general political conditions in the country as a whole. The first cohort, at the end of the 1980s, contained a high proportion of schools that were threatened with merger, closure or other problems. Writing in 1993, Fitz *et al.* (p. 38) recorded that 'For those schools for which we have data, nearly a half (107/227) were identified by their LEAs in connection with reorganisation schemes.'

Interestingly, the largest number of early opt-outs came from within Conservative-controlled county councils. Subsequently, during the run-up to the 1992 general election, there was a decline in the number of ballots, and an increase in the proportion of ballot results that went against opting out. Following the Conservative victory in 1992 there was a surge of opt-out applications, reaching a peak in the autumn of that year. During 1993 however, the rate of applications dropped rapidly – a trend that was likely to have been associated with the country-wide loss of power by the Conservative Party in the May 1993 local elections. The 1993 Education Act, published in the autumn of that year, was clearly intended to restore the popularity of GM status. It obliged governing bodies to give explicit consideration to an opt-out at least once in every school year. In practice, however, a brief spurt was quickly followed by a further slump, and the number of secondary schools seeking grant maintained status was very low in after mid 1994. Table 6.1 shows the pattern of successful opt-outs.

Another interesting feature of the school sector is that the opt-out mechanism necessarily involved a vote by 'ordinary' local people. The governing body of an LEA school, if it wished to opt out, was obliged to hold a ballot by first passing a formal resolution to do so. Every person appearing as a parent on the admissions register of the school was eligible to vote. A secret postal ballot was held organised by the Electoral Reform Society. If more than 50 per cent of those eligible to

Table 6.1   Creation of new GM secondary schools, by term

Term	Secondary Starters	Cumulative Total	Term	Secondary Starters	Cumulative Total
Autumn 1989	18	18	Spring 1990	2	20
Summer 1990	10	30	Autumn 1991	14	44
Spring 1991	6	50	Summer 1991	12	62
Autumn 1991	35	97	Spring 1992	33	130
Summer 1992	52	182	Autumn 1992	42	224
Spring 1993	37	261	Summer 1993	127	388
Autumn 1993	127	515	Spring 1994	39	554
Summer 1994	40	594	Autumn 1994	21	615
Spring 1995	7	622	Summer 1995	9	631
Autumn 1995	4	635*	Spring 1996	6	641
Summer 1996	3	644	Autumn 1996	6	650
Spring 1997	3	653	Summer 1997	5	658

*To give some perspective to the cumulative total, at the beginning of 1996 there were 3594 (GM and LEA) secondary schools, that is, GM schools represented about 18 per cent of the total.

Source: Figures supplied by the Department for Education and Employment.

vote did so they a simple majority result was conclusive. If fewer than 50 per cent voted (or the result was an exact tie) then a second ballot had to be held within 14 days, and the result of that second ballot was taken as decisive, irrespective of what percentage of the eligible 'electorate' participated.

The situations in healthcare and housing were different. In the NHS, as we have seen, there was no tradition of active local accountability and no provision for anyone to vote for or against the move to trust status. In many hospitals there were *de facto* votes – usually within the consultant body – but these were not determinative. Votes by patients and/or prospective patients were rare and played no part in any of the cases we examined. In housing, tenants' votes were mandatory and very influential. This was therefore closer to the balloting of parents on GM opt-outs, except that in the latter case the parents were making a choice not so much for themselves as on behalf of their children.

Before moving to an analysis of the particular experiences of the schools that participated in our research there is one further general issue that deserves mention: size. Much of the theoretical literature on organisations indicates that size is an important variable that extensively influences a number of other factors (such as the degree of formalism, the degree of specialisation and so on – see Donaldson, 1985, p. 161). Secondary schools were by some margin the smallest type of service delivery organisation we examined. For example one of the schools in our study had an annual budget of £2.2 million and employed about 70 staff. Compare this with one of our NHS trusts (not the largest), which had an annual budget of £45 million and employed 2 700 staff. One of the housing associations we looked at owned capital stock worth nearly £50 million, employed a staff of more than 180 and managed more than 8000 separate properties.

It is interesting to speculate what kind of effects these differences of size might have had. Larger organisations tend to be more differentiated and to face the challenge of coordinating a wider range of functions and occupational groups (this is certainly true for hospitals). Such coordination tends to lead to the development of a more formalised and elaborate set of internal rules and procedures. Smaller size may also mean that, *ceteris paribus*, an organisation is more permeable to outside influences. Thus in a secondary school most of the staff are quite close to the 'outside world', and are therefore more likely to notice when there is a change in the messages coming from parents and students. Almost every member of the staff of a school will meet a number of 'outsiders' every day, whereas there are many parts of hospitals that deal mainly or exclusively with other parts of the hospital, or other parts of the NHS. Likewise the 'grapevine' in a secondary school usually transmits important news very quickly. It is more difficult to get information around a hospital staff of upwards of 2 500, and by the same token it is easier for top management in a hospital to lose touch with rank and file staff. Furthermore schools tend to have a fairly well-defined and geographically concentrated 'clientele' – the vast majority of students will come from homes in a particular local catchment area – while the catchment areas for acute hospitals and housing organisations both tend to be considerably larger (and – for hospitals at least – are frequently less homogeneous).

The schools in our study

As with the hospitals in our study, we have given pseudonyms to those schools that were kind enough to give us research access. The four schools were as follows:

- *Rabbit*: a GM secondary school in the Midlands.
- *Dog*: a GM secondary school in a Midlands inner city area.

- *Fox*: an LEA secondary school in the same connurbation as *Dog*, but in a more prosperous suburban locality.
- *Badger*: an LEA secondary school in a prosperous Home Counties town.

Thus we worked within two GM secondary schools and two secondary schools that had remained within their respective LEAs. In each case we interviewed the head teacher and other senior teaching staff, plus a variety of other 'stakeholders', including parent governors, school secretaries, the chief education officer of the LEA within which two of the schools were located, several other LEA officials and the chairman of the Grant Maintained Schools Centre.

In the following sections we will review our findings with respect to various key aspects of opting out (or not opting out), including the reasons for the original go/no-go decision, the benefits and drawbacks of the chosen course and the assessment our respondents made of their current situation. We also asked for their definitions and assessments of their schools' performances. We shall supplement these particular local stories with references to the more general research literature on opting out, indicating where it appears that our particular findings either resonate with or depart from those of other studies. Last but not least, we shall reconsider the evidence in the light of the theories and concepts introduced in Chapter 2. How far do these theories and concepts enable us to understand the processes and outcomes of the restructuring of secondary education during the late 1980s and the first half of the 1990s?

Reasons and benefits

There was common ground among all four schools in terms of the arguments deployed for and against opting out. In each case the two crucial variables appear to have been the pre-existing relationship between the particular school and its LEA, together with the personal stance taken by the head teacher. In *Rabbit* and *Dog* the head teachers had been instrumental in organising the change process, despite vigorous campaigns against the change of status (indeed opinion had been neither uniformly against nor uniformly in favour of opting out at any of the four schools). At *Dog* the head had pushed forward despite a roughly 50/50 split of opinion among the staff. Also at *Dog*, relations

with the LEA appear to have been very poor. The school had believed
it had been unfairly under-resourced over a considerable period and a
number of staff (not all) had also been of the view that there was a real
threat of amalgamation or closure in the not too distant future. In this
situation, the head's vigorous leadership had been crucial. Although
the teaching staff had been split and the parents had initially been
somewhat 'mystified and unsure', both groups had eventually been
persuaded by the head. As a number of our respondents affirmed, he
was known and trusted by the local parents. The teachers had been
very concerned about what they saw as uncertainty about their future
conditions of service and pension rights. These fears had been accen-
tuated by pressure from the LEA, which (it was alleged by several
respondents) had implied to teachers that they would not get jobs in the
future in other schools within that authority. Despite these misgivings,
in the end the teaching force had come to the view that 'the whole thing
would go through anyway'. As one member of staff put it: 'even if staff
were against the principle of opting out they had a mortgage to pay and
responsibilities to fulfill'.

At *Rabbit* there had definitely been fear of amalgamation, or even
closure. Competition from a local City Technology College had been
regarded by a number of staff as a serious threat. Again, the staff had
been concerned about the proposed changes, with about half of them
initially voting against a GM application. The head himself was not
personally a believer in the principle of opting out, and had been fairly
critical of the general tenor of the government's education policy at the
time. Nevertheless, under the particular circumstances faced by his
school, he had judged that GM status was the best route to survival.
After some debate the staff had accepted this argument – a second
ballot had resulted in an 80/20 vote to make an application. The
chairperson of the governing body had resigned, but without any
public animosity. This is an interesting case of a school that went for
and achieved GM status despite considerable initial reservations by
almost all the principal stakeholders. It did so because a strategic
analysis of its local situation indicated that to hold back might damage
its long-term status and viability.

At both *Badger* and *Fox* the respective heads had decided that
caution was in order. At *Badger*, relations with the LEA had been
good and both the head and the deputy head told us that there had
been little or no educational or political desire on the part of staff,
governors or parents to opt out (except for the occasional individual
who had seen things another way). At *Fox* the senior management

team in the school had been in favour of opting out, but the local political climate had seemed to be against it and the head had been reluctant to risk alienating parental opinion. A vote against opting out could have created a serious rift between the school and the parents. For both these LEA schools there was evidence that the LEA had become somewhat more responsive and supportive following the introduction of opting out as new strategic possibility. Fresh LEA investment had taken place at both schools and there were references to LEA services becoming more efficient and responsive.

Reference to investment brings us directly to a further important factor in the decision to opt out. At both *Rabbit* and *Dog* we found extensive evidence of improved resourcing following the decision to go grant maintained. At *Dog* we were told that the school had been able to 'introduce IT across the curriculum, in a way that could never have been facilitated under the LEA system'. Another respondent at the same school referred to a 'massive injection for IT resources'. A third claimed that before opt-out the school had had an average of one computer for every 70 pupils, but after the achievement of grant maintained status this ratio had soon changed to one computer for every seven pupils. Other benefits that were referred to included greater investment in the reading and resource area, new equipment in the textiles area, the speedy setting up of a work experience abroad scheme and quicker and cheaper purchase of supplies and materials than under the previous arrangements, when the LEA supplies organisation had to be used. Respondents at the LEA schools also frequently referred to injections of extra cash as a prime presumed benefit that would have flowed from GM status, had they sought it. At *Badger* one respondent mentioned a need that had existed for cash to improve the school buildings and how the LEA had moved to provide £150 000 to support specific projects. At *Fox* financial advantages plus a presumed gain in managerial freedom had prompted eight out of nine members of the senior management team to vote in favour of submitting the idea of GM status to the governing body, despite ideological reservations about the whole policy. Subsequently, however, and despite a favourable vote from the governors, the head, after consulting all the staff, did not proceed with an application.

Our findings about the reasons for opting out, or refraining from doing so, are in the main echoed by other researchers. For example Fitz *et al.* (1993, pp. 35–8) identified the threat of reorganisation schemes as an important reason for applying for grant maintained status and tracked how increases in financial incentives boosted the number of ballots. They also produced evidence that capital allocations by the government were heavily skewed in favour of GM schools (ibid., p. 29). However the relative financial advantage of GM status has declined since the two schools in our research opted out:

> Largely because of the progress of Local Management of Schools (LMS) there is now very little overall difference in the funding available whether grant-maintained or LEA-maintained. However, this was not originally the case, and most of the schools which opted out earlier enjoyed considerable financial advantages which are no longer available. (Local Schools Information, 1996, p. 15)

There was, therefore, a 'one-off' aspect to the benefits of opting out. Whilst the two GM schools *Rabbit* and *Dog* had been able to buy computers, build libraries and purchase other specialised equipment, the advantages of these investments depreciated as time went by (and as the LMS freedoms accorded to LEA schools were extended). Research by Levačić (1994) and others has revealed widespread evidence of improved flexibility and efficiency in resource use, consequent on the introduction of LMS. Our work reinforces those findings.

The thesis that the relative freedom enjoyed by a GM school and an LEA school with LMS had become quite similar was to an extent supported by the examples of autonomy given by respondents at the two types of school. Respondents at LEA/LMS schools also offered a range of examples of welcome, practical improvements that they believed LMS had enabled them to make. They were not very different from those that had been made at the GM schools. At *Fox* the groundsman had been able to undertake some landscaping work around the school playing field and it had also been possible to provide new fencing and a car park. At the same school a number of new computers had been bought and staff had been able to choose the model they wanted rather than following LEA guidance (as they believed they would have been obliged to in the past). A school nurse and a school gardener had been appointed, and again it was claimed that LEA rules would previously have prevented this. At *Badger* the science laboratory had been refurbished and funds had been allocated to complete a reroofing project. The purchase of new textbooks had proceeded quickly and without fuss, and one member of staff told us about the rapid construction of a set of cupboards for one classroom, which, it was said, would probably have taken months under the old system.

Overall, therefore, one might say that the relative advantages of GM and LEA status varied considerably, both over time (with detailed changes to GM and LMS regulations) and by location (influenced by relations between the individual school and the LEA and between the individual school and other schools in the locality). Indeed other researchers, working with a larger set of schools than we investigated, have suggested that:

> The prediction that, if one school opts out, this will have a 'domino effect' on others in the same area has been borne out in practice. Of the first 60 LEAs to 'lose' a school to the GM sector, 25 had four or more opted-out schools operating within their boundaries by the beginning of 1993. (Fitz *et al.*, 1993, p. 39)

A related point is that 'as market forces increase, schools are likely to emphasise new management characteristics' (Ranson *et al.*, 1997). These 'new management characteristics' include internal structural reorganisations and a strengthening of control by governors, the head and senior teachers. Competitive pressures can even subordinate financial interests: 'In some cases, particularly when a school's future is threatened by its LEA, the issue of finance may hardly figure at all; what matters most is to survive' (Fitz *et al.*, 1993, p. 38).

The drawbacks of opting out

The majority of our respondents at the GM schools – including some who were enthusiastic about the overall effects of opting out – were easily able to identify the potential and actual disadvantages of their new freedom. The problems were perhaps most cogently expressed by a teacher at *Dog*: 'The local authority has cut us off.' Other respondents referred to the lack of access to resources and backing that only a larger organisation such as an LEA is able to provide. There was also a sense of isolation, and sadness and resentment at the fact that teachers were being 'snubbed by other teachers and by other schools'. In addition teachers wondered what would happen if their GM school suffered a fire or a major boiler failure. In the old days the LEA would have rallied other schools to help, and put in resources of its own.

A second focus for concern was the increase in administrative duties and the possibility that these might exceed the capacity of the schools' upper echelons to manage. Several respondents referred to the problems posed for the governing board, who as 'a group of amateurs' were expected to manage the finances. of the school and determine whether or not they were paying the right salary for the most senior posts. Respondents in the LEA schools also mentioned lack of business and management expertise as a reason why they had been nervous about going for GM status. One LEA officer cited two local schools outside our fieldwork and said that 'frankly [they] are rubbish and are failing as GM schools just as badly as they did when they were with the LEA. The only difference is that we might have helped them to survive, at least in part.' Generally speaking, teachers expressed regret at their reduced contact with other teachers in other schools and with LEA specialist support services. However a minority of respondents maintained that there had been no drawbacks whatsoever to GM status and much appeared to depend upon the LEA's willingness to try to keep good relations alive.

A third major drawback – mentioned especially by respondents in the LEA schools, but also by few in the GM schools – was diminishing equity in the local school system. We shall deal with this in a later section, but the important point here is that, from the perspective of the GM school, this disadvantage – if it exists – is essentially an externality.

Concepts of performance

We asked everyone we interviewed what signs they would look for that their school was performing well and, in contrast, what the warning signs of a poor performance would be (see Appendix 2 for the interview schedule). There was no systematic difference in the responses of the GM schools and the LEA schools. Most of our respondents were readily able to name three, four or five of what they regarded as key indicators. Most regarded these indicators as symmetrical that is, a bad performance was simply the opposite of a good one. The indicators that were most often mentioned included the following:

- Examination results.
- Standards of basic literacy and numeracy.
- Standards of pupil behaviour.
- Levels of pupil attendance.
- The rate at which pupils were excluded from a school.
- Staff attendance and sickness rates.

- Parental involvement and interest in the school (as measured by attendance at parent–teacher association meetings, the annual general meeting and so on).
- The range of extra curricular activities provided by the school.
- The state of school buildings (cleanliness, absence of graffiti, general evidence of care for the physical environment).

Many respondents used the term 'atmosphere' and some offered more holistic comments, for example that the aim of the school was to produce 'whole human beings' or that the performance of the school could be 'seen in the eyes of the children and in their body language'. A substantial number of respondents stressed that the 'performance' of a school against any of these indicators had to be weighted by social and economic factors. This point was made with particular frequency by the staff at *Dog*, which probably had the most socially deprived catchment area of the four schools.

In order further to explore our respondents' ideas about performance, we asked them about the factors that, in practice, they thought were most conducive to performance improvement. We followed this up with a supplementary question about the applicability of individual incentives and penalties within the school setting. In response to the first of these questions several factors were mentioned, but one stood out above all the others in terms of the frequency and fervour with which it was proposed. This factor was 'leadership', which was mentioned by almost everybody. Some simply used the term without elaborating much on its meaning. Others developed the concept, most commonly linking it to the process of establishing and communicating high expectations to pupils, teachers and parents. This kind of explanation was common to all four schools. Thus, for example, one teacher at *Badger* said that leadership was the most important factor and that it consisted of being able to 'sell the school to outsiders and ensure that teachers have an awareness of the school's goals'. Another teacher at the same school spoke of leadership as having a clear sense of 'where you are going and what you want as an organisation'. At *Dog* teachers referred to leadership as the fundamental principle behind improved performance and referred to the need for management to set standards and have high expectations of staff and pupils. The head explained that teachers needed to be increasingly aware of the demands and requirements placed upon them, and to be able to communicate this to the pupils. He said that the kind of cultural changes that were required came from good leadership and sound organisation. Some of our respondents saw leadership as coming from 'management' (meaning the head and senior teachers), while others identified leadership in a very personal way with the head: 'The key to all of this is the head teacher. The head teacher should continue to raise the expectations of parents.' Or 'A school needs a clear view of what is required for its children and this comes from the head teacher. Leadership is the most important factor in improving performance' (both these teachers were at *Rabbit*).

It was interesting that, while many of the people we talked to appear to view performance improvement as mainly having to do with relations between the head teacher, the teachers and the pupils, several respondents also stressed the significance of raising parents' expectations. This view was most succinctly stated by a teacher at *Dog*: 'No significant change in performance can take place in a school without the backing and commitment of the children's parents.' He went on to explain how the school management had put considerable effort into trying to 'sell the school to parents in order to get their involvement', and how this had paid off in terms of increased attendance at parents' evenings and other forms of participation.

It was noticeable that virtually none of our respondents connected our questions about the requirements for performance improvement with our earlier questions about performance indicators. No one suggested that performance indicator information could be used to improve performance. On the contrary, performance improvement was articulated very much in terms of 'leadership', 'expectations', 'commitment' and 'motivation'.

The reaction to our subsidiary question about the applicability of individual rewards and penalties was quite vigorous. The great majority of teachers rejected this idea. It was repeatedly described as 'divisive', and it was pointed out that teaching was a team activity that would be disrupted by the rewarding or sanctioning of individuals. We were told that penalties and incentives could 'destroy' teachers and that it would be neither practical nor ethically desirable to use cash incentives. The whole idea was referred to as 'perverse', and we were told that 'teachers become teachers because it is their vocation and not for rewards'. These comments were voiced equally in all four schools in our sample.

However, despite the fact that outright rejection was the most common response, there was also a substratum of qualified acceptance. Whilst only one or two people spoke in favour of financial incentives, a number conceded that, for example, 'some sanctions were necessary in order to impose discipline', or that penalties already existed in the form of fear of losing one's job. Quite a few respondents emphasised that the most important incentives were praise and recognition. A teacher at one of the LEA schools commented that the governing body had been prepared to introduce an incentive scheme for good classroom performance but had been forced to abandon the idea. He went on to argue that the concept of incentives was more profitably interpreted in terms of acknowledging good performance through status and recognition.

At the outset of our research we had wondered whether we would find a more hard-edged attitude towards both performance indicators and performance incentives/penalties in the schools that had opted for GM status. In the event our interviews and observations yielded no indication of any systematic difference between the two types of school.

Performance in practice: the use of performance-related information by schools

Although we had encountered open readiness to talk about the *concepts* of school performance (see the previous section), we subsequently discovered quite widespread vagueness about what performance data was actually collected and how it was used. Many of the rank and file teachers indicated that they were not sure what information was collected or how it was used. Unsurprisingly, head teachers and senior teachers were rather different in this respect – they were generally able to give a clear account of the use of performance information in their schools. There were some signs that a sharper focus on these issues was developing. The head at *Dog* explained that he was on the point of introducing indices that would show the number of disciplinary reports, recorded lateness and health-check information for individual pupils. A new computer system had been installed that, *inter alia*, kept a running check on attendance levels. Several respondents at the same school said that they could see that management was now moving towards more thorough data collection that would permit the setting of targets. There was widespread awareness that the school had improved its examination results over the preceding few years and increased pupil recruitment. At *Badger*, expected GCSE results in Year 11 were projected on the basis of the academic profile of each year group. It was claimed that these projections were very accurate, and that consequently the school knew what the results were likely to be as much as four years ahead. At *Fox* the curriculum development committee now set standards for the number of C grade GCSE passes, including targets for individual subject departments.

Our question about the use of performance information by parents revealed an interesting divergence of views. A number of teachers asserted that parents took a close interest in the public domain information about examination results and attendance levels. At *Dog* a couple of teachers suggested to us that the availability of this information had been influential in increasing applications for places at the school and in motivating individual transfers from other schools. However a number of other teachers – at all four schools – said that parent interest in performance data was both unsophisticated and fairly limited. Some of the comments by teachers seemed to indicate that, although they believed that many parents had a strong interest in (at least) examination results, these same parents rarely addressed comments or questions to the schools on this issue. Sometimes the contrast in perceptions about the extent of parent interest was quite sharp: at *Badger* two different teachers, in successive interviews, told us, first, that not much interest had been taken in the published information and, second, that there was a great deal of local interest in the information, both in terms of parental reaction and the local media.

One of our most unrewarding questions was whether the performance data collected to satisfy the publication requirements of the government's Parents' Charter had held any surprises for the schools themselves. Almost everyone we met told us that there had been no surprises. Overwhelmingly the claim was that the published figures carried information that had already been thoroughly familiar to the schools concerned. Whether this was in fact the case, or whether a certain amount of 'hindsight' bias was involved, we were unable to tell (Fischhoff, 1975).

Overall, therefore, the relationship of the schools in this study to what one might term the 'performance culture' was ambiguous. Although everyone was aware of the government-imposed school league tables, and although a good deal of effort was being made to try to improve the score on the two public domain indicators – examination results and attendance rates – the general attitude of staff towards quantitative performance measurement appeared to be negative. It was noticeable that remarkably few figures or statistics were volunteered to us during our interviews, and even when specifically discussing 'performance', the language used was overwhelmingly that of relationships – leadership, motivation, commitment and so on. The business of the school was usually seen as tending a complex network of personal relationships, rather than achieving specific targets or goals. In this context the idea of specific and individualised incentives or (even more so) penalties was regarded with considerable suspicion. Yet at the same time, some symptoms of change were beginning to become visible. Heads and senior management teams had started to formulate targets and to look for patterns in quantitative data relating to health, absenteeism, behaviour and so on. This process seemed to have gone slightly further in the two GM schools than in their LEA counterparts, but the difference was not striking. Nowhere did the role of parents in relation to performance data seem particularly prominent. Whilst it was generally acknowledged that parents were interested in examination results, there was little evidence of vigorous parental enquiry or (still less) campaigning. Collective action by parents did not seem to exist – the occasional enquiry about examination results or attendance rates was the most that heads had to face. In short, systematic and quantified performance data was still in the background rather than the foreground of most aspects of school life.

To conclude this section, it may be worth taking note of the national picture. According to the Chief Inspector of Education's 1996 Annual Report:

> Inspection shows that pupils' standards of achievement and the quality of teaching are very similar in GM and LEA secondary schools. In GM schools the average GCSE points score per pupil in 1996 was 37.3 compared with 33.8 in LEA schools. When schools with comparable intakes are compared, this difference between the sectors is reduced. (HM Chief Inspectorate of Schools, 1996, paragraph 59)

Although the difference between the performances of GM and LEA secondary schools was small, Conservative ministers did their best to make the most of it. Thus in a written parliamentary answer on 17 December 1996 it was claimed that:

> 46% of pupils in GM comprehensive schools achieved five or more good GCSE passes compared with 40% in LEA schools. Analysis of the GCSE performance tables from 1992 to 1996 shows that GM schools have made rather more progress than comparable LEA schools in raising standards year on year. (House of Commons Debates, 17 December 1996, Column 486)

Unlike the tables in the chief inspector's annual report, the minister's answer made no allowance for socioeconomic factors (commonly measured by the percentage of pupils eligible for free school meals).

Fragmentation, system coherence and equity

Prior to the 1988 Education Act (and always excepting the private schools sector) secondary education had been delivered through a series of local systems, with each system being planned and coordinated through an LEA. As pointed out by numerous critics of the 1988 Act (by no means all of them Labour Party supporters), the new ability of secondary schools to opt out from the control of their LEA threatened the previous pattern in various ways.

First, if a number of secondary schools within a given LEA jurisdiction opted out, it might become difficult for the LEA to plan sensibly over the whole area, given that it would no longer control most of the schools. Second, it was alleged that new inequities would now grow and flourish. From the beginning there would be inequities in funding: 'We have made no secret of the fact that grant maintained schools get preferential treatment in allocating grants to capital expenditure' (Prime Minister John Major, quoted in Bates, 1991).

Beyond this, however, lurked the potential for deeper inequities. From the beginning there was a suspicion that GM status would be used as a route through which academically selective admissions policies could be reintroduced. At the time of our research this had not materialised (Fitz *et al.*, 1993, pp. 111–12), however during the run-up to the 1997 general election various government pronouncements made it increasingly clear that academic selectivity was indeed on the cards, and it probably would have been introduced, if the Conservatives had won a fifth successive term. The possible introduction of selectivity in GM schools was mentioned by a number of our interviewees. For example a chief education officer for an area that contained two of our schools stated that 'I don't feel very strongly about who owns the buildings; I do feel strongly about equity of access. To whom are the grant maintained schools accountable for the principle of equity?' Overall, however, academic selectivity was not a prime topic of discussion for the majority of the teachers in the schools themselves.

In contrast, real or perceived financial inequities were frequently mentioned. A teacher at *Fox* expressed the view that the funding advantages of GM status were morally indefensible and divisive. 'Naturally enough, parents, teachers and pupils attending grant main- tained schools are bound to want to defend the advantages that they enjoy, whilst it is clearly unfair to those who did not get the same advantages.'

Because our fieldwork focused mainly on the schools themselves rather than LEAs, the amount of testimony we received concerning possible problems with systems coherence was limited. Nevertheless such comments as we did receive from LEA officials pointed towards the existence of a real problem. One chief education officer mentioned an example of a GM school that, by changing from a boys only school to a coeducational one, had destabilised a nearby LEA girls' school. However, in another LEA an official told us that a powerful relation- ship had been created between the authority and the GM schools within its area – that there was 'a basis upon which to develop the service'. Funds were now used more efficiently and the LEA had become a more responsive provider of services to both its own schools and GM schools. This respondent argued that these improvements in efficiency and responsiveness could have been achieved without creat- ing the disruption that accompanied GM opt-outs. Although our evidence is limited, it seems clear that LEAs had a choice as to the extent to which they co-operated with the GM schools in their midst. In the case of one of our LEAs the relationship had been mainly antagonistic – the GM school had been shut out from LEA events and there had been a range of other actions that had clearly signalled distance and disapproval. In the case of another LEA, however, the GM–LEA exchanges had been warmer, with both sides striving to maintain as 'normal relations' as possible. We were even told how keen the LEA was to sell its services to the GM schools, because they tended to have more money to spend!

Others who have researched the issue of system coherence on a wider scale assess the impact of the creation of GM schools as very significant:

> It became very clear to us in the course of our visits to LEAs that many of their reorganisation plans had either been abandoned or temporarily shelved in the wake of schools seeking or having achieved GM status. This outcome was reported by almost two thirds of the LEA officers we interviewed. (Fitz *et al.*, 1993, p. 54, reporting on in-depth interviews with 24 LEA officers)

This same research lent weight to the notion that most LEAs were attempting to cooperate with GM schools rather than 'punish' them. Even among Labour-controlled LEAs, where doctrinal resentment might have been expected to be at its strongest, the most common responses were apparently 'pragmatic as opposed to political' (ibid., p. 58).

In general, we would agree with the broad conclusions of a recent survey of relations between local authorities and 'non-elected agencies' (a generic title given to NHS Trusts, Training and Education Councils, Urban Development Corporations, GM schools and further education colleges). According to this research, 'NEAs were perceived to have had a negative effect on co-ordinated local service delivery, yet had not conspicuously weakened the tendency for public service agencies to co-operate with one another.' And 'One major effect of their existence [that is, NEAs] is inevitably the fragmentation of local service delivery that ensues. A significant development, though, is how such fragmentation is increasingly leading to the emergence of voluntary local alliances and networks, in an attempt to re-establish co-ordination of activities over related fields' (Painter *et al.*, 1996, pp. 5, 11).

Accountability

When we interviewed Sir Robert Balchin, chairman of the Grant Maintained Schools Foundation, he argued that GM schools were in fact *more* accountable than LEA schools. He suggested that the LEA system should be abolished because in practice it operated to the advantage of politicians and local authority officers, but was not accountable or helpful to parents. He would prefer all schools to become grant maintained and directly accountable to parents, who were the 'customers of the system'.

During our fieldwork in schools we found few staff who would agree with Sir Robert's analysis – even within the GM schools themselves. Whilst our respondents in GM schools rejoiced at their escape from 'local authority control and bureaucracy', the accountability dimension was very seldom mentioned. Staff were much more concerned about the possible loss of specialist advisory services and support from the LEA than about loss of accountability to elected councillors. In not a single instance did a teacher or head teacher cite the latter as a major drawback of opting out. Only among LEA officials themselves did we hear strong words on this point. An official in *Badger*'s LEA was bitingly critical. He said he believed that GM schools were not truly accountable to the community and were a manifestation of 'middle class snobbery':

> The schools themselves are trying to be something they are not, and appeal to parents who want to send their children to a school that is a cut above the rest, but don't have the money to send their children to private schools. It's what I call the 'oak panelled brigade'.

Another line of criticism was developed by Local Schools Information (1996, p.5):

> There is a thin dividing line between independence, autonomy and autocracy: the head teachers of GM Schools are in a very powerful position. In the absence of an LEA, governors become very dependent on the head teacher as a valuable system of checks and balances is removed.

Although this is clearly a theoretical possibility, we heard no echo of this at either of our GM schools. It could also be pointed out that the existence of LEA supervision does not necessarily restrain the instincts of autocratic head teachers. Autocrats are known to have existed under LEA control and it would be difficult to demonstrate (and as far as we know no one has done so) that a tendency for autocracy was more prominent under GM than LEA arrangements!

It is noticeable that, while both teachers and the public are evidently very concerned about equity (at least in the sense of equal opportunities) within our system of secondary schooling, they do not connect this with elected political supervision. It could, perhaps, be said that it is a significant issue for the legitimacy of local democracy that it occurs to so few people that councillors might be a route to equity and fairness.

Finally, it was the case that, although accountability to the interests of parents featured prominently in the rhetoric of heads and teachers, we found little evidence of any systematic research into what parents' perceptions of their interests actually were. Our findings mirror precisely those of a larger-scale project: 'However, it is apparent . . . that in general enthusiasm for finding out what parents want is considerably less than for promoting the school to parents and the wider community' (Glatter and Woods, 1994, p. 66).

Explaining school governance: concepts

In this final section we will apply the theories and concepts developed in Chapter 2 to explain our findings about the decentralisation of secondary education. First, in terms of our main organising concepts it is clear that a mixture of administrative and political decentralisation has taken place in the secondary sector. Administrative decentralisation has occurred in both GM and LEA schools insofar as they have been given greater managerial autonomy, in particular over their spending and purchasing decisions. There has also been an element of political decentralisation to the extent that power has been transferred to the governing bodies of GM schools. These governing bodies are made up of:

- Five elected parent governors.
- At least one but no more than two elected teacher governors.
- The head teacher.
- A number of other governors greater than the total of those in the above categories.

Thus governing bodies are a mixture of elected and appointed individuals, though the majority are appointed.

As far as the distinction between competitive and non-competitive decentralisation is concerned, both the creation of GM schools and the extension of LMS freedoms to LEA schools are essentially non-competitive. No competition for a contract is held. Nevertheless, these two forms of decentralisation have, in practice, led to some indirect growth in competitive decentralisation in the sense that schools (both LEA and GM) are now themselves able to contract out certain activities, typically including grounds maintenance, repairs and the purchase of specialist training and advisory services. Both types of school recorded some satisfaction with their new-found flexibilities in these respects. A number of respondents indicated that the schools now had more 'clout' when dealing with these matters, whereas it had formerly, been the LEA that had either provided the services itself or held the purse strings in the matter of paying contractors. Now the boot was often on the other foot – LEAs had to compete in order to sell their specialist services to schools. Both teachers and LEA officers acknowledged that this shift had given a different tone to the relationship between schools and LEAs.

Moving on to the third of our original distinctions, the creation of a GM school is the strong form of decentralisation that we term 'devolution'. This is because opting out involves the transfer of legal authority from one organisation (an LEA) to another (the school). However it has also involved the creation of a potentially powerful new government quango – the Funding Agency for Schools.

Our fourth distinction within the general concept of decentralisation is that between vertical and horizontal decentralisation. Our research showed clear evidence that management had become a more prominent and time-consuming function in both LEA and GM schools. We have also commented on the particularly crucial role that the head teachers played in guiding the debate on opting out at all four of the schools where we conducted fieldwork. It seems to us quite likely that there has been some incremental movement towards horizontal *re*centralisation, that is, a strengthening of the relative power and authority of head teachers. However we cannot systematically document it, and it needs to be borne in mind that head teachers already embodied a potent combination of professional experience and managerial authority, long before the 1988 Education Act.

As far as performance is concerned, we have shown that the predominant conceptualisation of performance is still in terms of creating a set of mutually supportive relationships between teachers, pupils and parents, rather than anything more quantitative or managerial. Whilst quite a few teachers were eager to tell us about improvements in the efficiency with which schools could purchase services (both under LMS and under GM status), there was actually very little efficiency or effectiveness data available at any of the four schools we visited. Statistics on input–output ratios were simply not on the lips or at the fingertips of most of the teachers, even those who were members of senior management teams.

Rhetoric on 'quality' was not particularly prominent in schools. Insofar as it could be inferred from what teachers and governors told us, the implicit notion of quality seemed to embody a mixture of producer notions (adherence to professionally determined standards) and concepts of responsiveness to parents as users. If there was any conflict between these potentially divergent producer and user definitions, we did not come across it. Of course this may have been because parents had not yet learnt the art of articulating or had the opportunity to articulate their own expectations and desires. Yet perhaps there was just a hint of divergence in the two or three cases where teachers referred, in an ever-so-slightly-disparaging way, to the unsophisticated approach parents took to school league tables and to their over-concentration on examination results. But we would not want to exaggerate this – on the whole the picture we were given was one of extensive agreement between teachers and parents as to the character-istics they wished to see displayed within the school community.

Explaining school governance: theories

Turning to our three main theoretical perspectives, it must first be said that the application of rational choice theory to the management of schools is by no means simple. As in the case of NHS trusts, it is hard to see Niskanan's budget-maximising bureaucrat within the walls of most secondary schools. Heads and senior management teams may enjoy considerable discretion as to how they spend their school's budget, but they can generally exert only very limited influence over the size of the budget. They are at the bottom of a ladder of grant-giving/resource-allocating institutions. For GM schools the Depart-ment for Education and Employment allocates funds to the FAS, which then allocates funds to individual schools. LEA schools depend upon the local LMS formula, which is devised by the LEA and has to be cleared by the Department for Education and Employment. The amount going into the top of the formula is decided by the local authority, but very much within the context of that year's local government spending settlement, as fixed by central government. Obviously, most heads are anxious to maintain and improve the 'image' of their school, which can lead to more parents choosing the school and therefore to a larger budget. But this is a fairly long and complicated sequence of events, and for most schools, whatever the head teacher may try to do in the short term, radical alterations in the size of the school are unlikely.

Thus while we have certainly found head teachers exerting them-selves to safeguard their schools from perceived external threats, it seems a considerable distortion to classify all this activity as simply budget maximisation. Indeed endless budgetary growth is neither a plausible nor even necessarily a particularly desirable objective for a professional teacher. If we analyse our interview records we can find little or no basis for the proposition that budgetary maximisation is a driving motivation in the day-to-day life of schools. As elaborated in our earlier discussion of the concept of performance, head teachers and teachers simply do not conceive of their activities in these terms.

The more sophisticated theory of bureau shaping is also difficult to apply. Most head teachers are not in a position to alter the functions of their schools, to hive off activities or in other ways 'shape their organisations into different formats. Perhaps the bureau-shaping model was never intended for organisations such as schools. After all, these are essentially professional organisations with strong local connections. The satisfaction obtained by the staff seems to have much more to do with the intrinsic quality of their work – including the quality of their relationships with children and parents – than with extending the power of their institution or shedding 'operational' tasks in order to take on more policy-making and regulative functions. And yet perhaps something can be salvaged from this theoretical approach. Dunleavy (1991) postulated that:

- Top-level staff would be most interested in boosting the prestige of their organisations and improving relations with clients or contractors.
- Top-level staff would concentrate on strategy making and diplomatic relations with other bodies, since these were high-status, high-discretion tasks.
- Senior officials in service delivery agencies were likely to push for programme budget increases because in service delivery the core budget tends to take up most of the programme budget.
- Leaders of service delivery organisations are likely to indulge in extensive internal reorganisation and transformation of working practices, partly with the aim of increasing the proportion of high-status work undertaken at the top of these organisations (thereby pushing routine work down to lower-level staff).

In a way it could be argued that each of these hypotheses has been borne out in the case of GM schools. The head teachers we met certainly spent a lot of their time safeguarding the status of their institution – indeed preserving one's school from merger or takeover was widely recognised as a common motive in the first wave of opt-outs. Furthermore, a source of satisfaction that came through in the interviews was that GM status had given schools more 'clout' in dealing with contractors (since the contractors now knew that the schools no longer had their hands tied by LEA control). There was also a sense in which head teachers and senior management teams appeared to be increasing the effort they put into strategy development: consciously steering the school towards an improved performance. Certainly the days of the head teacher spending a substantial amount of time in the classroom were over: head teachers had become managers and strategists. It was also the case that head teachers were indeed to be found arguing for increases in the programme budget. It is worth remembering that the initial cash boost figured significantly in opt-out decisions, and that, once the opportunity to opt out existed, the remaining LEA schools were effectively able to exploit it as a lever to persuade their LEAs to delegate a higher and higher proportion of the LEA budget through LMS. Finally, it was true that GM head teachers had launched internal reorganisations and, to a limited extent, attempted to alter working practices within the schools, for example by employing new categories of staff especially to help schools with their new administrative and external relations tasks.

Even so, this sort of explanation and characterisation of changes in the secondary school sector strikes us as somewhat superficial. If we look at the four hypotheses more closely, it can be seen that in each case the 'fit' with the evidence is questionable. Head teachers have always been interested in boosting the prestige of their schools, and in external relations generally. It is hardly surprising that during the sometimes fraught process of opting out, they were obliged to pay a great deal of attention to these aspects, whether they wanted to or not. Equally, the increasing amount of strategy making and administration was regarded by many of the teachers we spoke to as a distinctly mixed blessing. They felt obliged to spend more time on it, but they didn't necessarily want to. Within the cultural environment of most schools, to excel at the process of teaching itself remained a high-status ability, and increased 'administration' was regarded as something of a necessary evil. Most head teachers had abandoned any attempt to retain a presence in the classroom long before 1988. As indicated earlier, the idea of 'hiving off' routine work does not easily fit the context of a secondary school. The main routine work is classroom teaching, and this remains absolutely central to the life of the school. For all practical purposes it cannot be contracted out.

Moving on to the question of pressure for programme budget increases, it is hard to see this as in any way a new feature of school life. Throughout the 1980s, individual schools and teaching unions complained vigorously to government that the education system was being starved of investment and that teachers were underpaid. These issues have remained on the agenda in the 1990s. Lastly, the prediction that leaders of service delivery organisations are likely to indulge in extensive internal reorganisation and transformation of working practice is not a satisfactory representation of what occurred in the schools we visited. The sense was very much of reorganisation being *imposed* by pressure of circumstances and government action. Probably the largest amount of reorganisation in all these schools had to do with the introduction of the national curriculum – a profoundly centralising feature of the 1988 Education Act. The effects of this innovation touched almost every aspect of the internal life of schools.

But perhaps there is another way of thinking about the possible application of the bureau-shaping model at the level of individual schools. Whilst it is not open to a school to redesign itself as something other than a delivery agency, it can nevertheless try to shift its 'market niche'. One way would be 'via manipulating its client base . . . to try to make itself into a "boutique bureaucracy"', that is, to become a fashionable, sought-after place to go (Dunleavy, 1997). The development of selective admissions policies would be a crucial step in any such attempt, but there are myriad of smaller ways in which a school can attempt to reshape its image: adopting a school uniform, establishing new discipline or homework codes, inventing new ceremonies and so on). This could be seen as maximising feasible utility, in the sense that, if such a strategy were successful, the teachers would get to work in a higher-status establishment, teaching 'a better class of pupil'. Some of the attitudes we encountered in our fieldwork seemed to lend support to this kind of interpretation. The comments about the 'oak panelled brigade' fit neatly here, as do certain detailed changes in the ways in which some of the schools were attempting to present themselves to parents. Yet even this more refined version of bureau shaping still lies uneasily within the overall picture that emerged from the four schools we looked at in depth. Part of the problem is that the rational choice approach assumes that most behaviour is self-interested, and directed at maximising the utility of those individuals who hold positions of power. Whilst it would be pointless to deny that self-interested decisions are sometimes taken, and that head teachers and senior teachers would like their schools to grow in prestige, at the same time we are dealing here with organisations that are dominated by a profession whose ethics accord great salience to the provision of certain kinds of services to children and young people. In other words, the school community is erected on the assumption that teachers will regularly behave in ways that serve the interests of others. To exclude the possibility of such other-directed behaviour from one's model would seem to be either a declaration of fundamental scepticism about most of the self-representations of the teaching profession or a serious limitation on the analysis. It would also – as argued above – construct a picture of the world in which the proportion of strategic, calculative behaviour is rather higher than the mixture of uncertainties, muddling along and occasional bouts of longer-term thinking that seemed to come out of the accounts offered by the interviewees.

At this point, however, we need to make a distinction between 'normal times' and 'turning points'. When we were undertaking our fieldwork the schools were returning to 'normal times'. The decision to opt out or to refrain from opting out had already been taken. 'Business as usual' – albeit a modified and reformed version of business as usual – was in place once more. Yet 'turning points' are precisely those occasions when the leaders of organisations are forced to think in a more calculative or strategic way. So it was quite evident that the heads of all four schools had given the question of opting out very serious thought, and that in doing so they had considered the dynamics of the relationship between the school, parents, the LEA and other schools in the locality. The 1988 Education Act certainly provided a 'critical juncture' (Bengtsson, 1995) at which the rules changed, reshaping the areas of discretion available to head teachers. Thus the application of the concepts of game theory may be quite fruitful. For example it could be argued that in the case of *Dog*, the head teacher and a number of the staff conceptualised their relationship with the LEA as essentially a zero sum game. In contrast, at *Rabbit* the head teacher and the LEA seemed less polarised and more willing to look for bargaining possibilities, including the continuation of certain relationships after opting out had taken place. This opens up the intriguing possibility that different players in the same local situation may perceive the nature of the current game in fundamentaly different ways. This is one way in which 'history' can have an important effect: if the relationship between a school and its LEA was close and communicative in the years before the 1988 Act, then (as we have seen) this was likely to reduce the probability of a decision to opt out or – if it was decided to opt out – to reduce the amount of conflict and punitive behaviour associated with the process of opting out itself. If, in contrast, the previous relationship had been cool or antagonistic, then even coming to some agreement about what the nature of the 'game' was would be more difficult.

If there were 'bureau shapers' at work during the implementation of the 1988 Education Act, they were not in the schools or the LEAs, but were firmly located in Whitehall. It would be a distortion to picture head teachers as strategic actors, cleverly manoeuvring their schools in order to decrease the amount of routine work, increase the programme budget and transform internal working structures and practices. What our evidence shows is that head teachers struggled to preserve their schools in the face of a highly uncertain climate, being obliged to respond to a series of government initiatives (the national curriculum, school league tables) and somewhat reluctantly taking on a more strategic leadership role. Furthermore the differences between the experiences of GM and LEA schools seem to have been relatively modest. Both gained considerably more financial management freedom; both had to reorganise in response to the introduction of the national curriculum, and the overwhelming majority of staff at both believed that the decentralisation of secondary education provision had gone far enough, and that the remaining apparatus of local coordination and system coherence needed to be retained. Only a handful of our respondents wished for the demise of LEAs and the universal propagation of GM status.

Last but not least, we are faced with the brute fact of the modest number of opt-outs nationally. By November 1996, GM secondary schools still accounted for fewer than one fifth of all secondary schools. Margaret Thatcher's wish for most secondary schools to become GM had clearly not been realised. If opting out offered head teachers the opportunity to take on a much more bureau-shaping role, only a modest number seemed to be interested in taking up this challenge.

Moving on to the new institutionalist approaches, we can certainly find elements to assist us in understanding the experiences of secondary schools since 1988. In a number of ways these approaches shed light on both the evidence we derived from interviews and on the wider findings of the research literature. However, as noted in Chapter 2, it is hard either to confirm or to falsify the new institutionalist approaches because, unlike rational choice theory, they seldom generate specific and readily testable propositions. One might say that the main value of this approach lies in its general resonance with much of the evidence, rather than yielding any specific forecasts of behaviour.

March and Olsen suggest that most organisational behaviour is directed towards goals of 'appropriateness' – that is, it seeks to satisfy prevailing norms rather than to maximise some quantum of utility. Their view is that the internal character of organisations is, in most circumstances, likely to change only slowly. Our research in the schools sector bears this out. The advent of GM status, LMS, the national curriculum and a number of other reforms collectively represented what might be thought of as a revolution in school life. Yet in all the schools we visited the basic norms and character of everyday decisions and actions appeared relatively unchanged. If the traditional values of school life were under pressure, they had not yet cracked. As already noted, a new 'performance culture' had not arrived. In a sense it is remarkable that, in the midst of such a maelstrom of change, the schools of the 1990s remained so recognisably similar to the schools of, say, the 1970s. In the light of our findings we would support the new institutionalists in their emphasis on the significance of history and continuity. As a group of researchers into local educational markets expressed it:

> The market in education is not simply a product of the 1988 Education Reform Act and LEA decision-making; markets in particular settings have long and complex histories. Those histories are part of the local folk-knowledge that parents draw upon when choosing schools. Those histories construct and confer reputations upon schools. (Ball *et al.*, 1994, p. 92)

The new institutionalists also stress the importance of legitimation in organisational life. This finds some echoes in our fieldwork. The concern of the two heads of the GM schools to justify their actions, and to explain them as ways of preserving the true educational interests of their children and parents, was quite prominent. Di Maggio and Powell (1991, pp. 67–76) identify three mechanisms for 'institutional isomorphic change'. The introduction of GM status (and LMS) appear to have been an interesting combination of all three. First, Di Maggio and Powell refer to 'coercive isomorphism', in which superordinate organisations insist on specific changes in the structures and procedures of subordinate organisations. There were definite elements of coerciveness in the secondary sector, at least in the sense of the government's insistence that LMS be 'rolled out' to all LEAs and that the formula each LEA intended to use for allocating resources to schools within its jurisdiction must be submitted to Whitehall for approval. Thus while GM status was optional, LMS (in some form or other) was effectively mandatory.

GM status was, in principle, a voluntary matter. In Di Maggio and Powell's terms, many opt-outs could be seen as a form of mimetic isomorphism, in which schools that feared closure or amalgamation followed what rapidly became a recognised route for escaping from the effects of LEA reorganisation schemes. However this was a highly orchestrated form of mimesis. It was not so much a question of some pioneer schools finding a new model of organisation and then others imitating them, because the new model was rather carefully specified and, in effect, heavily advertised by the government. So this situation was nothing like the one that Di Maggio and Powell seemed to have had in mind when they wrote: 'Models may be diffused unintentionally, indirectly through employee transfer or turnover, or explicitly by organisations such as consulting firms or industry trade associations' (ibid., p. 69). Indeed, what we have in the case of the GM schools programme is perhaps a hybrid form of isomorphism where the new model, instead of evolving spontaneously, is carefully specified and supplied by a superordinate authority, which furthermore tilts the playing field in order to encourage 'volunteers' to try the new format.

Di Maggio and Powell's third category is 'normative pressures', which they strongly link with processes of professionalisation. Although at first sight one might be tempted to say that both GM status and LMS came from the government and not from the teaching profession, this would be an oversimplification. LMS, in particular, had been significantly influenced by professional considerations. LMS had been piloted in the mid 1980s in two LEAs, where the head teachers and professional educational administrators had played an influential role in shaping the arrangements that were subsequently generalised as government policy. Thus LMS, at least, can be seen partly as a development influenced by 'the growth and elaboration of professional networks that span organisations and across which new models diffuse rapidly' (ibid., p. 71). It also commanded wide support among teachers (Levačić, 1994).

GM status seems to have been rather different in this latter respect. Prior to the 1988 Act it had not been widely discussed or piloted within the education community. Although it clearly commanded the support of some teachers, it was deeply controversial within the profession and (as we saw in our fieldwork) provoked doubt and hesitation even among the staff of those schools that had been led into opting out. But perhaps a different kind of possible legitimation was one of the attractions of GM status. The government had some success in associating the notion of GM status with a particular set of social values. These included an emphasis on discipline and self-discipline, achievement through competition and a particular form of localism – the more parochial localism of a school catchment area rather than the broader and more abstract localism of a local authority jurisdiction. The caustic remarks by an LEA official about the 'oak panelled brigade', whether fair or not, reflect this desire for enhanced stability and reputation.

The new institutionalist emphasis on legitimation, normative conformity and symbolism also finds some support in the relatively weak focus most of our interviewees seemed to have on the details of the measured efficiency of school management and the quantified changes in examination results (or, more ambitiously, 'value added'). It would be true to say that, while our interviews yielded no shortage of statements about GM and LEA schools acquiring a new 'focus', hard evidence of significant changes in educational outcomes was conspicuous by its absence. The currency of debate was much more that of anecdotes about physical improvements, shifts of mood and crucial meetings than it was about quantitative evidence of change in the educational process itself.

Overall, therefore, it could be said that those elements of the new institutionalist approach that we have applied generate a general picture of organisational life that fits reasonably well with what our fieldwork yielded. Whether this approach adds very much to our ability to *explain* the changes is another question. The new institutionalist approach seems to provide a reasonably rich set of descriptive concepts with which to capture and taxonomise much of what the interviewer hears and the researcher of school and LEA documents reads. To this extent it is useful. What it does not appear to do, however, is to generate a coherent explanation of why certain schools opted out and others did not, or how head teachers and senior management teams (and LEAs) managed the resulting novelties and disruptions.

Finally, we shall consider what insights rhetorical analysis can afford. Of course we must reiterate the 'health warning' given earlier, that is, what is offered here is by no stretch of the imagination a rigorous analysis of texts or conversations. It is no more than an impressionistic interpretation of the most persistent assumptions, themes and metaphors that characterised the many conversations and responses that constituted our programme of interviews.

The first point to make is that teachers and parents spoke of the decision to opt out or to remain under LEA control on two very different levels. One of these was very concrete – statements were made about what other schools in the neighbourhood were doing, about the attitude of the LEA, about job security and pension arrangements might be affected by opting out, and so on. The other level was more general and abstract, and involved an appeal to general principles or values. Thus, for example, the head of *Dog* insisted that the resource allocation policies of the LEA had been 'unfair', while the head of *Fox* asserted that using salary increases as a reward for good teaching was not 'ethically desirable', and argued that praise from the head teacher was a more appropriate incentive. On the whole the majority of the arguments we encountered were of the former type (that is, specific and concrete) rather than the latter, though this may have been partly a function of the type of questions we asked (see Appendix 2 for the interview schedules). This is not to say that concrete and specific arguments are somehow free of more general or abstract considerations. They are not: rather it is that the general values and principles that underlie these more specific statements have to be inferred or exhumed through further questioning.

What is immediately clear from any inspection of our interview material is that the most salient justification deployed by heads and other senior teachers was that the course of action that had been followed had been in the best interests of pupils and parents. Understandably, this was used as if it was the 'clincher' argument. It was deployed equally by those heads who had taken their schools to GM status and those who had decided to stay with their LEAs. It was striking that none of the heads justified the particular trajectories they had chosen in terms of either the correctness or the incorrectness of national policies in favour of opting out. The most enthusiastic supporter of GM status was probably the head teacher at *Dog*, but even he, though envisaging a general spread of GM schools in future, did not specifically justify his own opt-out in those terms. The decision was rather presented as one of safeguarding the interests of the particular local community in the face of alleged discrimination and neglect on the part of the LEA. Yet although the interests of pupils and their parents played a central role in the rhetoric, it was noticeable that we were offered very little in the way of a direct analysis of what these interests were. *Dog* was perhaps nearest to being the exception to this rule, in that the head teacher and several of the staff there complained about the way in which the LEA had starved the school of resources (which was obviously not in the pupils' interests) and went on to show how opting out had significantly increased the school's resource base. At *Rabbit*, it was stated that the main intention of opting out had been to avoid the effects of an impending LEA-driven reorganisation. The head teacher spoke of a 'psychological response to a perceived danger', but exactly why a reorganisation would be a danger was not spelled out – presumably the intention of the LEA had been that the reorganisation would actually result in improvements, at least across the locality as a whole. One thing that was therefore conspicuous by its absence from most of the verbal reasoning was any acknowledgement that different parents and different pupils – even within one school – might have different interests or preferences. 'Parents' were normally referred to as an aggregate category, and we were never offered quantitative breakdown of the views and interests of the parent body. One can see that this sort of disaggregation could be rhetorically very dangerous for head teachers and teachers, since it had the potential to undermine a central plank in their argument, namely that the school was a relatively homogeneous community that was bent on preserving its qualities in the face of dangerous pressures and currents flowing in from the external environment. On more than one occasion we wished that our research design had permitted a more extensive and direct analysis of the values and expressed interests of the pupils and parents themselves.

Next we come to the question of the identity of the audience. In terms of the intended audience, most of the senior staff of the four schools seemed to think that the parents were the principal audience rather than the LEA, central government or the wider public. At other times fellow teachers appeared to be the audience. Whilst appealing in its specificity, the focus on the parents of the school's pupils implicitly downgraded or ignored the possible interests of other parents and pupils in the area, that is, those who attended neighbouring schools. Naturally enough, this equity point was strongly made by one or two of the LEA officials. This very parochial and specific orientation was more pronounced than in the case of the hospitals, where senior managers, although sometimes seeming to address themselves to an audience of local service users, more commonly developed managerial lines of argument, attuned to the world of NHS managers and civil servants.

As far as metaphors and other analogies were concerned, it was noticeable how infrequently head teachers, teachers and governors made use of the managerial terms 'efficiency', 'flexibility' and 'quality'. This just did not seem a natural form of discourse for these groups. Terms that were much more frequently employed were 'stability', 'respect' (especially of head teachers), 'confidence' and 'leadership'. The most common negative terms were 'ideological', 'politics' and 'insecurity'. There was relatively little use of technical terms and no consistent or striking use of metaphors. In terms of the distinction between logos, ethos and pathos, a great deal of emphasis was placed on ethos, especially through the abovementioned device of referring to the interests of parents and pupils as fundamental.

Also noticeable was the paucity of reference to general organisational principles or arguments. If we consider the list of doctrines in Hood and Jackson's *Administrative Argument* (1991), we find a number that are potentially highly relevant to schools opting out or staying within an LEA system, but these were not arguments that we actually encountered much in use. In other words the head teachers and others associated with these decisions only rarely justified them in terms of the fulfilment of some organisational principle or doctrine. When we specifically questioned them about benefits and drawbacks they were certainly able to identify the uses to which the autonomy that came with GM or LMS status had been put, but on the whole the benefits cited had not been used to justify the original strategic decision. The decision was explained much less in terms of organisational principles than in terms of local relationships and pressures.

The incoming Labour government of 1997 nailed education high on the mast of its manifesto priorities. In general terms it promised closer cooperation with LEAs and an end to the perceived divisiveness of Conservative education policies. The specifics, however, pointed to the distinct possibility of further local–central tensions. The centralisation–decentralisation issue seemed particularly likely to rear its head. The league tables of school performance were to be maintained – indeed it appeared as though they would be made more prominent. Labour ministers repeatedly promised tough action (that is, government intervention) in cases where schools were seen to be failing. If a whole locality seemed to be having problems an 'education action zone' would be formed, to be governed by a forum involving the participating schools and business, community and voluntary organisations, as well as the LEA. It remains to be seen how far such fora become genuine partnerships – and how much good they can do.

There is also, of course, the issue of resources. The ink was scarcely dry on the new government's proposals before teachers were writing to the newspapers with a familiar refrain: 'Management is important, but the will to fund public (as opposed to private/privatised) education properly is the heart of the matter. It is becoming tragically apparent that this lot are no better at understanding this than the last lot' (letter to the *Guardian*, 12 January 1998, p. 8).

Finally, to judge from our research, one of the most difficult tasks facing the Labour government is to persuade the teaching profession to become more performance-minded. Despite continuing pressure from the Thatcher and Major Conservative governments, during our research we found little evidence that performance had become a concept that was integral to the day-to-day running of schools. It was still perceived mainly as part of an externally, imposed and fairly unwelcome agenda. On the one hand it could not be ignored, but on the other it could be – and was being – largely excluded from the normal vocabulary of teachers. Engineering a cultural change here would be an achievement of considerable magnitude for any government.

7 Decentralised Management of Socially Rented Housing

Introduction

The housing sector is particularly interesting for at least two reasons. First, unlike the schools and hospitals, the local authority housing departments that chose to transfer their housing stock to a housing association devised the transfer process themselves. They were, of course, responding to government policy, but they chose their own route out of the public sector to become autonomous service delivery agencies. This was not at all what the government had expected; as outlined in Chapter 4, the government's own opt-out strategy of tenants' choice was a policy failure, producing only a few transfers and leading to the eventual winding down of the Housing Corporation's initiative to promote it. Second, the transfers were not to a new type of agency but to a new (in a few later cases to an existing) housing association, which could take its place in a large and comparatively favoured subsector.

The housing association movement has a long history, for much of which it has been a philanthropic provider and largely independent of state funding and regulation. We could expect that under these circumstances, when compared with the health and education sectors, the transfer process ought to have been much more under the control of local service agencies, and to have to led to greater autonomy. This has been broadly the case. The Department of the Environment (DoE) has been mainly reactive, making up new rules to govern the transfers and, in response to Treasury pressure, limiting the number that can transfer each year. The pattern of opting out has been quite steady since the first transfer in 1988. There has been no shortage of applicants, and the DoE has approved around 20 applications a year.

From the start there were considerable incentives to transfer, which helped it to remain an attractive alternative even when the DoE altered the rules to make it less lucrative for local authorities, taking 20 per cent of the capital receipts for the Treasury. First, transfers have been the only way of stopping the constant shrinkage of the housing stock due to the 'right to buy' scheme. This has had most impact in those local authorities which have had semidetached and terraced housing, in reasonable quality and in areas with a buoyant housing market; it is no accident that most of the transfers have taken place in rural and suburban areas, and in small to medium-sized towns. Second, the transfers have enabled housing staff to move from a sector that is no longer allowed to build new housing to a favoured sector that, through the Housing Corporation, is receiving substantial government grants for new building (averaging over half the cost of a scheme) and is able to borrow on the private money market without this counting as public expenditure. For local authority housing departments, the combined effect of these two factors – the right to buy and the absence of permission to build – is that they have been managing a steadily reducing housing stock; not a comfortable position for local managers, even if they do not want to maximise their budgets, nor for local councillors, who have a statutory duty to house the homeless and are under constant pressure from constituents who are on the waiting list.

More particularly, pressures have arisen from the government policy changes brought in by the 1988 Housing Act and the 1989 Local Government and Housing Act. Early large-scale voluntary transfers (LSVTs) were aimed at avoiding the threat of tenants' choice, but when this was seen to have failed, the next threat was seen to be a large rise in local authority rents because of a new financial regime brought in by the 1989 Act. Then the threat of rent rises receded because new government guidelines were issued limiting them to about the level of inflation: Treasury officials were concerned that the rises were adding to housing benefit costs, since around 65 per cent of council tenants were claiming benefit. However, other pressures resulting from the 1989 Act were affecting housing revenue accounts, in particular a reduction in funding for maintenance and the fact that housing benefits had to be paid out of surpluses from the account, meaning that in effect some tenants were paying other tenants' benefits. These pressures did not apply to housing associations, which were largely free of government interference in their rent setting and use of surpluses.

The next threat was compulsory competitive tendering (CCT) of housing management, which was introduced in 1992 and set for implementation in 1996. This produced the greatest upheaval the housing management profession had ever seen. It involved the complete specification of the tasks of housing managers, the splitting of purchaser from provider within the housing department, and an attempt to create a market by tempting private and voluntary sector agencies to compete for contracts. With hindsight we can see that, like the tenants' choice legislation, the impact of this policy was not as great as was feared. In the first round of tendering few contracts went to the private sector, and those housing departments that set out to win contracts usually did so. However, unlike tenants' choice, there was a hidden impact within the local authority, with enormous amounts of work going into specifying and pricing contracts, and departments having to accept cuts in their budgets in order to win tenders. Voluntary transfer was the only alternative, except for transfer of management to a tenant management organisation (TMO). So great were the pressures that this option became the focus of keen interest, and one London authority (Kensington and Chelsea) transferred its entire housing stock to a new TMO.

As we noted in Chapter 3, at the back of all these pressures was the feeling that the government no longer wanted the local authorities to be in the business of providing housing directly. The 1987 White Paper on Housing, which remains the most substantial explication of Conservative housing policy, made clear that the local authorities were to move towards an enabling role and to withdraw from the provision of council housing. Housing managers became disheartened by the feeling that they were no longer seen as legitimate. Conservative councillors took the new role seriously, in some cases embracing the liberal market ideology behind it, and in most cases pragmatically searching for a way to safeguard the interests of the authority and tenants in the face of the government's determination to question their role. There was a powerful incentive for housing managers and professionals to transfer to the housing association sector, whose political legitimacy was not being called into question.

The housing agencies in our study

We focused on four cases. Two, which we shall call *Pike* and *Carp*, were LSVT housing associations that were created to buy out the whole of the local authority's housing stock. The other two, *Trout* and *Flounder,* were local authority housing departments where transfers had been rejected by the tenants (in one case in a formal LSVT ballot, in the other by a preliminary testing of tenants' views). At *Trout* the situation was complicated by the need to prepare for compulsory competitive tendering of housing management and maintenance, and by the forthcoming results of the local government review, which could mean merger with another local authority. At *Flounder* the situation was complicated by a radical decision to go for voluntary competitive tendering (VCT) of the housing service for the next five years, without the in-house team being encouraged to make a bid. The outcome was that at the time of the fieldwork a private company was about to take over the management of the department; a case of devolution of management but not of ownership. All four case studies were typical of the type of authority that was most interested in transfer: Conservative-controlled district councils in the south-east of England, with relatively small council housing stocks in good repair.

Reasons for opting out

All four of our case study agencies at some point wanted to go down the LSVT route, for some or all of the reasons noted above. At *Carp* the transfer was driven by the officers, who wanted more autonomy, to 'get out of the clutches' of central government, and the opportunity to provide a more focused service. But the catalyst for the decision was the ring-fencing of the Housing Revenue Account, which might have resulted in rents being put up by 110 per cent. For the councillors there was the fact that, though their local authority was still building council houses, this was about to be stopped. The 'enabling' role was not wanted here, because it meant not being able directly to house the homeless. The councillors were also attracted by the cash release of an estimated £10 million. While all of these reasons were important, the main consideration had to be the tenants' interest, particularly in rent levels, and the councillors sanctioned it for this reason. The case must have been quite compelling, because in an initial ballot the tenants' vote came out at 66 per cent against, and other authorities at this point tended to give up. It was the rents issue that spurred the councillors to proceed to a full vote. As one tenant representative put it, 'there was a lot of negative support; tenants were frightened the rents would be horrendous if they stayed with the council'. On the other hand, she admitted to a more positive reason, that the image of a housing association was 'quite posh' so the tenants felt they were taking a step up in social status.

At *Pike*, the reasons for pursuing the transfer were the threat of privatisation through tenants' choice, the government directive about authorities moving to an enabling role, the prospects for capital receipts to finance the construction of new housing, and the threat of rent increases. Within this last point were two other fears: of a reduction in maintenance spending, and of the impact tenants paying for other tenants' housing benefits might have. The councillors pursued the transfer for all these reasons, but it seemed clear that the senior officers were the power behind the transfer. As one interviewee admitted, they 'worked to a plan, holding a lot back and phasing the release of information'. The chair of the new housing association commented that 'the tenants required a great deal of information and direction in order to make up their minds. Eventually the senior management team convinced them of the advantages and the tenant vote was won easily.'

There was no pretence of fairness to both sides of the argument here. The top managers had their own priorities: they were just waiting for the chance to move into the development of new housing. The development director commented that the housing department was 'always different from the rest of the local authority, more commercially minded'. The situation was unusual in that this housing department had its own in-house architects, surveyors and even construction staff. They worked for other departments as well as housing, but until recently had still been building council homes. They wanted to transfer to the association as well – no wonder that they, and outside observers, referred to it as 'development-led'.

The junior staff were not so keen at first, because of fear of the unknown. However as one director put it, they were 'always a fairly loyal staff', and 'we made sure staff were happy with it and they contributed greatly'. In other words the staff would have faith in the transfer because it would be steered by people they trusted. When the Liberal Democrats 'started getting funny' about the proposal, the officers talked it over with them and regained their support. Clearly, whatever the councillors' rhetoric about concern for the tenants, the transfer was officer-led. On the other hand, because officers had to put in a substantial amount of extra time to attend meetings, much of it unpaid, their support was crucial. In this case, teams of four staff each went out to knock at the doors of 200 tenants in order to discuss the proposal. As one director said, 'If the staff are not for it, no LSVT will be achieved'. Unlike *Trout*, where the campaign failed, partly through 'too much honesty', here 'our business was to convince the tenants'.

Yet the politicians had to be seen to be driving it: the staff would still have to run the service afterwards if it failed, and therefore could not be seen as too partisan.

Because this was an early transfer the rules were just being formulated by the DoE, and did not yet demand a strict separation of those who were to transfer over to the new association (and therefore had an interest in the result) and those who were to lead the ballot process. The finance director joined the staff of the new association half-way through, and the process of negotiating over the transfer price had to begin again. The tenants were persuaded to vote in favour of the transfer because they wanted to retain the *status quo*, and the transfer was represented as doing this, as well as improving the housing stock and, in the long run, providing more opportunities for the children of tenants to be housed.

At *Trout*, the transfer bid was again officer-driven, with strong support from the ruling Conservative group. The managers saw advantages for themselves in opting out: more autonomy and a secure future with an expanding housing stock. There were short-term benefits for the tenants in the rent guarantee, but the tenants did not really understand the complex set of issues and were content with the *status quo*. The assistant director pointed out that it did not help that the campaign was run in 1989, at the time of the poll tax demonstrations, and the government was very unpopular. An honest campaign was run that, unlike some early transfers, put both sides of the argument to the tenants. All was going well until the Conservatives shattered a fragile all-party consensus on the transfer, by letting it be known that the small number of local authority places on the eventual board of directors would all be nominated by the ruling Conservative group. The district's one Labour councillor then ran a well-organised anti-transfer campaign, helped by the larger Labour group in a nearby district council who opposed the whole idea of transfer. This meant that the tenants, faced with conflicting signals, voted against the transfer. The balanced way in which the campaign was run was also a factor: DoE researchers are reputed to have said that it was 'too honest'. The chair of the Housing Committee interpreted the results positively as a vote of confidence in the council, and a projected rent rise of 54 per cent over five years was cushioned by the fact that 60 per cent of tenants were on housing benefit. Generally it was felt that voluntary transfer would not be on the agenda again.

At *Flounder*, again it was the officers who were originally interested. Most of the staff supported the idea because it would mean a continuation of what they were doing, but with a little more freedom from what one interviewee called 'political shenanigans'. The main reason for not proceeding with a transfer campaign was a lack of consensus among the councillors, and in particular a small group of Labour councillors who were against the idea. This was just before the 1992 election; if it had happened afterwards the Labour members might not have been so negative. A voting paper was sent to every tenant in a pre-voluntary-transfer ballot and a resounding 'no' came back. If there had been political will on the Conservatives' side they could have countered it, but they were not a cohesive group. There were a few 'true ideological Tories', but most were just local members with parochial interests and a tradition of independence.

The benefits of opting out

At *Carp* the results soon vindicated the decision to opt out. The immediate benefits were tangible: rents were pegged at 1 per cent above inflation for three years while rents in neighbouring authorities went up by around 5 per cent. Three million pounds of catch-up repairs were guaranteed. Their aspirations with regard to development were, as the chief executive put it, 'never particularly high', but within two years they had built nearly 250 new homes and planned to build 200 a year. On the management side, they felt they could now pinpoint the exact relationship between rent levels and levels of service, and had been able to cost the improvements demanded by tenants. They had also changed the organisational culture by setting up a customer care strategy and they planned to obtain British Standard quality accreditation for the whole service. All the staff were put on performance-related pay. Structural change came after a year, with reorganisation into four teams. The development director commented that the staff now felt that they 'owned' their jobs, and had a more generic team to relate to. The directors met as a management team every Monday morning, and were aware of the need for good communication and fluid boundaries between the teams. Further structural changes were planned, with decentralisation to area teams and eventually regional boards.

The finance director commented that 'taking the housing stock out of the political arena' was a major benefit. The customer services manager went further and said that local authorities 'get in a rut, its all got too cosy'. This underlines the importance of organisational culture and the chance to change it. He explained that formerly the staff had tried to get out of doing things, but since the tenants had voted for them they had developed a sense of obligation. He called it 'rethought training', and gave as an example the fact that they had established response time indicators for repairs before the Housing Corporation had asked for them.

The positive results of greater autonomy and the change in culture included the reduction of rent arrears to 0.8 per cent (the Audit Commission's target was 2 per cent). The reletting time was down to three weeks, which is about as low as it can ever get. It had been feared by some that rent increases would be severe after the end of the rent-guarantee period, but in this case it was held to 6.5 per cent. Response times for repairs had also improved. Although it was not part of the original reason for transferring, *Carp* was now free to bid for new building schemes over a much wider geographical area; it was already working in two neighbouring districts, replacing faulty systems-built houses and developing special needs accommodation for the young homeless, students and hospital staff. The association still had a recognisably local identity, though how long this would last was uncertain.

There had also been improvements in accountability to tenants. For one tenant representative the main benefit was that the tenants now had a say, with a tenants' forum and three representatives on the board. She confirmed the sea-change in staff attitudes: 'They used to give the impression that the money came out of their own pockets' but now see the tenants as the clients, 'putting the staff's wages in their pocket'. They now had a complaints system, a clearer tenancy agreement and an improved repairs service, and were looking forward to an unusually generous four-year maintenance cycle of exterior painting.

At *Pike*, the immediate benefits were that the authority became debt free and there was £10 million to spend on new development. This was enhanced by a payback arrangement, whereby the DoE returned the money spent on the local authority housing association grant so that the interest on it could be used again. They were committed to spending over £18 million on backlog repairs and the modernisation of existing stock, including the demolition and replacement of concrete houses. Soon all homes were expected to have new roofs, windows and central heating, after which they planned to move on to kitchen improvements. They were building for several local authorities and had a development programme of 500 homes per year. Already they had expanded so fast that three regional offices had had to be opened. Under the 'housing market package', a short-term measure to boost the housing market, the association had bought nearly a thousand homes. This package was offered only to the biggest associations, confirming *Pike*'s high status with the Housing Corporation. They also participated in four business expansion schemes, managing nearly 400 homes on an agency agreement from business expansion scheme companies, and aiming to buy these once the scheme's four-year tax break was over – they had sufficient assets to cover the purchase price even if they did not receive a housing association grant for it. With over 7 000 council homes bought at sitting-tenant valuation, they had an enviably strong asset base and had instantly become one of the top players in the housing association world.

The tenants' rents had been pegged for three years, but then they had begun to rise steeply, with a recent 10 per cent increase. Critics of LSVT had pointed out that new tenants would have to pay dearly to keep the association financially secure, and that a slump in 'right to buy' sales might financially endanger the associations. In some cases these predictions proved true, although in *Pike*'s case, the surpluses made in the first few years were used to keep down the rents to new tenants, and the shortfall in sales did not seriously affect the business plan. The top-level staff felt there was much more job satisfaction and that they were delivering a better service, which was substantiated by a tenants' survey in which most tenants said they had seen an improvement. The main cultural change seemed to be the staff's closer identification with the association, and eventually a heightened sense of identification from tenants as well, due partly to its being a single-purpose organisation, and partly because they now had more direct contact with staff who could make decisions and make them quickly. The new association had changed to some extent towards the housing association culture, but had also changed that culture, being seen to be unusually aggressive within the movement. The development director said of the traditional housing association attitude: 'Everything took for ever – three years to do development schemes. We had a competitive, aggressive feel, compared to traditional housing associations, who are a complaining bunch of people. We did not go out of their way to upset them but suddenly we were everywhere, spreading out.'

Those in the management team felt they had been different even within the local authority culture, that they had been a typically ambitious and single-minded before the transfer. Since then their attitude towards the job had permeated throughout the lower-level management, helped by the recruitment of a number of new staff members from the private and association sectors. Most line managers had been put on 'spot' salaries, based on an annual appraisal. The structure of the new association had been changed immediately upon transfer: the housing management staff had been decentralised and 'patch-based', unlike those at the local authorities *Trout* and *Flounder,* where cost-consciousness precluded such tight working arrangements.

The emphasis on housing development might have meant the neglect of day-to-day housing management, and there was some evidence of this. There was some tenant dissatisfaction with the repair and maintenance service, and *Pike* had set up a working party with tenant representatives to look at the problem. Rent arrears had increased to nearly 2 per cent because some staff had been diverted to run the housing market package. Hence there was some cost attached to the heavy emphasis on development, but not so much that the tenants would notice. A tenant representative confirmed that tenants were now 'a lot happier' with the service, and were being encouraged to participate and feel a greater sense of responsibility. 'The whole organisation is more customer based and friendly.'

At *Trout*, the consequence of not transferring was that rent rises were even higher than predicted, rising by 68 per cent over four years. In some cases of tenants voting against transfer, there had been accusations that the authority concerned had punished them for not voting 'yes' by deliberately raising their rent, but *Trout* did it in order substantially to improve the housing stock. They installed central heating and cavity wall insulation and refurbished a systems-built estate, but at a higher cost to the tenants than was the case with the transferred associations. At *Flounder*, having decided against the idea of voluntary transfer, a radical 'bureau-shaping' group of top managers decided to go for a voluntary competitive tender, well in advance of the compulsory tendering to be imposed from the centre. Interestingly, having got the cost savings they wanted from a private contractor, they, and a new group of councillors, still found the benefits to be had from opting out compelling: a year after our research finished they began to prepare for voluntary transfer.

We have noted that the desire for autonomy was one reason for opting out, but not a major reason. At *Carp* the chair of the association felt they had gained autonomy in a struggle against the local authority culture, but that they now had a new set of masters in the funding bodies that had loaned them a massive £34 million. The finance director agreed that the funders were their 'main bosses'. In contrast to traditional associations, they did not see the Housing Corporation as a serious check on their autonomy. The Housing Corporation had been criticised for being a funding and regulatory agency in one, but, the directors of *Carp* were rather complacent about regulation, because in its other role the Housing Corporation was dependent on the larger associations to carry out development. The directors certainly had no fear of the Housing Corporation's performance auditors. At *Pike*, according to the finance director, the transfer had resulted in a 'different world', allowing them the freedom to act entrepreneurially and without the restrictions of the public sector. Decision making was much quicker: as long as the four members of the management team reached agreement, decisions could be made in a day. Like the management of *Carp*, they too saw the main pressure as coming from the funding agencies – which required tight financial management and adherence to an annual business plan – and were complacent about the Housing Corporation's monitoring.

The drawbacks of opting out

In our case study organisations, few interviewees were able to identify drawbacks from opting out. At *Carp*, even one member who had retired after 44 years could only see good things coming from the move. According to the finance director, 'there could be no better deal for the tenants and the local authority'. There were, however, what might be called problems of success. At *Pike*, there were signs that the association was suffering from too rapid a change and too much growth, and the interviewees were looking forward to a period of stabilisation. In the opinion of the chair of the board, it had been growing too rapidly and needed to set up a new regional structure in order to be able to provide localised management. The director admitted that 'We have been papering over the cracks'. They were tempted to expand all over the south-east but were not going to do so, and decided to stay in the areas currently covered.

Compared with existing housing associations, these new associations did not see the Housing Corporation's 'regime' as a drawback. This is not surprising, since it guaranteed them a place in a competitive system for development grants in which they soon became powerful players. Even though the Housing Corporation monitored the new associations closely at first, and a few managers did complain about excessive form-filling, they were confident that they had handled this well and would be regulated more lightly in the future. Perhaps when the initial sense of release from local authority bureaucracy wore off they would come to see the Housing Corporation as another controller. The Corporation went through something of a crisis in the early 1990s, in which it had to ward off bids by the Audit Commission and the National Audit Office to take over its monitoring role. As a result its monitoring system was made less detailed and mainly consisted of financial appraisal, which was more suitable for the large associations.

Concepts of performance

In the social rented housing sector there are two systems for reporting performance, one for local authorities and one for housing associations, and there are different statutory requirements in each case. LSVT housing departments move from one to the other, and it is by no means clear that the move makes for more measurement and greater use of performance data; it may well be the reverse. The council housing sector has to provide two levels of performance data. The first is a general set of measures, identified by the Audit Commission (1992), which have to be provided to the public in some form. The set consists of throughput measures for dealing with the public: length of time taken to answer the telephone and letters; number of complaints to the ombudsman; handling of complaints; and so on. Basic information has to be provided on the housing stock: number of dwellings managed; number adapted for the disabled; number of flats in blocks of three storeys or more; and so on. There are several measures of allocations and lettings, including the highly visible statistic of homes left empty, and measures of effectiveness in housing repairs and maintenance. Rent collection is another highly visible area, with the percentage of council tenants in arrears often being used as a key measure of how 'soft' the council is on its tenants. Levels of rents and capital expenditure on major repairs have to be set out somewhere, and there are several key statistics on homelessness. This is a long list of measures, but they are all easily found in the Housing Investment Programme forms or the Housing Revenue Account. What is missing from these is any reference to new building, which is one of the main indicators of success for housing associations.

In addition, Section 167 of the Local Government and Housing Act 1989 requires performance data to be published annually for tenants. Called the 'Reports to Tenants', it is considerably longer than the above list. It adds a wider context to the basic information, such as the degree of concentration of the stock and the age and ethnic profile of the tenants. It shows the range of rents charged, as well as the average; describes the contractual arrangements and priority categories for repairs; and presents rent arrears in six bands ranging from under four weeks to over a year. Similar levels of detail have to be provided for housing allocations, housing benefit, homelessness and so on. Some of the requirements go beyond what the local authorities can actually provide, and they are struggling to make their computer systems produce such sophisticated data as the costs of management per week per dwelling, with separate figures for the amounts charged by other departments and a breakdown of costs over an incredibly detailed list of 24 different functions.

Housing associations are not required by law to provide all this information, but the Housing Corporation introduced equivalent requirements in its monitoring forms and through instruction circulars. In addition, associations have a range of performance indicators on the development of new and rehabilitated property. They are major borrowers of finance for housing, and therefore have financial indicators to collect as well, including (since the Housing Corporation insisted on their moving to plc accounting) the value of and return on their assets. While local authority housing departments have three 'customers' for performance data – the DoE, local citizens and tenants – housing associations have at least five: partner local authorities, private lenders, the Housing Corporation, local communities and tenants.

Despite this detailed statutory framework for collecting and publicising performance indicators, as in the schools and hospitals studied, it was difficult to discern more than a superficial commitment to a 'performance culture'. All the organisations were familiar with basic indicators such as rent arrear levels, void turnover and timing, average repair times, and number and type of tenant complaints, and all four had begun to conduct tenant satisfaction surveys. However, when asked what would indicate to them that something was going wrong, managers in the opted-out agencies identified a wide range of indicators that bore little relationship to the published data. At *Pike*, managers were sensitive to adverse press publicity, tenant representatives cited the quality of the relationship between staff, and board members believed they would be alerted by general feedback received from staff, tenants and the public. At *Carp*, the first indication was felt to be in tenants' complaints and arrears information, and in deteriorating relations between tenants and front-line staff. In all our cases, as in the schools, the quality of relationships was cited almost as often as hard indicators: realistic expectations among the tenants; the relationship with the partner local authorities (if the association is performing well the 'councillors will be happy'); the relationship with the Housing Corporation (whose development allocations reflect the relationship); and signs that the staff were becoming tense, an indicator that for those who managed in the old-fashioned way was exemplified by 'walking about'.

There was some scepticism about the use value of the standardised performance indicators required, particularly of the annual report to tenants, which was met with indifference. One regular item that was taken seriously at the opted-out agencies was a quarterly review of the business plan, which was agreed by the board and sent to the Housing Corporation and funding bodies. In general there was a relaxed attitude towards performance information, because even though so much of it was required and made public, in contrast to hospital waiting lists and school league tables it did not generate much comment or criticism from tenants or the public. There was not much difference between the attitudes of staff working for the opted-out associations and those working for the non-opted-out agencies, except that local authority staff were more aware of levels of homelessness as a key statistic.

Performance in practice

In housing, though there was greater awareness than in the schools about what data was collected, there was the same vagueness about the uses to which it was put. For instance at *Carp* the chair of the board emphasised the need for performance indicators, saying conventionally 'If you can't measure it you can't manage it'. Yet what dominated the discussion were not routine measures but a specific set of promises made to tenants before opting out, and for these it was felt crucial to measure performance: rent increases, progress with major improvements to the homes, removal of the need for further loan facilities, and so on.

At *Pike*, not surprisingly given their emphasis on the construction of new buildings, development targets were set and their progress was monitored, but even on this crucial topic monitoring was 'by exception'. Managers acknowledged that regular indicators had been neglected in favour of rapid expansion through development, measured by development statistics. As the development director said, 'development and housing have been belting ahead without administrative backup' – no one had been taking responsibility for it. They were hampered by reliance on an 'ancient' computer system inherited from their days as a local authority department. They had some basic information, but relied on 'seat of the pants' intuition that things were going well. Unlike at *Carp*, there did not seem to have been any pressure from the board to rectify this.

At *Trout*, the managers had to deal with councillors who sometimes picked up on the data provided at committee meetings. At *Flounder*, the process of contracting out meant that they were able to write a higher level of performance reporting into the specification. Of course, in a client–contractor relationship, performance information is a crucial part of the process, and they were planning monthly meetings between client and contractor at which performance would be reviewed. With penalties for poor performance and the threat of cancellation of the contract if things went badly, this indicates that the 'performance culture' flourishes best not in fully opted-out agencies but in that half-way house between decentralisation and devolution: competitive tendering of housing management.

Fragmentation, system coherence and equity

The move from local authority housing departments to associations can be seen as a fragmentation of responsibilities, especially in provision for the homeless and new building. At *Trout*, a quite traditional local authority housing department, managers expressed concern that the system would lose overall coherence, specifically that the local authority would remain responsible for the homeless and yet be reliant on other agencies to meet the housing need. This issue has been raised by all transferees, and their business plans have tended to include a detailed commitment to becoming an agent for the local authorities in housing the homeless, with a certain percentage of new lettings reserved for this purpose. There has been concern that these agreements are voluntary, and may not be so easy to guarantee in the future, but research has shown that the arrangements have generally worked well (Mullins *et al.*, 1995). The local authorities' role has been growing at the regional level, and they have a considerable say in which associations may work in their areas; they still ought to be able to drive a bargain in relation to their statutory duties as a housing authority.

The loss of influence by the new associations has often caused problems. In one instance a chief executive had to resign when the local authority representatives on his board accused him of becoming too independent from the authority. In another the opposite happened, and all the councillors on the board resigned. In our case studies, at *Pike* the relationship with the local authority had become quite fraught. As the chair of the board put it, at first there was 'great bloodletting and friction' while they gained their independence. The Housing Association grant can be channelled directly through the Housing Corporation, or through a local authority via its housing investment programme. For the first two years of its life, *Pike* was dependent on the latter and it was 'like walking on eggshells': the association had to prove its independence yet relied on the local authority for development. At first, both tenants and councillors found it difficult to 'let go of the apron strings' – the chair of housing was in tears at the handover ceremony. As *Pike*'s own chair put it, they had to 'throw off the mantle' of local authority thinking and take responsibility, and they were helped in this by the retirement of the authority's chief executive, who had steered the transfer process. Resentment was fuelled by a decision not to take over the local authority architects', with the result that the architects were made redundant, and by a decision to change the name to one not based on the locality. It is interesting that of the three local authority representatives on the board one could not adapt and resigned, to be replaced by a more forward-looking councillor. The housing director reckoned the councillor members were now an asset, having realised that the relationship had to be one of partnership rather than domination. This was just as well, because after a modest start the association expanded well beyond its original boundaries in an aggressive bid to become a large, regional player in new housing development.

Carp avoided these problems by having much more modest development goals and staying within the locality. Even so the Housing Corporation was exerting pressure on them to expand into the territory of neighbouring authorities – the strong asset base of LSVT associations means they can do development work more cheaply than the traditional local associations. It will soon be the case that any coordination of the LSVTs' work with that of other providers will be done by the Housing Corporation and the DoE at the regional level, and the local authorities will completely lose control. Whether this will result in the fragmentation of planning for new buildings and of provision for the homeless will depend on how well the Corporation carries out its tasks, and on whether the local authorities are effective in their new role of enabler (see Goodlad, 1993). What is certain is that monopoly supply by a single local landlord has gone. So has the goal of building up local housing associations and giving them the task of managing local housing estates; there will be a plethora of associations with a 'pepper pot' of small estates, some owned locally, some by more remote regional and national agencies. Whether this will lead to poor-quality housing management will depend on the ability of these large associations effectively to decentralise. This may in turn lead to higher management costs than would have been the case if a local association or housing department were responsible.

Unlike schools and hospitals, where the question of equity has been crucial, in housing there has been little discussion of possible inequities, except that between existing and prospective tenants: the new associations have been charged with securing their financial viability at the expense of new tenants. In our case study the managers and boards were aware of such criticism even if they did not voice it openly – one of their aims was to reduce the difference between the two rent levels as soon as possible.

Accountability

One major criticism has been that the new associations are less accountable to their tenants and the public. The local authorities provided access to decision making through councillors. It was an indirect route, which was itself criticised for allowing housing managers to be complacent about the rights of tenants and for not distinguishing properly between consumers and citizens (see Birchall, 1992). Yet the local authorities had developed quite sophisticated and varied forms of tenant participation, often along with decentralised structures for service delivery.

Housing associations are a mixture of two traditions: philanthropy and mutual aid. While early in their history a serious attempt was made to involve tenants in their ownership and control (Birchall, 1996), it has been the philanthropic model that has dominated. As industrial and provident societies, associations have a membership base that ranges from a small group of the 'great and the good', who elect a board on which consumers are hardly represented, to a large group representative of the local community. Since the 1970s a challenge has been presented by housing cooperatives, which own and control their own housing, and by management cooperatives, which act as agents for the landlord in carrying out their own management (Birchall, 1988). The move after 1988 towards concentrating development on large, regional and national associations has led the Housing Corporation to emphasise the need for tenant participation. It is now one of the Corporation's requirements that associations have a policy on tenant participation.

In our cases, at *Carp* the question of accountability was not raised, probably because they had six active tenants' associations and three elected tenant representatives on the board. Nor had councillors reacted adversely, because the association was still firmly based in their local area, although it was gradually being persuaded by Housing Corporation officials to work outside. It had already signed up 160 members, mainly tenants, who could exercise control over the association at the annual meeting. So there is potential here for a real alternative to the kind of participation offered by the local authority as landlord. The main limitation on managerial autonomy was the 15-strong board. In contrast, at *Pike* there were only 40 members, and little organised tenant participation. The director admitted that pressure from below was non-existent; the tenants were generally satisfied and habitually passive. Among the transferred tenants, after trying for two or three years to get representatives from each area, they had had to write to every tenant asking for nominations. They planned to form consultation committees in each area, which would elect four tenants to each of the four regional committees. These regional committees would then elect up to three tenants to represent them on the main board. At the time of interviewing there was only one tenant on the board, elected not by the tenants but by the members. Two more places were reserved for tenant representatives but had not yet been taken up. In such a situation it would have been easy for the management team to run ahead of the accountability structures of the association, and this may account for the muted unease shown about the issue of accountability. The chief executive at *Pike* could not remember whether the board met quarterly or every two months, and referred to the weekly management meetings as the 'board'. One manager admitted that, though the politics of the local authority had held them back, they had experienced a loss of sharpness because accountability to councillors had been replaced by a more 'cosy' relationship with the board. Another commented that, although there had been a loss of accountability 'in the political sense', there was now more tenant involvement, so accountability to their 'market' had made up for the democratic deficit.

Clearly these agencies had moved from one rather unsatisfactory form of accountability to another. It remains to be seen whether the more direct involvement of tenants on their boards will lead to an improvement.

Transfer to LSVT associations: concepts

How can we understand the case of housing in terms of the conceptual apparatus developed in Chapter 2? A first and rather obvious point is that both administrative and political decentralisation have occurred. However this is not as radical as it seems at first sight. *Administrative decentralisation* has been to a body that essentially consists of the same group of managers and front-line staff, doing much the same tasks and dealing with the same group of tenants. In this respect it is not as radical a change as internal administrative decentralisation, which usually means the setting up of area or neighbourhood offices and the giving of substantial budgetary and managerial powers to local staff. Compared with the radical decentralisation effected by many authorities – Islington, Birmingham and Tower Hamlets, to name but the most well known – this kind of decentralisation (from the perspective of customers and front-line staff) means business as usual. *Political decentralisation* has had more radical effects: the new bodies have been restricted with regard to the proportion of councillors they may have on the board and they have restricted the number of tenant representatives, and so the result has been a mixed form of governance, including board members chosen for various types of representativeness or expertise. Despite attempts by councillors to hold on to power, most of the new associations have grown out of their initial role as a local authority housing association.

Our second distinction is between *competitive and non-competitive decentralisation*. The decentralisation of housing has been non-competitive because, like the hospital trusts, new housing associations have been formed to take over from existing housing departments, and the exercise has been marked by cooperation rather than competition. The transfer of some new town housing stocks illustrates that such a process can be competitive, with local authorities competing with housing associations and tenant-led bodies to take over new town corporation housing stock (see Birchall, 1992). However in this case tenants have not been given a choice between competing agencies, merely the choice of whether or not to opt out. It is ironic that, since 1993 at least, this process has enabled the new associations to avoid a different form of competitive decentralisation – the compulsory competitive tendering of council housing. One form of decentralisation has been used to avoid another – more radical – form.

Within the agencies studied there was little evidence of a taste for further competitive decentralisation. At *Pike* the chief officer claimed that they 'market tested' their services, but in practice had not put anything out to competitive tender. Like other large housing associations, *Pike* had its own in-house development team and was able to gain a considerable competitive advantage by keeping the profits from design and development in-house.

There is no doubt that this is *devolution*: the new agencies are separate legal entities. Even more than grant maintained schools and health trusts, the new housing associations are independent agencies. With a rental income and the ability to borrow money on the strength of their asset base, they are not just creatures of statute, nor are they dependent on public funding for their continued existence. They are independent both legally and financially, and if they choose not do any further development work (as many small housing associations have done), they will be free from all but the lightest regulation.

The fourth distinction is between *vertical* and *horizontal decentralisation*. With regard to vertical decentralisation, it could be argued that in becoming housing associations these new agencies have come under government control, via a powerful quango, the Housing Corporation, which regulates them and makes the rules in the competition for development funding. It is certainly true that, in return for becoming the favoured developers of subsidised housing, housing associations have become less autonomous (Langstaff, 1992). However, considering the cumulative effects of government restrictions on council housing and the relative freedom of housing associations, the idea of *recen*-tralisation does not seem to apply. However, as in the schools, there has been a strengthening of top management and probably (though this is hard to quantify) some recentralisation of authority to the chief executive. Previously the buck stopped at a higher level in the local authority – at the assistant chief executive and then the chief executive and the leader of the council, rather than just at the housing director – while the new association directors are accountable, on a day-to-day basis, only to the chair of their board of directors.

Nor has there been much horizontal decentralisation. The freedom to engage in housing development has meant that the new associations have hired specialist development staff who tend to be at one remove from the traditional housing management hierarchy. However, to see them as a new breed of autonomous professionals would be to exaggerate their difference; they tend to be well integrated via a development director into the associations' management teams, and in any case good practice demands that they liaise closely with housing management staff in the planning of new estates or the refurbishment of old ones.

The concept of *performance* tended, in our case studies, to be dominated by tangible outputs from housing development, partly due to the sheer novelty of being able to build houses again, partly because the associations, whether they intended to or not, rapidly became key players in the Housing Corporation's regional strategy. Performance in the day-to-day business of housing management was dominated by the need to balance the books in relation to the banks that had funded the transfer, and again this may turn out to be a short-term preoccupation (though one shared with the health trusts, in their concern to achieve the requisite return on capital). There was evidence of interest in a user-oriented concept of quality, hampered by an almost total lack of mechanisms of tenant involvement under the previous local authority regimes, but given some urgency by the need to find ways of choosing tenant representatives for reserved places on their boards of directors.

Turning to *accountability*, as they lack the diversity and complexity of the health service, housing agencies have been more readily able to identify to whom they are accountable: funding agencies, the Housing Corporation, their own board of directors, their tenants, and the local authorities in whose areas they work. In our case study we could find no evidence that these forms of accountability were regarded as onerous, and there was some unease that they did not keep the managers in check to the extent that the old local authority system had done.

Finally, what of *quality*? In this sector the managerial notion of quality has been accepted more readily than in the other sectors. Unlike the health trusts, with their organisational complexity and competing professional definitions of quality, and unlike the schools, with their emphasis on the quality of personal relationships, housing agencies have been more likely to embrace a managerial concept. The housing association sector generally seems receptive to ideas of total quality management and quality standards, and one of our cases, *Carp*, was not untypical in pushing ahead with plans to have recognised quality standards in every area of its work.

Transfer to LSVT associations: theories

How far do the theories presented in Chapter 2 illuminate this case study? First, there is little evidence of budget maximisation. The transfers were seen as a way of protecting budgets, or at least the sphere of influence of housing managers. Also, there was a keen expectation of expansion into housing development. There was, in behind-the-scenes discussions among managers, anticipation of higher salaries and better-quality company cars, and so in this sense they were maximising their own utility. However we should not overestimate the individual self-seeking behaviour of local authority housing managers. Like doctors and teachers, they were interested in the quality of their work, and this was manifested most clearly in new building and refurbishment schemes, and in the kind of interesting schemes they were able to put forward to solve particular local authorities' problems concerning homelessness, or structural problems on estates. Problem solving seemed to bring its own satisfactions. In relation to the housing management budget, the aim was not maximisation but value for money, with low rent increases being the main measure of success.

How far does the idea of bureau-shaping apply? Dunleavy's theory expects managers to undertake a major internal reorganisation aimed at insulating high-status policy and strategy-making functions. There was some evidence of this in our study, in that top management teams emerged that spent more time on strategy than they had when under local authority control. This may have been more a consequence of being autonomous than a positive decision. Chief executives, like the head teachers interviewed, spent more of their time safeguarding the organisation's status and paying attention to the local press, but this may be a reflection of the newness of the organisations in the early days. There were major internal reorganisations aimed at introducing new management techniques, but the pace of change in conventional housing departments was also increasing, and it is probably the case that reorganisation would have happened anyway.

As we have noted, there was a reluctance to hive off routine tasks by contracting out. Like teachers, the housing managers recognised that day-to-day routine work was the stuff of the organisation, providing its income and its legitimacy. It remained central to the managers' conception of themselves. In the previous chapter we noted how in the case of schools the bureau-shapers were not in the opted-out organisations but in central government. In the case of housing it remained with the local authorities to develop an 'enabling' role in liaison and partnership with local housing associations. There is some evidence both from our study and from others that chief officers who oversaw the transfer and stayed with the local authority thought they would have more influence over the resulting organisation than actually turned out to be the case. They were not able to shape these new 'bureaus' for very long after their birth.

A second prediction is that managers will want to set up sophisticated monitoring systems. We found no evidence of this, merely a recognition that with new computer systems comes the capacity to generate more performance information. Third, there was an increase in the work of forming relationships with other key organisations, creating partnerships and managing the boundaries of the organisation. However local authority managers were also doing this, and it was not cited as a reason for opting out.

Fourth, we should expect managers to want to export low-status work but, as we have already noted, this is the stuff of housing management and the main revenue earner. The new housing associations were beginning to differentiate themselves in the kinds of work they did, but only at the margins on the development side, and in their different policies for growth and geographical expansion. Finally, we have already noted how the fifth option, contracting out, has no relevance because the transfers were made partly to avoid it.

So there was not much evidence of bureau-shaping, and what there was could also be identified in some local authority housing departments. As with the schools, transfer was only one of a number of strategies, and as shown by the minority who transferred, it was not one that appealed to all housing managers.

Game theory provides some illumination. Like the NHS and Community Care Act, the 1987 White Paper on housing marked a critical juncture, which was followed by a radical rewriting of the 'rules of the game'. However, while in health and education there was a discernable trend in strategies from a zero-sum through bargaining to a cooperative game, in this case there was bargaining from the start. Local authorities took the lead, and waited for central government to catch up with their initiative and impose rules controlling the financial payoffs, the limit in size of transfer association, and the number who were allowed to transfer each year. Remaining a local authority housing department, on the other hand, was seen as definitely zero-sum, with the government having had the best of the game, introducing one disadvantage after another for those staying with the council. The new game had to be cooperative, because the government had the power to say 'no'. At the local level, the game was risky, the outcome uncertain, and there was a genuine desire to do the best for the tenants (or if not, a need to create a convincing rhetoric that amounted to almost the same thing). Unlike in the schools sector, at the local level there was no antagonism between those wanting to opt out and the centre; with only one housing department in each local authority, there had to be a great deal of cooperation between the chief executive's department and the councillors if the transfer was to go ahead. In relation to the tenants, the game plan of the landlord was to persuade them that the change was really necessary if 'business as usual' was to be preserved. At any sign of organised opposition, tenants tended to vote against the transfer – at the local level it had to be a cooperative game.

New institutionalist approaches are also helpful in this case. We have noted how they are good at emphasising stability and continuity, and this confirms what several of our interviewees stressed, that the transfer was a conscious attempt to protect existing norms of professional housing management, the public service ethos and care for one's tenants in the face of a hostile central government. They were attracted by the idea of transfer because it was seen as a different, but more effective, way of doing what they were already doing.

On the other hand, as in the health trusts there was incremental adjustment to the new situation, in this case to the slightly different housing association ethos. The creation of so many large new housing associations provoked interesting reactions from traditional associations, with accusations of the newcomers being too agressive, too competitive for the association sector. Eventually they settled down and there was more acceptance of shared norms, though there has been a two-way adjustment, with the traditional associations having to adjust to a more competitive system (instituted by the Housing Corporation in 1988, independently of the transfers), and the new-comers moderating their stance. Underlying these differences there was always a set of shared understandings about what social rented housing and the role of the housing manager were all about.

As in the schools, the basic norms and the nature of everyday life at the front line remained relatively unchanged. There was evidence of pride in the new associations among tenants and staff, but the former still had the same needs, and the latter still did much the same kind of work as before. There is support here for the new institutionalist emphasis on tradition and continuity.

Were the transfers an example of isomorphism? There was mimesis - the copying of new trends and fashions – but it was certainly not coercive. It was orchestrated by the housing policy community itself, and was a genuine learning process, in contrast to the situation in the schools and hospitals. But we must not overestimate the cultural change that the transfers represented. The housing profession was never united behind the idea, and it was not required even of progressive housing managers to believe in it. Unlike in the schools sector, opting out was never associated with a particular set of values but was a pragmatic response to government restrictions.

The rhetoric of transfer almost completely ignored the vocabulary of the new managerialism. In relation to transfers, a conventional rhetoric was used to argue that the transfer was (or was not) in the best interests of the tenants. As in the schools, this tended to be deployed as a 'clincher' argument, again not as political rhetoric – government policies for the most part being taken as a given, as part of the organisation's environment – but as a pragmatic argument about rent levels and housing quality. In the transfer process it was tempting for the organisers to put across the pro-transfer message too strongly, and as noted in Chapter 4, early on in the development of the policy the government began to impose rules, insisting that a counter-rhetoric be communicated, and that a 'tenants' friend' be hired to provide what might be called an interpretation of these on the tenants' behalf (see Mullins *et al.*, 1995). Although we speak of rhetoric, this does not mean that the arguments were at a high level of generalisation; they remained for the most part concerned with rent levels, new building, opportunities for housing improvements, and the preservation of good landlord–tenant relations. In this case, general arguments about why service delivery agencies should opt out of the public sector were occasionally heard, but they tended to be submerged under more urgent arguments.

The language used by managers was still the language of housing management and development, overlaid with some more general jargon derived from business and inculcated in housing departments in the late 1980s through a programme of cultural change called 'customer care'. Unlike the clinical staff of the hospitals in our study, they were not bashful about using this business jargon in relation to tenants; seeing tenants as customers may have been controversial at the time, but managers generally came to see it as a healthy move away from the old paternalism. We have noted that there was a relatively weak use of arguments about efficiency and effectiveness, but this is explained by the fact that the managers were doing much the same work as before. They emphasised continuity in the quality of their own work. There was some unease about the difference between old and new tenants, because for the first few years of a new association's life the latter had much higher rent levels. There was a desire to see rent levels equalise as soon as possible. They were like schools in this, being uncomfortable when the interests of different tenants were disaggregated, and desiring the image of a homogeneous community. The rhetoric that remains is one of concern for the tenants, and this is reinforced, not contradicted, by the rhetoric of 'customer care'.

The advantages of opting out have been considerable and sustained over time by an accumulation of restrictive government policies. The advent of a new Labour government in 1997 has not really begun to level the playing field between local authority housing departments and housing associations. The phased release of capital receipts for new building will not mean local authorities can begin to build council houses again. The rules on what is and what is not public spending will not be changed, so the basic structure remains skewed towards the association sector. Voluntary transfers continue, and in proposals for 'local housing companies' the idea is being adapted to include inner city authorities that still have outstanding debt on their homes and therefore need to continue to receive government grant aid even if they sell their stock. In the health sector, transfer to the new provider agencies is complete, but the autonomy of the health trusts is still in question. In the education sector, grant maintained schools have already been partly assimilated back into the old system. In the housing sector, the new government is busy creating a vehicle for large-scale transfers to the new agencies. When it comes to the need to borrow money in order to refurbish estates or build new ones, the pragmatic advantages of being a private rather than a public agency are still overwhelming.

8 Freedom, Performance and Accountability

Introduction

In this final chapter we return to the big questions we started with, and add a couple more. Thus we ask:

- Has decentralisation really taken place?
- What has been decentralised?
- What seems to have been the effect of decentralisation on the performance of the organisations concerned?
- What lessons can be learned from looking at different approaches to decentralisation in different settings and sectors?

These were the questions we posed in Chapter 1. The additional questions are:

- What messages does the experience of the reforms of the decade from 1987 hold for the organisation of representative democracy?
- How well do our chosen theoretical perspectives measure up to the task of explaining and interpreting the events of the period?

Has decentralisation really taken place?

This is a relatively easy question to answer. Substantial decentralisation has occured in all three of the sectors we investigated, and almost none of the managers we interviewed – even the disgruntled ones – thought it feasible or desirable to go back to the *status quo ante*. In this bald sense the policies of the Thatcher and Major Conservative administrations can be said to have achieved what they set out to achieve.

However, what is equally clear is that the degree of decentralisation – especially in the case of the NHS – was less than originally envisaged by its most enthusiastic proponents, and that – especially in secondary schooling and the NHS – the decentralisation was accompanied by significant measures of centralisation. As we have explained, there is nothing contradictory in this: it is perfectly possible to decentralise or devolve authority over certain issues (for example, school budgets) whilst simultaneously centralising authority over other issues (for example, the curriculum). Hence the paradox that, while extensive decentralisation has taken place, it is simultaneously correct to maintain that the UK state, already known to comparativists as one of the most centralised in Western Europe, became even more centralised during the late 1980s and early 1990s. Above all it was the level of local representative government that was 'hollowed out', with its powers and authority being transferred both 'downwards', to local units such as trusts and GM schools, and 'upwards', to central government and its quangos (Housing Corporation, Funding Association for Schools).

Furthermore there is the horizontal dimension to consider as well as the vertical. In all three sectors there was evidence that 'managerialism' – the doctrine and practice that overall control by managers is necessary and desirable – was on the increase (see, more generally, Pollitt, 1993). As local service-providing units became more autonomous there seems to have been a general acceptance that they needed strong central leadership if they were to remain 'afloat' in the uncharted but potentially competitive waters of quasi-markets. Thus head teachers and NHS and housing association chief executives all needed to begin to think strategically, to position their organisations in their local and regional marketplaces, and to ensure that the dead wood among their staff were not allowed to damage the attractiveness or productivity of their organisations. Of course different individuals took to these duties with greater or lesser skill and alacrity, but in each case there was a recognition that greater external freedom implied tighter internal control.

What has been decentralised?

The two principal freedoms – across all three sectors – have concerned the ability to spend budgets according to internal priorities and to organise internally with whatever structures and procedures local management deems most appropriate. Beyond this, however, there has been a considerable difference between housing on the one hand, and the NHS and education on the other. While health care and education have experienced strong central control over capital spending and the size of revenue budgets (and have also been subject to other forms of strong central control such as the national curriculum and the Patients' Charter league tables), housing has enjoyed a much broader range of freedoms. Housing associations have been able to raise capital, adjust rents and expand their operations beyond their original geographical jurisdictions.

The new endowments of authority have certainly been put to work. Budgetary and organisational freedoms have been exercised to redecorate entranceways, purchase more computers or books, speed up repairs and maintenance, build new houses, hire key staff at premium salaries, and redefine internal roles and structures. Such activities had given evident satisfaction to many of the staff we spoke to.

It is clear that the sense managers and other staff have of the tangibility of their new freedoms has depended to some extent on the overall budgetary climate. This has been chilliest in the case of the NHS, where many of our interviewees questioned the reality of trust freedoms under circumstances where there was little money available for new developments. At the other extreme the particular housing associations we looked at were relatively buoyant, replete with new projects and service improvements. Somewhere in between came the secondary schools, where achievement of GM status brought an early boost to cash and capital, albeit on a one-off basis.

What seems to have been the effect of decentralisation on the performance of the organisations concerned?

Regrettably, it will never be possible to give clear and precise answers to general questions about the effects of decentralisation on performance. Even if everyone could agree on what the key dimensions of performance should be (unlikely), there are a number of practical and methodological barriers in the way of achieving 'hard answers'. Whilst there is an abundance of anecdotes, there is little systematic before and after data. The reforms were simply not set up or implemented in such a way as to permit rigorous evaluation and attribution of performance changes. Either *ex ante* data was not collected, or it was collected on a different basis or key aspects of performance have still not been measured (for example many aspects of clinical quality), and even where reliable data on performance change is available, it is difficult to attribute it to specific measures of decentralisation or devolution because there were other important changes going on at the same time (one of us argues that this is a general problem with 'new public management' reforms all over the OECD world – Pollitt, 1995). The anecdotes themselves, though much beloved by politicians and the media, are frequently open to attributional objections. Was the improvement in waiting times in accident and emergency department due to better management consequent upon trust status, or to additional funding being put in, to the completion of a new building or to the retirement of the rather crusty old senior consultant and his replacement with a more managerially-minded and nurse-friendly successor? More often than not insiders are able to cite a series of possible causes rather than just one alone.

The requirements of strict causality are therefore both onerous and rarely satisfied (not at all in any of the 12 organisations in which we undertook fieldwork). If, however, we are prepared to relax the rigour slightly, and speak of plausible attributions and the 'balance of probabilities', then there are some things that, suitably festooned with qualifications, we can say about the performance of self-governing local service delivery agencies. Most obviously the pace of activity has intensified in all three sectors. This can be expressed in an endless variety of ways – more finished consultant episodes per consultant, falling lengths of stay in hospital, quicker average repair times, lower unit costs, rapid absorption of the ever-changing requirements of the national curriculum by schools, and so on. Furthermore the monitoring of this activity has become more transparent and comparative – public domain league tables have become a feature of life in all three sectors, and most of the measures they contain are essentially of activity (or, to a lesser extent, quality). These are considerable achievements, but (and here comes the first major qualification) it is by no means clear that self-governance has been the major factor boosting activity. Indeed two of the most important contributory factors have been the centralised imposition of 'league tables' of performance indicators and the centralised imposition of quasi-market competition. Paradoxically there was a sense in which many local service delivery organisations had to be forced to be free, then forced to compete! The rhetoric may have been mainly on the side of 'letting the managers manage' but the practice was more towards 'making the managers manage'.

The picture with respect to other important dimensions of performance – including effectiveness and equity – is less clear. There is some evidence that LSVT housing associations are providing housing more effectively than their local authority predecessors, but evidence of final effectiveness for schools and hospitals is conspicuous by its absence. This is not meant as a criticism of the staff at these institutions – it has long been recognised that to measure the final outcomes of either healthcare or education is a ferociously difficult task. Nevertheless it is perhaps worth stressing that any claims that decentralised self-govern-ance has resulted in better outcomes for patients and pupils should be treated with great caution. As for equity, we saw in Chapters 5 and 6 that this has not been a principal focus of concern either for ministers or (with a few exceptions) for the senior staff in the institutions themselves. Evidence is therefore patchy, but there are at least *prima facie* grounds for believing that GP fundholding (in the NHS) and the creation of GM schools (in education) have each resulted in some equity losses.

What lessons can be learned from looking at different approaches to decentralisation in different settings and sectors?

The broad policies of self-governance outlined in Chapter 4 may be thought of as general mechanisms. When implemented, these mechan-isms are applied in a series of different sectoral and local contexts. That such contexts affect the outcomes produced by the mechanism is one of the oldest findings of both the implementation literature and the programme evaluation literature (for example Pressman and Wild-avsky, 1973; Pawson and Tilley, 1997).

   There appear to be at least two sets of contextual factors that have a major influence on the ways in which national policy mechanisms actually work out at local level. The first set may be termed 'locality characteristics' and the second 'service characteristics'. Locality char-acteristics include such variables as the state of local party politics, the degree of competition and overlap existing between local service-providing institutions and the socio-economic profile of the particular area. Thus of our 12 case study sites, it mattered whether one was in an area of sharp political competition or local one-party dominance; it mattered whether a school was serving a well-to-do, middle-class area, or a deprived inner city zone; and it mattered whether an institution was basically a local monopoly provider or whether it was always looking sideways at rival providers to see what they were doing. Examples of these influences are strewn throughout Chapters 5, 6 and 7.

Service characteristics are also important. The nature of modern medical technology and the economics of operating and staffing it, tends to mean that hospitals are quite large and occupationally diverse institutions. As we have noted, this gives them a different set of characteristics from the more monoprofessional, low-technology schools. It is also a characteristic of the education process that it tends to work with groups of users (classrooms of students), whereas secondary and tertiary healthcare is focused on a series of individually differentiated patients. All these factors affect the way in which a new policy mechanism can be implemented and disseminated. The high degree of autonomy enjoyed by hospital consultants is one, but far from the only, example of such influences on the implementation process.

Others have written perceptively about the importance of such service characteristics. For example Stewart (1992) has shown how services may be delivered for all or selectively, and may be provided as an option or on a mandatory basis (for instance clean air would be an example of a mandatory service provided for all). He has stressed the significance of distinctions that differentiate between our three services, such as the time scale of the relationship (long for schools, usually short for hospitals), or the requirement for equipment (moderate for schools, high for hospitals).

It is when we look at the housing sector that we perhaps see the most striking example of the influence of service characteristics upon policy implementation. Unlike healthcare and education, housing is a service that provides (literally) bricks and mortar rather than (as for education and healthcare) intervention in the minds or bodies of service users. It is middle or low tech, but considerably more capital-intensive (less labour-intensive) than the other two services. Furthermore (and this could be said to be a mixture of service and local characteristics), public housing has always been supplied alongside a large and vibrant private housing market – proportionately much larger than either the private healthcare sector or the private education sector. Taken together, these housing service characteristics have made it considerably easier for the government to promulgate policies of a more market-orientated, non-governmental kind in the housing sector than in education or the NHS. Direct provision of socially rented housing by local authority housing departments, unlike direct service provision by LEAs or the NHS, is becoming a minority activity – a residual rump set within the wider panorama of provision by private developers and housing associations.

What messages does the experience of the reforms of the decade from 1987 hold for the organisation of representative democracy?

The decentralisation reforms described in this book have each reduced the influence and control of locally elected representatives – radically so in the case of GM schools and LSVTs, incrementally so in the case of LMS, and marginally so in the case of NHS trusts (because under the 1990 Act local authority representatives were removed from DHAs, and in any case DHAs lost their direct hierarchical authority over trust hospitals). What our research has shown is that the senior staff of these housing associations, schools and hospitals are largely indifferent to this loss, or even welcome it. What are the implications of this finding for the theory and practice of democratic government? Are we, as some critics have argued, now facing a severe 'democratic deficit' (Stewart, 1994), or is it that, as the Conservative minister with responsibility for civil service reform boldly claimed: 'The fact is, there has *not* been such a loss. Rather there has been a [democratic] *gain'* (Waldegrave, 1994, p. 84). There are a number of strands to Waldegrave's claim. First, he says that accountability has been gained by the provision of better information to service users – in particular he cites the publication of the results of national curriculum testing for school children and strategic purchasing plans and Patients' Charter quality indicators within the NHS. Second, he argues that:

> The key point in this argument is not whether those who run our public services are elected, but whether they are producer-responsive or consumer-responsive. Services are not necessarily made to respond to the public sector by giving citizens a democratic voice, and a distant and diffuse one at that, in their make up. They *can* be made responsive by giving the public choices, or by instituting mechanisms which build in publicly approved standards and redress when they are not attained.

He concludes by offering and then dismissing some fairly unpalatable alternatives – either having 'judge-led systems', where the performance of public services becomes a matter for the courts, or going back to the 1970s, 'when we let producer interest dominate consumer interest' (Waldegrave, 1994, p. 86). He also cites the findings of a survey conducted in the County of Cleveland, which found that 68 per cent of respondents said that 'responding to local people's wishes' was an important aspect of local services; 54 per cent rated 'cost and quality' as important but only 28 per cent thought that 'accountability' was important.

There are at least four problems with Waldegrave's position. First, he unhelpfully merges the notions of managerial accountability for operational results and political accountability for broad strategies and for the structure of institutions (Day and Klein, 1987). In effect, most of his argument is that the Conservative government put in place mechanisms for ensuring the better accountability of managers for operational results. This may be true (although we have referred to the inadequacy of performance 'league tables' at some length) but it is not really a satisfactory answer to the concern about the lack of political accountability. It is rather like saying that people shouldn't worry about the apple shortage because the supply of pears has been increased.

Second, mirroring the confusion between political and managerial accountability, there is a tendency to assume that the interests of the users of public services are identical to those of the citizens as a whole. But this is by no means necessarily true, even in the case of popular, broad-based services such as education and healthcare. In short, making better operational information available to users may seriously neglect the wider, collective interests of the citizenry as a whole.

Third, Waldegrave appears to put an unwarranted amount of weight on a very particular reading of the results of the survey in Cleveland. A more recent and broader-based survey, which was specifically directed towards issues of accountability and control, gives a rather different picture (Miller and Dickson, 1996). Briefly, this seems to show that, while the members of the public are not unduly disturbed by the multiplication of local bodies with no direct accountability to elected representatives, they want these bodies to be monitored (although not controlled) by elected local authorities, and in any case they have significantly more trust in elected local authorities than in locally appointed bodies.

Fourth, it is noticeable that Waldegrave is largely silent about what the probable future role of local authorities should be. There is an absence – perhaps not surprising in view of the generally antagonistic relations that existed between the Conservative government and local authorities – of any principled defence, or even acknowledgement, of the idea of local democracy.

Although there may be substantial weaknesses in Waldegrave's arguments, the defenders of local democracy can take only limited comfort from this. They have to confront serious problems of their own. In addition to the oft-cited issue of low turnout and national orientations in local elections (Stoker, 1997), our research has shown a decided absence of enthusiasm for local political control among the managers and professionals who deliver key local services. This sceptical attitude towards the value of local politics was expressed by a group that, in the main, was speaking on the basis of considerable experience. Taking all this evidence together, it would seem that fairly substantial changes will be needed if the value of the direct element in local governance is to be more widely recognised. This is too large a topic to take very far here, but from the particular perspective of management of local service-providing institutions, at least two issues have emerged that seem worthy of further consideration.

The first is that of how locally elected representatives can work in harmony with directly participating service users (parents, tenants and so on). New models are needed that will balance and combine these two different forms of political representation, each of which appears to have a substantial rationale of its own. The second is hinted at in the survey work by Miller and Dickson. It would appear that the members of the public can draw a distinction between monitoring and control. They are keener on the idea that elected local authorities should *investigate* the activities of local service-providing bodies than they are on the idea that they should *control* them (Miller and Dickson, 1996, p. 15). This perhaps points the way to the evolution of a new, scrutinising and publicising role for local authorities in relation to otherwise self-governing entities such as GM schools or NHS trusts. This would not be so much the 'enabling authority' that was envisaged by the Audit Commission and others during the late 1980s as a 'democratic watchdog', with the authority to obtain information, ask questions and explain and communicate significant issues to the local public. Whether such a watchdog would be best placed at the traditional level for English local government, or at the regional level (where developments are promised by the new Labour government) is a matter for further debate.

How well do our chosen theoretical perspectives measure up to the task of explaining and interpreting the events of the period?

In Chapter 2 we introduced selected prominent theorists from within three broad perspectives. It is clear that each perspective – collective action/rational choice, the new institutionalism and rhetorical analysis – has the potential of making a significant contribution to the understanding of those ideas and events upon which this book has focused. Game theory is particularly promising, though the data requirements of applying it rigorously appear formidable. The new institutionalism is perhaps disappointingly vague – at least in the hands of the authors we have cited. Yet somehow we retain the suspicion that more could be done here, that the general observations about symbolism and legitimacy could perhaps be developed into some more precise models of particular types of organisation or organisational change. Rhetorical analysis appears to have considerable possibilities and to possess the advantage of being accessible to the lone, desk-based researcher. However, like rational choice theory, it may be at its strongest on quite a small scale, where a limited volume of textual material and a small number of rhetors and audiences may be analysed in great depth. When much larger and more diverse sources are under scrutiny it becomes more difficult to be confident that one's sample is adequately representative.

This is not the place to reiterate the specific advantages and disadvantages of each perspective (this was done in general terms in Chapter 2 and then demonstrated at greater length in Chapters 5, 6 and 7). Nevertheless one broad-scope reflection may be in order. For a topic of the kind that we have been investigating, the most obvious general limitation to these perspectives is that none of them appears to furnish adequate models of local and service characteristics. Yet in many ways these are the crucial parameters within which the key decisions are taken and the implementation of national policies is shaped. They are not questions of individual utility, nor are they principally questions of behavioural norms, organisational symbols or political or professional rhetoric although, of course, local and service characteristics may certainly have an influence on norms, symbols and rhetoric).

To put it directly, the theories we are working with possess considerable subtleties and advantages but, both individually and cumulatively, they are weak in modelling socio-technical contexts. To complement them, therefore, there is a need for some sort of theory of what might be termed 'implementation habitats'. The principal elements of such a body of theory have been briefly indicated in the preceding discussion of local and service characteristics. Here we will take matters a little further, suggesting what kind of a theory might be constructed from such components.

Modelling implementation habitats: some building blocks

The full development and application of a theory of implementation habitats – or receiving locations for reform – will have to await later research. The significance of such habitats was, in a sense, a finding of our research to date, one that now needs to be elaborated and tested in further work. In one way the need for some modelling of local and service characteristics is glaringly obvious. The implementation of a reform could be likened to improving the design of an electric plug – if the reform is the modernised plug it may possess excellent characteristics, but if it is taken to another country and does not fit the local sockets, the potential improvement will never be realised. Hence the need for some theory or model, or at least typology, of sockets as well as of plugs. The scope of any theory of implementation habitats will almost certainly run wider than just the issue of decentralisation. It should be possible to develop a theory that would be relevant for the implementation of quite a range of managerial and administrative reforms, not only those with – as in our case – decentralisation as a major theme.

We are far from the first to have perceived this need. In one way or another, and at different levels, a number of writers have wrestled with it already (for example Hood, 1976; Pollitt and Summa, 1997; Stewart, 1992). If we have anything to add here it is probably the observation that it is often the *interaction* between local characteristics (which are spatially specific) with service characteristics (which are service specific) that determines the overall limit to, or constraint upon, reform.

To take the spatially specific locality characteristics first, our research points to at least three significant variables. First, there is the current socio-demographic composition of the local community. This is likely to have a range of effects, both direct and indirect. If the population is mainly affluent and well-organised, then *prima facie* they are in a stronger position either to support a reform or to offer what Hood (1976, pp. 21–2) terms 'recalicitrance' (Hood refers principally to recalcitrance among administrators, but clearly a local population can offer resistance as well). If, in contrast, citizens are internally divided and beset with the problems of multiple deprivation, they are in a weaker position to make their views felt. None of this is remotely new. Socio-demographic characteristics tend to interact strongly with certain service characteristics, so that 'human services' types of service are strongly influenced by the character of the population with which they have to deal. A change in the pattern of home visiting in healthcare, or parent–teacher communications, or housing counter services, may be fairly smoothly implemented in Gerrards Cross but lead to all sorts of problems in an intensely multicultural community such as Newnham, where there is a wider variation of expectations and far greater linguistic diversity.

Within our research, the implementation of the housing reforms had clearly been influenced by socio-demographic factors. Historically, local characteristics have always had a major effect on the way in which national housing policies have been implemented (Daunton, 1984). Over the previous two decades council housing had become more and more 'residualised'. When LSVTs came along they were concentrated in rural and small town locations, where there existed reasonable-quality housing stock. The seriously run-down inner city estates with severe social problems were left to one side. Now the Labour government is trying to develop the concept of the Local Housing Company to address the problems of these neglected localities.

A second local characteristic is the degree and nature of party political competition. It might be thought that this would only affect local authority services, and that the kind of opted-out organisations we have been mainly concerned with would have escaped such influences. In practice, however, the boundaries of party politics as an activity have never neatly coincided with the formal boundaries of local councils and their directly provided services. Local councillors and local MPs tend to get involved with virtually every type of local development of any consequence, so those running NHS trusts or grant maintained schools or housing associations still need to keep local politicians 'onside'. This is easier to do in some circumstances than others. If the local political scene is highly conflictual and the major parties are in campaigning mode, any change in local services risks becoming a political football (as occurred with at least one of our GM school applications). If, at the other extreme, elections are some way off and one party is routinely dominant, or alternatively that local party leaders have evolved modes of cross-party cooperation, then reform may be an easier process. The willingness and capacity of local politicians constructively to support and work with partly or fully autonomous local service-delivery agency varies considerably (Painter *et al.*, 1996). In the specific case of decentralisation, much is likely to depend upon perceptions as to which parties may gain or lose control of the organisation or function in question. If a Labour local authority 'loses' an LEA secondary school through an opting-out process designed by a generally anti-local-authority Conservative government, that is one thing. If a strong, new Labour government introduces education action zones, in which LEAs become only one partner among several, that may be perceived by the same local authority politicians as something rather different.

A third local characteristic emerged from our analysis as particularly significant. The degree of potential competition for a local service-providing organisation appears to have a major influence on its attitude towards decentralisation. A local service-providing minnow may not want more autonomy if that means that the shark in the same locality will have the freedom to operate without control by superior levels in the hierarchy (we found that this phenomenon existed for both schools and hospitals). However, if there is no serious competition in sight, then greater autonomy looks much more attractive. Also, the incentive to use decentralised authority to improve one's services increases to the extent that one fears rivals may be 'getting ahead'. Whether all such improvements are optimal from the point of view of the whole community is another question. When, in a budget-restricted situation, several local service-providing units are attempting to develop the same types of facility, unnecessary duplication and the missing of other opportunities may be the result. This appeared to be the case for hospitals in at least one of the areas in which we conducted research. Again, much depends upon the skills and attitudes of senior managers and local politicians as to whether cooperative or zero-sum solutions are pursued.

Turning to service characteristics, we can list a number that are likely to influence the receptivity of a given organisation to particular types of administrative reform:

- The size of the organisation.
- Whether contacts with users are remote, face-to-face but episodic, or continuous and close.
- Whether the service is universal (open to and used by all or most citizens) or selective (some services are obviously highly selective, for example primary education for the deaf and hard of hearing).
- Whether the service is 'consumed' on an optional or a mandatory basis.
- Whether a service is capital-or labour-intensive.
- Whether a service is closely wedded to and dependent upon a particular technology, or fairly flexible and 'low tech'.

Each of these may influence how the organisation concerned regards and adapts to a proposal for decentralisation (or any other kind of reform). Size, as stated earlier, consistently shows up as an important variable in organisational studies (Donaldson, 1985). In relation to decentralisation the additional administration required may be proportionately much larger for a small primary school than a big secondary school. Indeed scale factors were recognised by the Conservative governments, both in relation to applications for GM status and for GP fundholding status (though the size minima were progressively reduced in both cases). Size also influences market power, so that in general terms a large organisation may have more ability, in a competitive situation, both to 'do deals' with other providers and to survive temporary market downturns. Even in the tightly managed NHS quasi-market, it was clear that in two of our research areas the biggest hospital was seen as the 'playmaker', able to exert its weight in a way that was denied to smaller rivals. On the other hand size is not an undiluted benefit. As we saw, the internal promulgation of a reform can be much more difficult and time-consuming within a large and highly differentiated organisation than a small one. The head teacher in a small school can call in all the staff for a lunch-time or after-school meeting in a way that is impossible for the chief executive of a large hospital.

The nature of an organisation's contacts with its users is also significant. In a school, where teachers see the children and many of the parents every day and for prolonged periods, changes in the running of the organisation will need to be explained and their impact on local relationships will no doubt become, at least temporarily, the focus of much face-to-face discussion. The situation is different in a hospital, where most patients are brief visitors, and any changes in the status of the organisation may seem both obscure and irrelevant to their more pressing concerns. In competitive contexts, organisations that provide services involving extended face-to-face contact with users have built-in opportunites to build up 'brand loyalty' in ways that are not available to organisations that provide services remotely, or that see their users only briefly and spasmodically. On the other hand prolonged face-to-face contact can transmit bad news as well as good, so that any internal malaise in the organisation is likely to leak out to users more rapidly and comprehensively. In these senses schools are very intensive 'implementation habitats' where it is hard to keep secrets, while housing associations, though not as remote as, say, an air pollution inspectorate, are less intensive environments in which it may be possible to implement some administrative reforms 'at a distance' from the majority of service users.

The scale running from universal services (almost everyone visits their GP from time to time) to selective services is perhaps less relevant for decentralisation than for other types of administrative reform. Yet it was not without influence. Our three sectors ranged from 'tending towards universal' (hospitals and schools) to fairly selective (socially rented housing). The echos of selectivity could be heard in the perception, by some tenants that the transformation from local authority tenant to housing association tenant was a gain in social status (housing associations do not have some of the negative connotations historically attached to living in a council house). This may have influenced their willingness to consent to the change, although there were others who, in contrast, were anxious about leaving the shelter of the local authority. More importantly perhaps, any change in the rules for selecting tenants (consequent upon decentralisation) might have had major consequences for potential tenants. However those who might have been ruled out by such a change would also have tended to lack a voice, and in any case would not have been captured by our research design, which focused on tenants and their representatives, not on potential tenants or disappointed non-tenants.

The optional–mandatory distinction was not very prominent for the services we concentrated on, although it may be much more important in other implementation habitats. All three of the services we analysed were broadly optional (going to school is not normally optional, but there is in principle some choice of school, and in any case the service is normally seen as desirable and beneficial for the recipients). If, however, one were to study decentralisation in, say, a police force, or in the use of child protection orders by social workers, or in the administration of environmental health regulations, then the 'mandatoriness' of the service might well be seen as a more significant feature of the situation. On might imagine that, for mandatory services with a high control component, citizens would be very concerned to ensure equity, and therefore those wielding the control power would be subject to some higher authority and appeal processes would be readily available. The discovery that, because of decentralised powers, child protection orders were being administered more harshly in Leeds than in Luton would presumably be a source of public concern (whichever city the public happened to think was 'right'!)

We have already made some observations about the distinctions between more and less capital-intensive/labour-intensive services.

Housing is the most capital-intensive of our three sectors, and we noted how the LSVTs were concentrated in localities where the housing stock was in reasonable condition, avoiding run-down urban estates where large investments would be required. In general one could predict that radical decentralisation might be more difficult for highly capital-intensive services since, on a local scale, there would be the obvious problem of raising (or even acquiring the skills to raise and manage) the requisite resources. Decentralisation in social work is easier than decentralisation in telecommunications because social workers require hardly any capital and telecommunications networks require a great deal. It is obvious that this service characteristic connects to a number of others. Consider, for example, a computerised tomography scanner. It represents such a substantial capital investment (or at least it did when the technology was in its youthful stage) that it makes no sense, in a context of severe capital rationing, for a town to have more than one or two. This in turn tends to mean that local competition in the provision of such a service will be limited, except in the larger connurbations. On the other hand a very labour intensive service, with a large workforce and perhaps both horizontal divisions and vertical divisions between different types of occupational group, provides the classic scenario for reaping the benefits of decentralised management.

Finally, we should mention the technological 'embeddedness' of a service (Stewart, 1992). Where a service is heavily dependent on a particular piece of technology (a particular model of fire engine for a fire service, a particular design of switching gear for a telephone service), then a great deal will depend upon periodic decisions to renew or change that technology. It will be very important to get those decisions 'right', and therefore to call upon the views and knowledge of all the main stakeholders (users, field operatives, managers) as well as the technological experts themselves. One consideration in such a debate might certainly be how far a particular piece of technology permitted or encouraged a decentralised mode of operations. For example it has sometimes been argued that it is a drawback of civil nuclear power that, for security reasons, it requires hierachical and authoritarian organisations to support it (Flood and Grove-White, 1976; Royal Commision on Environmental Pollution, 1976, p. 82; Winner, 1977). None of the three services we examined happened to be particularly 'technology-embedded', at least not in the sense that decentralisation was glaringly inhibited by the requirements of servicing a piece of centralised and centralising technology. Nevertheless the technological dependence of a service would need to feature in a more general theory of implementation habitats.

These, then, are the components of a possible theory of implementation habitats – a theory that could help predict the ease or difficulty a particular type of managerial reform would face in a particular context. The next step would be to derive a series of propositions for combining the components in different ways, and then to go out and test the propositions in a sample of carefully selected empirical contexts. However that is for the future. The present task is to bring to a close our investigation of the Conservatives' large-scale experiments with decentralisation.

Concluding reflections

As we saw in Chapter 3, the rhetoric of Conservative ministers told a story of growing enthusiasm and personal responsibility among public service staff, clearer lines of accountability, enhanced efficiency and cost-consciousness, the fostering of leadership and innovation and, last but by no means least, higher-quality, more responsive services for the public. Our story, whilst not unrecognisably different, is much less uplifting – it is more complicated and is not topped off with the unwaveringly happy ending that Conservative ministers understandably preferred.

An alternative story is told by Clarke and Newman (1997, p. 159) who write that: 'Where champions of the managerial state have celebrated its dynamism, our analysis leads us to a different view. What we see is the unstable oscillations of a former state that cannot reconcile the social contradictions and conflicts of contemporary Britain within a managerial calculus.' But this is not quite our story either. We recognise the point that Clarke and Newman are making. Certainly, in some sectors the late 1980s and 1990s did witness a helter-skelter succession of different organisational formats, a new one seemingly being invented long before any rational assessment could be made of the success of its predecessor. In the education sector, as we have seen, city technology colleges, grant maintained schools and LMS all arrived fairly close together, and there were also continuous modifications of detail within each of these formats, so the rules of the game were never stable for long. In the socially rented housing sector, too, several different arrangements were tried one after another. In this sense, therefore, it is entirely appropriate for Clarke and Newman to refer to 'oscillations'.

But the story we want to tell is slightly different again. If it avoids managerial triumphalism it also somewhat downplays the drama of 'unstable oscillations'. For the two elements that showed up most regularly and clearly in our research were, first, the extent to which the government was able to orchestrate the whole process, and yet, second, the surprising degree to which public service professionals were able to preserve and protect their own conditions and styles of work within the organisational formats that were changing all around them. There was an element of 'dynamic conservatism' in much of what we saw, that is, housing managers, doctors and teachers were able to accommodate themselves within new organisational formats in ways that minimised the disturbance to their day-to-day practices. Indeed in the case of LSVTs, housing managers were able to some extent to retrieve former freedoms, and to build upon them further.

To begin with, therefore, we would stress the degree to which it was a powerful central government that drove along the whole experiment in decentralisation. On the whole, schools and hospitals were reluctant volunteers – 'choosing' self-governing status because they felt threatened or because they saw themselves as having little alternative. In this, as in other aspects of the process, housing was different. LSVT was keenly sought after, but then it was a policy invented more by local government than by central government, and one that took place against a background of ever more harsh conditions being placed upon local authority housing departments. Even when self-governing status was attained, NHS trusts and GM schools were still subject to a fairly tight regime of central government monitoring and regulation. So autonomy was real, but limited. The controls that were removed were mainly those which had hitherto emanated from local government, while central government strengthened its grip.

The intensification of activity, gains in efficiency and the spreading and deepening of cost consciousness were all tangible benefits that accompanied the process of decentralisation. Whether they were caused by that process is another question. As we have seen, the attribution of some of these developments is by no means clear. What is more certain is that the drive towards decentralisation, performance management and greater competitiveness was squeezed into different formats by the particular combination of service and local characteristics in each sector and at each locality. The characteristics of socially rented housing permitted the development of genuine market-like behaviour, at least in certain localities. The rather different characteristics of hospital care and secondary schooling placed tighter constraints on the development of entrepreneurial self-governance. Very few staff in these two sectors expressed any desire for substantial further increments of autonomy (although they certainly indicated a wish for more generous budgets).

As we have been writing, a new Labour government has settled into power. What lessons should it take from the decentralisation reforms of 1987 to 1997? Perhaps one lesson is that, if it summons all its formidable power, central government in the UK can force even the most unwilling horses to water. The creation of trusts and GM schools was achieved in the teeth of fierce opposition from the respective professional establishments. Yet in the end the horse could not be forced to drink – or at least, not enthusiastically or deeply. On the whole, freedoms were used cautiously – if they were not constrained by the nervous central government itself. Perhaps because of this caution, fragmentation, though real enough, has also been limited. Emerging new behavioural norms have embodied some of the older threads of appropriate conduct. Professional cultures have shifted, but have not been wholly transformed. Enormous institutional resilience and inertia have metamorphosed what some ministers intended as a revolution into a mere reform. LSVTs showed what could be achieved by working with the grain and supporting reform with access to enhanced resources. The NHS reforms showed what could be achieved by central government working against the grain in a tight resource climate. These two examples – with the reform of secondary schooling somewhere in between – marked the two ends of a scale of recalcitrance.

What our study does not include, however, is an example of large-scale political decentralisation from central to local or other subnational governments. This kind of change – which was common in continental Europe during the period – was almost entirely absent from UK reforms between 1979 and 1997. The Blair government, however, has moved quickly to set up Scottish and Welsh assemblies. It has also shown signs of fulfilling its promise to work more sympathetically and closely with local authorities than did its predecessors. The challenge for Labour will be to find a way of retaining the benefits of managerial freedom whilst simultaneously re-energising subnational political institutions. Under Thatcher and Major we gained a new breed of public service manager. The question now is whether, under Blair, we will see a new breed of local public service politician. If we do, it will be intriguing to see how well the new politicians and new managers get along together.

Appendix 1 Research Design and Methodology

The research design that supported the fieldwork reported in Chapters 5, 6 and 7 was essentially a set of holistic multiple case studies (Yin, 1994). The 12 service-providing institutions each constituted a case study in its own right. This set of 12 studies was intended to be used for a variety of purposes:

- To test the hypotheses that lay behind those decentralist doctrines of the Conservative Government that are discussed in Chapter 3. That is, to attempt to confirm or falsify the proposition that certain distinct types of benefit (for example greater efficiency and responsiveness to users) would flow from the reforms described.
- Within the first objective above, to assess whether experiences at the newly self-governing institutions (that is, GM schools, LSVT housing associations and early-wave NHS trusts) were significantly different from those at the non- or less-self-governing institutions. For this purpose we chose two self-governing institutions and two non-self-governing institutions (or, in the case of the NHS, late trust applications) within each sector to provide points of comparison.
- To provide a set of ordered case study materials that would permit us to test the usefulness of alternative academic theories of organisational change (particular varieties of rational choice and new institutionalist approaches, plus rhetorical analysis – see Chapter 2).

In adopting this design we had very much in mind the guidance offered by Robert Yin (1994). He is one of a number of scholars who have argued that case studies may be considered not merely as a data collection tactic but rather as a comprehensive research strategy in their own right. In particular, case studies are useful in circumstances where the need is for a study that: '(a) Investigates a contemporary phenomenon within its real life context, especially when (b) the boundaries between phenomenon and context are not clearly evident'. The case study approach served our purposes because it copes with the technically distinctive situation in which there are many more variables of interest than data points. As a result of this it (a) relies on multiple sources of evidence with the data converging in a triangulating fashion, and (b) benefits from the prior development of theoretical propositions to guide data collection and analysis (ibid., p. 13).

The project was based mainly, but not excusively, on intensive, semistructured interviewing and documentary analysis carried out at 12 fieldwork sites. More than 160 interviews were carried out, averaging over an hour in length.

The bulk of these were conducted between late 1994 and mid 1995. A smaller number of interviews were completed between September 1995 and February 1996. The purpose of the second round of interviews was to provide a longitudinal check (had anything changed since the first round?), to explore certain key issues in greater depth (especially concepts of performance and accountability) and to secure a measure of respondent validation for the picture formed of the organisation's circumstances during the first round of fieldwork.

A semistructured interview schedule was designed and piloted for the first round and a different, more focused schedule was created for the second. The interviews were concentrated at fairly senior levels – the research was never intended to focus on the 'rank and file'. In each hospital we approached the chief executive, other executive directors and a sample of other senior managers and consultants. We also sought interviews with the main local purchasing authority, with non-executive directors and, where appropriate, with the local GP fundholders and the Community Health Council. These latter interviews helped to give us an 'outside-in' perspective to complement the main thrust of the research, which was essentially concerned with an 'inside-out' perspective. In the secondary schools we interviewed the head teacher, other senior teachers, governors and, in some cases, officers of the LEA. In the housing associations we interviewed chief executives and their top management team, plus members of the board (the chair, councillor and tenant representatives). In the non-opted-out housing departments we interviewed deputy chief executives, directors of housing and their management teams, together with councillors on the Housing Committee and tenant representatives. Foreseeing the amount of data the interview programme would generate (approximately 3 000 separate responses) we decided at an early stage to pre code our questions and employ software (Textbase Alpha) that would permit us to sort out themes and patterns automatically.

The 12 fieldwork sites were carefully chosen. We selected two pairs (four in all) in each of the three sectors (healthcare, education and housing). To give a reasonable geographical spread, each pair was drawn from a different part of the country, although we excluded Greater London on the ground that the capital suffered from some unique problems (at least in degree) that we did not see as central to our research. One factor that posed a problem for our original research design was the rapid emergence within the NHS of a position where virtually all hospitals were becoming trusts (this had not been the original intention). This meant that we could no longer pursue our plan of contrasting a pair of acute trust hospitals with a pair of directly managed units that had not opted to become trusts. We therefore selected two 'early' trust applicants (second wave) and two 'late' trust applicants (fourth wave).

In addition to our interview programme, we collected a large number of institutional documents (annual reports, Citizen's Charter publications, accounts, management handbooks and so on) and conducted a general literature search on the subjects of managerial autonomy, decentralisation and devolution in public service contexts.

Appendix 2   Interview Schedules

Set out below are the interview schedules used for the main phase of the fieldwork. There were separate versions for:

- Case study organisations that had become self-governing (that is, early-wave NHS trusts, GM schools, LSVTs).
- Case study organisations that had not chosen to become self-governing, or had done so only late in the day (that is, fourth-wave NHS trusts, LEA schools, local authority housing departments).
- Other actors (for example, NHS purchasing authorities, GPs, LEAs).

Because of our use of Textbase Alpha software the numbers of the questions are not always in sequence.

Interview schedules for use in structured interviews: version for self-governing units

Identifying underlying goals and values

1. When trust status/opting out/voluntary transfer was first discussed, what were the main intentions?
2. How widely were these shared? [Follow-up supplementary questions to establish identities of any groups with different values/goals.]
3. What were the main considerations influencing the drafting of the submission? [For trust status/grant-maintained status/voluntary transfer and so on.]

Benefits and drawbacks of self-governance

4. What do you see as having been the main benefits of [grant-maintained status/trust status/voluntary transfer]?
5. Can you give examples of these benefits having been realised in practice?
6. Have there been drawbacks?
7. Can you give examples of the drawbacks?
8. What further changes do you envisage in the longer term?

[*Prompt*: ask for both benefits and drawbacks if both are not offered.]

9. Are there areas where, in your view, more autonomy is obviously desirable? If so, what are they?
19. Has autonomy made any difference to the organisation's relationship with important external bodies?

Respondent's concept of performance

10. What signs would you look for as indicators that a [GMT/NHS trust/ voluntary transfer] was performing well?
11. What would be the warning signs indicating that it was performing badly?
12. Is this information [that is, the indicator data referred to by the respondent in answering the previous two questions] actually collected by management?
13. Has the performance data for this unit contained any surprises?
14. What happens to the performance data that is collected? [Follow up with more detailed questions on this to discover whether such information is fed into key decision-making processes, and into divisional or personal objectives. Also, are there any declared standards or targets for these dimensions of performance and are there any incentives or penalties connected to such standards/targets?]
15. How much of such performance information is published or otherwise released into the public domain?
16. Who, if anyone, takes an interest when it is released?

Models of performance change

17. What are the main requirements if a [GM/NHS trust/voluntary transfer] is significantly to improve its performance? [Then develop this with subsidiary questions exploring whether the respondent considers environmental, resource, organisational or personal/leadership factors to be the most important.]
18. Is there evidence that specific incentives or penalties have improved performance?

Interview schedule for use in structured interviews: version for units that are non-self-governing or latecomers to self-governance

Identifying underlying goals and values

1. What were the main reasons for not making an early bid for trust status/ grant maintained status/voluntary transfer?
2. How widely were these shared? [Follow-up supplementary questions to establish identities of any groups with different values/goals.]

Benefits and drawbacks of self-governance

3. Have you made gains in flexibility and autonomy even without this status? If so, what are they?
4. Can you give examples?
5. What would have been the main benefits of grant-maintained status/NHS trust status/voluntary transfer?
6. What would have been the main drawbacks?
7. What further changes do you envisage in the longer term?
8. Are there areas where, in your view, more autonomy is obviously desirable?
19. Has autonomy made any difference to the organisation's relationship with important external bodies?

Respondent's concept of performance

9. What signs would you look for as indicators that a [LEA school/NHS trust/housing department] was performing well?
10. What would be the warning signs indicating that it was performing badly?
11. Is this information [that is, the indicator data referred to by the respondent in answering the previous two questions] actually collected by management?
12. Has the performance data for this unit contained any surprises?
13. What happens to the performance data that is collected? [Follow up with more detailed questions on this to discover whether such information is fed into key decision-making processes, and into divisional or personal objectives. Also, are there any declared standards or targets for these dimensions of performance and are there any incentives or penalties connected to such standards/targets?]
14. How much of such performance information is published or otherwise released into the public domain?
15. Who, if anyone, takes an interest when it is released?

Models of performance change

16. What are the main requirements if a [LEA school/NHS trust/housing department] is significantly to improve its performance? [Develop this with subsidiary questions exploring whether the respondent considers environmental, resource, organisational or personal/leadership factors to be the most important.]
17. Are specific incentives or penalties required to achieve lasting performance improvement, and if so, what form should they take?

Interview schedule for use in structured interviews: version for other actors

20. Have you noticed any changes in the performance of the [trust/school/housing department] since it acquired trust status?

21. What has been the nature of any such changes?
22. To what do you attribute these changes [wholly or partly to trust status, or to something else – if so, what?]
23. What would you look for in a model or ideal relationship between a trust and a purchasing authority/GP fundholder? [This question is designed to bring out the dimensions of performance that the GPs believe to be the most important.]
24. How does the actual performance of the [trust/school/housing department] measure up to the model developed above?

References

AUDIT COMMISSION (1986) *Managing the Crisis in Council Housing* (London: HMSO).

AUDIT COMMISSION (1992) *The Publication of Information (Standards of Performance) Direction* (London: HMSO).

AUDIT COMMISSION (1996) *What the Doctor Ordered* (London: HMSO).

BAILEY, G. (1987) *New Life for Old Estates* (London: Conservative Political Centre).

BALL, S., R. BOWE and S. GEWIRTZ (1994) 'Schools in the market place: An analysis of local market relations', in W. Bartlett, C. Propper, D. Wilson and J. Le Grand, *Quasi Markets in the Welfare State* (Bristol: School for Advanced Urban Studies), pp. 78–94.

BARTLETT, W. and J. LE GRAND (1994) 'The performance of trusts', in R. Robinson and J. Le Grand (eds), *Evaluating the NHS reforms* (London: King's Fund Institute), pp. 54–73.

BATES, S. (1991) 'Major admits opt-out schools get extra to encourage the others', *Guardian*, 7 August.

BENGTSSON, B. (1995) 'Housing in game-theoretical perspective', *Housing Studies*, vol. 10, no. 2, pp. 229–43.

BIRCHALL, J. (1988) *Building Communities: The Co-operative Way* (London: Routledge).

BIRCHALL, J. (1992) 'Council tenants: sovereign consumers or pawns in the game?', in J. Birchall (ed.), *Housing Policy in the 1990s* (London: Routledge).

BIRCHALL, J. (1996a) 'The hidden history of housing co-operatives in Britain', in A. Heskin and J. Leavitt (eds), *The Hidden History of Housing Co-operative* (Davis: University of California Press).

BIRCHALL, J. (1996b) *Decentralisation of Local Government Services: Some Emerging Paradigms*, paper presented to the International Symposium of New Frontiers of Theories and Practices in Local Government, Honolulu, November.

BRIGHT, J. (1988) 'Taking stock', in *Housing Magazine*, October.

BRINDLE, D. (1996) 'The internal market, warts and all', *Guardian*, 24 April.

BURNS, D., R. HAMBLETON and P. HOGGETT (1994) *The Politics of Decentralisation: Revitalizing Local Democracy* (Basingstoke: Macmillan).

CARTER, N., R. KLEIN and P. DAY (1992) *How Organisations Measure Success* (London: Routledge).

CLARKE, J. and J. NEWMAN (1997) *The Managerial State* (London: Sage).

CLARKE, K. (1991) speech to the North of England Educational Conference, November (quoted in Fitz *et al.*, 1993, p. 13).

CLARKE, K. (1992) interview on BBC Radio 4, *Today Programme*, 12 March.

COLEMAN, A. (1985) *Utopia on Trial: Vision and Reality in Planned Housing* (London: Hilary Shipman).

DAUNTON, M. (ed.) (1984) *Councillors and Tenants: Local Authority Housing in English Cities, 1919–1939* (Leicester: Leicester University Press).
DAY, P. and R. KLEIN (1987) *Accountabilities: Five Public Services* (London: Tavistock).
DEPARTMENT OF THE ENVIRONMENT (1987) *Housing: The Government's Proposals* (White Paper) (London: HMSO).
DEPARTMENT OF HEALTH AND SOCIAL SECURITY (1976) *Sharing Resources for Health in England: Report of the Resource Allocation Working Party* (London: HMSO).
DEPARTMENT OF HEALTH AND SOCIAL SECURITY AND THE WELSH OFFICE (1979) *Patients First: Consultative Paper on the Structure and Management of the National Health Service in England and Wales* (London: HMSO).
DEPARTMENT OF HEALTH AND SOCIAL SECURITY (1989a) *Working for Patients*, Cmnd 555 (London: HMSO).
DEPARTMENT OF HEALTH AND SOCIAL SECURITY (1989b) *Working for Patients: Self-Governing Hospitals*, Working Paper no. 1 (London: HMSO).
DI MAGGIO, P. and W. POWELL (eds) (1991) *The New Institutionalism in Organizational Analysis* (Chicago: University of Chicago Press).
DONALDSON, L. (1985) *In Defence of Organisation Theory: A Reply to the Critics* (Cambridge: Cambridge University Press).
DOUGLAS, M. (1987) *How Institutions Think* (London: Routledge & Kegan Paul).
DOWDING, K. (1991) *Rational Choice and Political Power* (Aldershot: Edward Elgar).
DOWDING, K. (1994) 'The compatibility of behaviouralism, rational choice and "new institutionalism"', *Journal of Theoretical Politics*, vol. 6, pp. 105–17.
DUNLEAVY, P. (1991) *Democracy: Bureaucracy and Public Choice* (Hemel Hempstead: Harvester Wheatsheaf).
DUNLEAVY, P. (1997) personal communication, 20 June.
DUNSIRE, A. (1978) *Control in a Bureaucracy* (London: Martin Robertson).
DUNSIRE, A. (1995) 'Administrative theory in the 1980s: a viewpoint', *Public Administration*, vol. 73, no.1 (Spring), pp. 17–40.
ELCOCK, H. and S. HAYWOOD (1980) *The Buck Stops Where? Accountability and Control in the National Health Service* (Hull: Institute of Health Studies).
ELSTER, J. (1983) *Sour Grapes: Studies in the Subversion of Rationality* (Cambridge: Cambridge University Press).
FERLEY, E. (1994) 'The evolution of quasi-markets in the NHS: early evidence', in W. Bartlett, C. Propper, D. Wilson and J. Le Grand, *Quasi-Markets in the Welfare State* (Bristol: School for Advanced Urban Studies), pp. 209–24.
FERLEY, E., L. ASBURNER, L. FITZGERALD and A. PETTIGREW (1996) *The New Public Management in Action* (Oxford: Oxford University Press).
FISCHER, F. and J. FORESTER (eds) (1993), *The Argumentative Turn in Policy Analysis and Planning* (London: UCL Press).

FISCHHOFF, B. (1975) 'Hindsight does not equal foresight: the effect of outcome knowledge on judgement under uncertainty', *Journal of Experimental Psychology: Human Perception and Performance*, vol. 1, pp. 288–99.

FITZ, J., D. HALPIN and S. POWER (1993) *Grant-Maintained Schools: Education in the Market Place* (London: Kogan Page).

FLOOD, M. and R. GROVE-WHITE (1976) *Nuclear Prospects: A Comment on the Individual, the State and Nuclear Power* (London: Friends of the Earth).

GLATTER, R. and P. WOODS (1994) 'The impact of competition and choice on parents and schools' in W. Bartlett, C. Propper, D. Wilson and J. Le Grand, *Quasi-Markets in the Welfare State* (Bristol: School for Advanced Urban Studies) pp. 56–77.

GLENNERSTER, H., M. MATSAGANIS, P. OWENS and S. HANCOCK (1994) 'GP fundholding: wild card or winning hand?', in R. Robinson and J. Le Grand (eds), *Evaluating the NHS Reforms* (London: King's Fund Institute), pp. 56–77.

GOODIN, R. (1982) 'Rational politicians in Washington and Whitehall', *Public Administration*, vol. 62, no. 1 (Spring), pp. 23–41.

GOODLAD, R. (1993) *The Housing Authority as Enabler* (Harlow: Longman).

GRIGGS, E. (1991) 'The politics of health reform', *Political Quarterly*, vol. 62, no. 4 (October/December), pp. 419–30.

HALACHMI, A. and P. BOORSMA (eds)(1998) *Inter and Intra Government Arrangements for Productivity: An Agency Approach* (Dordrecht: Kluwer Academic Publishers).

HARRISON, S. (1988) *Managing the National Health Service: Shifting the Frontier?* (London: Chapman & Hall).

HARRISON, S. (1994) 'Working for patients: context, content and rationale', in S. Harrison and N. Freemantle (eds), *Working for Patients: Early Research Findings* (Leeds: Nuffield Institute), pp. 5–16.

HARRISON, S., D. J. HUNTER, G. MARNOCH and C. POLLITT (1992) *Just Managing: Power and Culture in the National Health Service* (Basingstoke: Macmillan).

HARRISON, S. and C. POLLITT (1994) *Controlling Health Professionals* (Buckingham: Open University Press).

HARSANYI, J. (1986) 'Advances in understanding rational behaviour', in J. Elster (ed.), *Rational Choice* (New York: New York Press), pp. 82–107.

HENNEY, A. (1985) *Trust the Tenant: Devolving Municipal Housing* (London: Centre for Policy Studies).

HER MAJESTY'S CHIEF INSPECTOR OF SCHOOLS (1996) *1996 Annual Report* (London: HMCI)

HESELTINE, M. (1980) 'Ministers and management in Whitehall', *Management Services in Government*, vol. 35.

HESELTINE, M. (1987) *Where There's a Will* (London: Hutchinson).

HOGGETT, P. (1996) 'New modes of control in the public service', *Public Administration*, vol. 74, no. 1 (Spring), pp. 9–32.

HOGWOOD, B. (1987) *From Crisis to Complacency: Shaping Public Policy in Britain* (Oxford: Oxford University Press).

HOOD, C. (1976) *The Limits of Administration* (London: Wiley).

HOOD, C. (1991) 'A public management for all seasons', *Public Administration*, vol. 69, no. 1 (Spring) pp. 3–19.

HOOD, C. and JACKSON, M. (1991) *Administrative Argument* (Aldershot: Dartmouth).

HUGHES, D. and DINGWALL, R. (1990) 'What's in a name?', *Health Service Journal*, 29 November, pp. 1770–1.

HUNTER, D. J. (1993) 'The internal market: the shifting agenda', in I. Tilley (ed.), *Managing the Internal Market* (London: Paul Chapman) pp. 31–43.

JOSS, R. and M. KOGAN (1995) *Advancing Quality* (Buckingham: Open University Press).

KICKERT, W. (1993) 'Complexity, governance and dynamics: conceptual explorations of public network management', in J. Kooiman (ed.), *Modern Governance: New Government–Society Interactions* (London: Sage), pp. 191–204.

KOOIMAN, J. (ed.) (1993) *Modern Governance: New Government–Society Interactions* (London: Sage).

LANGSTAFF, M. (1992) 'Housing associations, a move to centre stage', in J. Birchall (ed.), *Housing Policy in the 1990s* (London: Routledge).

LEVAČIĆ, R. (1994) 'Evaluating the performance of quasi-markets in education', in W. Bartlett, C. Propper, D. Wilson and J. Le Grand, *Quasi-Markets in the Welfare State* (Bristol: School for Advanced Urban Studies) pp. 35–55.

LINDBLOM, C. and D. COHEN (1979) *Usable Knowledge* (New Haven, CT: Yale University Press).

LOCAL SCHOOL INFORMATION (1996) *Guide to the Issue of Opting Out* (revised April 1996) (London: LSI).

LOWNDES, V. (1996) 'Varieties of new institutionalism: a critical appraisal', *Public Administration*, vol. 74, no. 2 (Summer), pp. 181–97.

MAJONE, G. (1989) *Evidence, Argument and Persuasion in the Policy Process* (New Haven, CT: Yale University Press).

MAJOR, J. (1995) 'Prime Minister's Speech to Grant-Maintained Schools Foundation', Birmingham, 12 September (press notice)

MALPASS, P. (1990) *Re-shaping Housing Policy: Subsidies, Rents and Residualisation* (London: Routledge).

MARCH, J. and J. OLSEN (1989) *Rediscovering Institutions: The Institutional Basis of Politics* (London: Free Press).

MARSH, D. and R. RHODES (1992a) *Policy Networks in British Government* (Oxford: Clarendon Press).

MARSH, D. and R. RHODES (eds) (1992b) *Implementing Thatcherite Policies: Audit of an Era* (Buckingham: Open University Press).

MAWHOOD, C. (1997) 'Performance measurement in the United Kingdom, 1985–1995', in E. Chelimsky and W. Shadish (eds), *Evaluation for the Twenty First Century: A Handbook* (London: Sage), pp. 134–44.

MILLER, W. and M. DICKSON (1996) *Local Governance and Local Citizenship: A Report on Public and Elite Attitudes* (Glasgow: Economic and Social Research Council).

MINISTER OF HEALTH (1945) Memorandum to the Cabinet, 5 October, Public Record Office, CAB 129/3.

MINTZBERG, H. (1979) *The Structuring of Organizations* (Englewood Cliffs, NJ: Prentice Hall).

MULLINS, D., P. NINER and M. RISEBOROUGH (1992) *Evaluating Large Scale Voluntary Transfers of Local Authority Housing – An Interim Report* (London: Department of the Environment, HMSO).

MULLINS, D., P. NINER and M. RISEBOROUGH (1995) *Evaluating Large Scale Voluntary Transfers of Local Authority Housing – Final Report* (London: Department of the Environment, HMSO).

NATIONAL HEALTH SERVICE MANAGEMENT INQUIRY (1983) *Report* (the 'Griffiths Report') (London: Department of Health and Social Security).

NISKANEN, W. (1971) *Bureaucracy and Representative Government* (Chicago: Ill.: Aldine-Atherton).

NISKANEN, W. (1973) *Bureaucracy: Servant or Master?* (London: Institute of Economic Affairs).

OECD (1995) *Governance in Transition: Public Management Reforms in OECD Countries*, (Paris: PUMA/OECD).

OECD (1997) *In Search of Results: Performance Management Practices* (Paris: PUMA/OECD).

O'TOOLE, B. and G. JORDAN (eds) (1995) *Next Steps: Improving Management in Government?* (Aldershot: Dartmouth).

ØVRETVEIT, J. (1995) *Purchasing for Health* (Buckingham: Open University Press).

PAINTER, C., J. ROUSE, K. ISSAC-HENRY and L. MUNK (1996) *Changing Local Governance: Local Authorities and Non-Elected Agencies* (Luton: Local Government Management Board).

PAWSON, R. and N. TILLEY (1997) *Realistic Evaluation* (London: Sage).

PERELMAN, C. and L. OLBRECHTS-TYECA (1971) *The New Rhetoric: A Treatise on Argumentation* (Notre Dame, IN: University of Notre Dame Press).

POLLITT, C. (1986) 'Beyond the managerial model: the case for broadening performance assessment in government and the public services', *Financial Accountability and Management*, vol. 2, no. 3 (Autumn), pp. 155–70.

POLLITT, C. (1989) 'Danger – demolition contractors at work', *Health Service Journal*, 9 February, pp. 165.

POLLITT, C. (1990) 'Performance indicators: root and branch', in M. Cave, M. Kogan and R. Smith (eds), *Output and Performance Measurement: The State of the Art* (London: Jessica Kingsley), pp. 167–78.

POLLITT, C. (1993) *Managerialism and the Public Services*, 2nd edn (Oxford: Blackwell).

POLLITT, C. (1995) 'Justification by works or by faith? Evaluating the new public management', *Evaluation*, vol. 1, no. 2 (October), pp. 133–54.

POLLITT, C. and G. BOUCKAERT (1995) *Quality Improvement in European Public Services* (London: Sage).

POLLITT, C., S. HANNEY, T. PACKWOOD, S. ROTHWELL and S. ROBERTS (1997a) *Trajectories and Options: An International Perspective on the Implementation of Finnish Public Management Reforms* (Helsinki: Ministry of Finance).

POLLITT, C., S. HANNEY, T. PACKWOOD, S. ROTHWELL and S. ROBERTS (1997b) *Public Management Reforms: Five Country Studies* (Helsinki: Ministry of Finance).

POLLITT, C., S. HARRISON, D. J. HUNTER and G. MARNOCH (1988) 'The reluctant managers: clinicians and budgets in the NHS', *Financial Accountability and Management*, vol. 4, no. 3 (Autumn), pp. 213–33.

POLLITT, C., S. HARRISON, D. J. HUNTER and G. MARNOCH (1991) 'General management and the NHS: the initial impact, 1983–88', *Public Administration*, vol. 69, no. 1 (Spring), pp. 61–83.

POLLITT, C. and H. SUMMAR (1997) 'Trajectories of reform: public management change in four countries', *Public Money and Management*, January/March, pp. 7–18.

POWER, A. (1987) *Property before People: The Management of Twentieth Century Council Housing* (London: Allen & Unwin).

PRESSMAN, J. and A. WILDAVSKY (1973) *Implementation* (Berkeley, CA: University of California Press).

RANSON, S., J. MARTIN, P. McKEOWN, J. NIXON and R. MITCHELL, (1997) 'Governing agreeements for the civil society: the new management of institutions', paper pressented to the ESRC Local Governance Programme Conference, Glasgow, 28–29 April.

RHODES, R. A. W. (1981) *Control and Power in Central–Local Government Relations* (London: Gower).

ROYAL COMMISSION ON ENVIRONMENTAL POLLUTION (1976) *Nuclear Power and the Environment*, Cmnd 6618 (London: HMSO).

SECRETARIES OF STATE FOR HEALTH, WALES, NORTHERN IRE-LAND AND SCOTLAND (1989) *Working for Patients*, Cmnd 555 (London: HMSO).

SECRETARY OF STATE FOR HEALTH (1997) *The New NHS – Modern, Dependable* (London: Stationery Office).

SHERMAN, J. (1997) 'Spending on NHS will be capped', *The Times*, 10 October, p. 1.

SMITH, B. (1985) *Decentralisation: The Territorial Dimension of the State* (London: Allen & Unwin).

STANYER, J. (1976) *Administration* (London: Fontana).

STEWART, J. (1992) *Managing Difference: The Analysis of Service Characteristics* (Birmingham: Institute of Local Government Studies).

STEWART, J. (1994) 'The Rebuilding of Public Accountability', in N. Flynn (ed.), *Reader: Change in the Civil Service* (London: Public Finance Foundation), pp. 75–9.

STOKER, G. (1997) 'Local political participation, in G. Stoker (ed.), *New Perspectives on Local Governance* (York: Joseph Rowntree Foundation), pp. 157–96.

SUMMA, H. (1992) 'The rhetoric of efficiency: applied social science as depoliticisation', in R. Brown (ed.), *Writing the Social Text* (New York: Aldine de Gruyter).

SUMMA, H. (1993) 'The rhetoric of bureaucracy', in P. Ahonen (ed.), *Tracing the Semiotic Boundaries of Politics* (Paris: Mouton de Gruyter).

THAIN, C. and M. WRIGHT (1995) *The Treasury and Whitehall: The Planning and Control of Public Expenditure, 1976–1993* (Oxford: Clarendon Press).

WALDERGRAVE, W. (1994) 'The reality of reform and accountability in today's public service', in N. Flynn (ed.), *Reader: Change in the Civil Service* (London: Public Finance Foundation), pp. 81–8.

WHITEHEAD, M. (1994) 'Is it fair? Evaluating the equity implications of the NHS reforms', in R. Robinson and J. Le Grand (eds), *Evaluating the NHS Reforms* (London: King's Fund Institute), pp. 208–420.

WINNER, L. (1977) *Autonomous Technology: Technics Out of Control as a Theme in Political Thought* (Cambridge, Mass.: MIT Press).

YIN, R. (1994) *Case Study Research: Design and Methods*, 2nd edn (London, Sage).

ZITRON, J. (1995) *Local Housing Companies: A Good Practice Guide* (Coventry: Chartered Institute of Housing).

Index